Globalizing Rights

Matthew J. Gibney is Elizabeth Colson Lecturer in Forced Migration at the Refugee Studies Centre, Queen Elizabeth House, University of Oxford and an Official Fellow on Linacre College, Oxford, He has written extensively on asylum, immigration, and the liberal democratic state.

The Oxford Amnesty Lectures 1995

Globalizing Rights

The Oxford Amnesty Lectures 1999

Edited by

Matthew J. Gibney

OXFORD
UNIVERSITY PRESS

OXFORD
UNIVERSITY PRESS

Great Clarendon Street, Oxford OX2 6DP

Oxford University Press is a department of the University of Oxford.
It furthers the University's objective of excellence in research, scholarship,
and education by publishing worldwide in

Oxford New York

Auckland Bangkok Buenos Aires Cape Town Chennai
Dar es Salaam Delhi Hong Kong Istanbul Karachi Kolkata
Kuala Lumpur Madrid Melbourne Mexico City Mumbai Nairobi
São Paulo Shanghai Singapore Taipei Tokyo Toronto

Oxford is a registered trade mark of Oxford University Press
in the UK and in certain other countries

Published in the United States
by Oxford University Press Inc., New York

British Library Cataloguing in Publication Data

Data available

Library of Congress Cataloging in Publication Data

Data available

ISBN 0–19–280305–0

1 3 5 7 9 10 8 6 4 2

Typeset in Bembo and Univers
by RefineCatch Limited, Bungay, Suffolk
Printed in Great Britain by
Clays Ltd., St. Ives plc

Contents

CONTENTS

Contributors

KWAME ANTHONY APPIAH is Laurance S. Rockefeller University Professor of Philosophy at Princeton University

HOMI K. BHABHA is Anne F. Rothenberg Professor of English and American Literature at Harvard University

B. S. CHIMNI is Professor of International Law at the School of International Studies, Jawaharlal Nehru University, New Delhi

NOAM CHOMSKY is Institute Professor in Linguistics and Philosophy at the Massachusetts Institute of Technology

SUSAN GEORGE is Associate Director of the Transnational Institute in Amsterdam and Vice-President of ATTAC France (Association for Taxation of Financial Transaction to Aid Citizens)

MATTHEW J. GIBNEY is Elizabeth Colson Lecturer in Forced Migration at the Refugee Studies Centre, Queen Elizabeth House, University of Oxford and a Fellow of Linacre College, Oxford

MICHAEL LIKOSKY is Lecturer in Law at Lancaster University

RICHARD RORTY is Professor of Comparative Literature at Stanford University

ALAN RYAN is Warden of New College, Oxford

JOSEPH E. STIGLITZ was formerly Chief Economist at the

World Bank and now holds a chaired professorship, jointly in the Graduate School of Business, the Economics Department of the Graduate School of Arts and Sciences and the School of International and Public Affairs at Columbia University

YOGI SIKAND is a post-doctoral researcher at the University of London

VANDANA SHIVA is the founder and director of the Research Foundation for Science, Technology, and Ecology in New Delhi

CHARLES TAYLOR is Emeritus Professor in Philosophy at McGill University, Montreal

Acknowledgements

I am grateful to the Committee of the Oxford Amnesty Lectures for inviting me to edit this volume. The task has proven difficult, challenging, and rewarding in equal measure. The balance, however, would have been less favourable without the intellectual and practical assistance of Chris Miller. His efforts made this book possible. I am grateful also to Wes Williams, Chimène Bateman, Andrew Linklater, and David Turton for advice and assistance. Finally, I would like to express my deep thanks to the scholars who agreed, often at short notice, to act as discussants for the chapters that follow.

Matthew J. Gibney

Introduction

Matthew J. Gibney

Not long ago I was talking with an American-based Chinese anthropologist who had just presented a paper on the changing relationship between the people and state authorities in China. To illustrate the new terms of this relationship, he explained how it was increasingly common for those under arrest in China to appeal to their 'rights' when confronted by the police. He attributed this development to the powerful influence of imported television crime dramas, like *Starsky and Hutch* and *Hawaii 5–0*, on the country's population. Taking their cue from the dubious characters apprehended by TV cops, the Chinese people were now vocally letting the authorities know that they too had rights. In a state renowned for its brutal suppression of freedom of speech, television had, ironically, elevated the 'right to remain silent' to popular prominence.

Scholars of globalization, by contrast, have shown little interest in exercising this right in recent years. Advocates, critics, and dispassionate observers alike have been responsible for a massive outpouring of work on the subject. A virtual 'globalization industry' has emerged, drawing participants from an array of intellectual and political perspectives, and finding its audience in politicians, business leaders, and journalists. The crosscutting appeal of the term 'globalization' admits no simple explanation. Certainly, the vagueness of the term's referent has been helpful, enabling diverse social, political, and economic phenomena to fit under its head. The ideological blandness of the term has probably also played a role. A term of neither obvious praise nor approval, 'globalization' has served as both, satisfying critics and supporters alike.

The roots of globalization's appeal are also found in something more substantive: the widespread need for a shorthand way of referring to a set of profound material changes that have increasingly impacted upon relations between societies in the last few decades. We can readily identify the outward signs of these changes: e-mail, the web, increasing immigration, transnational corporations, non-governmental organizations (NGOs) that operate globally, the World Trade Organization (WTO), fibre optic cables, the flourishing of commuter travel, and satellite transmission. But how can we best characterize what unites these changes? We can make at least some headway by returning to the example of TV cop shows in China.

What makes the Chinese case notable is not the fact that it illustrates the spread of rights across national boundaries. The idea of rights has long been an international traveller. The key events in the institutional codification of human rights in the US in 1776 and in France in 1789 were both marked by *Declarations*—statements of principle addressed not only inwards to a domestic audience but also outwards to European states. One could hardly make full sense of Edmund Burke's concern about 'the pretended rights'[1] of the theorists of the French Revolution without conceding the ability of these ideas to infect other states, disturbing the delicate fabric of social life. Not without reason was the spread of rights on both sides of the Atlantic in the 1790s referred to as 'Paine's yellow fever'.[2]

2

Rather, the distinctiveness of this example lies in what it tells us about the way the idea of rights is transmitted. Throughout most of the last 250 years, the 'culture of rights'[3] has spread, when and where it has, through a mixture of immigration, peripatetic advocates, the printed word, and as a result (often indirect) of Western colonialism. In more recent times, trade sanctions and aid conditionalities have been the instrument of choice for furthering the rights agenda. The Chinese case suggests, however, a new transmission mechanism: popular entertainment beamed across huge distances directly into the home (or village). This is not only a non-coercive way for a rights culture to expand; it is also a relatively unmediated one. For the vehicle of popular entertainment suggests the possibility that rights might percolate from the people up to transform the relationship between the governed and the governors. The globalization of the idea of rights suggests that the truths self-evident in 'Book him, Danno' might touch parts of the globe that the words of Jefferson or the Universal Declaration have hitherto been unable to reach.

But if this example raises the possibility of new modes of travel for rights, it also bespeaks their new audience: the globe in its entirety. Here, the case of China is particularly apposite. This is not only because the country's population and land mass are so vast that no social, economic, or political force could be considered truly global without having conquered them. It is also because China serves as a reminder of the 'mind-forg'd manacles'[4] of prejudice which have historically limited those deemed worthy of being part of the community of rights holders. Forty years ago, openly discriminatory immigration policies, such as the White Australia Policy and the US's National Origins Act, prevented the settlement of

Chinese immigrants in almost all English-speaking countries. A little less than 200 years before, white middle-class men, some of them slaveholders, signed the Declaration of Independence, declaring that all men are created equal. Exclusions of this sort are hardly past history. For many, however, globalization suggests the possibility of a world where the extension of rights signals the overcoming of not just geographical boundaries, but also the limits of our moral imagination.

One way of pinpointing what globalization is, then, is to see it as a way of describing how recent developments in technology and communications, such as the internet and satellite transmission, have fundamentally transformed both how ideas travel and the nature of their final destination. And, of course, not just ideas—also people, culture, images, crime, and, above all, goods, services, investment, and finance. The movement of the latter has enabled the emergence of a worldwide economy and the flourishing of transnational corporations that have come, quite understandably, to be synonymous with globalization. As for corporations, so for NGOs. The head of Amnesty International's US operations recently claimed that 'no development in the last five years . . . has been more important to the success of the human rights movement than the growth of the web'.[5] Confronted with a new, global stage and virtually instantaneous access to information—political, humanitarian, social, and religious—NGOs have become a ubiquitous part of international life.

Described thus, we might be tempted to join with Vaclav Havel in seeing globalization as 'morally neutral . . . depending on the kind of content we give to it'.[6] But this is hardly an adequate description. For it edits out of the picture the question of who owns and controls the means of technology and communications that are transforming the globe. It was Western-based multinational corporations not Human Rights Watch that laid, launched, and produced the cables, satellites, and video that have encouraged the spread of rights to China, though both groups are united in their concern with how events unfold there. The world's largest potential market for Sony televisions is, coincidentally, also the country with the greatest population of people living under authoritarian government.

Globalization thus has implications for established relations of power between rich states and poor states and people and their governors, and for minority groups and majority populations. The aim of this volume of the Oxford Amnesty Lectures is to consider the impact of globalization on the spread of and respect for human rights. At their core, human rights are tools for empowering and providing security to individuals. They serve these goals by setting minimal standards on how individuals may rightfully be treated (e.g. the right not to be tortured), what they are owed (e.g. the right to a minimum wage and safe working conditions), and what they are entitled to do (e.g. the right to vote in free and fair elections). The contributors in this volume all concern themselves, more or less directly, with the prospects for squaring the technological changes and economic developments associated with globalization with a universal respect for rights—what we might call the 'globalization of rights'.

The compatibility of human rights and globalization is an article of faith for most government and corporate leaders in the West. A globalized economy, enabled by technological innovation, is seen as not only congruent with, but also a necessary condition for, the spread of human rights. Participation in a world market brings benefits to the poorest and the richest countries, to huge multinational corporations, as well as to small family firms. Falling trade barriers ensure a global pool of buyers, sellers, employers, employees, investors, and lenders, maximizing the returns of all players. Market competition provides incentives for the spread of technology, education, and economic growth. The result is rising living standards across the globe. In recent years, according to the multi-billionaire Bill Gates, 'world trade has been the mechanism allowing poor countries to take care of their really basic needs like vaccination.' The lesson is clear: 'if you block [world trade] . . . the big losers are the poor people of the world.'[7]

And the benefits of globalization for developing countries go beyond the economic. Participation in a free, global economy corrodes repressive rule. The deregulation of industries, the acknowledgement of the legal force of contracts and private property, openness to external sources of information, ideas, and entertainment, and the empowerment of entrepreneurial elites, serve to constrain the power of national governments. Ultimately, these changes create internal pressure for publicly stated limits on state authority, including the codification of human rights. In a globalized context, states face more external scrutiny too. International organizations, NGOs, and media organizations are now able quickly and cheaply to acquire knowledge of systematic rights violations. The roving spotlight of the international community provides a new and growing deterrent to the systematic abuse of state powers.

This attractive picture of the fruits of globalization has not convinced everyone, however, even when garnished with caveats on the need for 'supportive and stabilizing policies'[8] to address globalization's more disruptive consequences. From

Seattle in 1999 to Davos in 2001, many critics have derided
the 'globalization of rights' as a cheap fiction constructed to
license the worldwide spread of Western capitalism. Some
Southern countries have been unimpressed by the promise of
increased material prosperity shared across poorer and richer
countries. According to the President of Tanzania, Benjamin
Mkapa, speaking at the World Economic Forum in January
2001, 'Globalization can deliver, just as Tanzania can play in
the World Cup and win it.'[9]

But just what is the case against globalization in its current
form? The chapters here by Susan George, Noam Chomsky,
and Vandana Shiva provide three different versions. By
redescribing globalization as neoliberalism gone global, a
manifestation of US economic and political hegemony, and
a continuation of Western colonialism, these authors show
why the threats to human rights posed by globalization far
outweigh its benefits.

In 'Globalizing Rights?' the activist and writer on global
poverty, Susan George, argues that 'neoliberal' globalization
works systematically to undermine the empowerment and
security of the majority of the world's population. Marshal-
ling an array of evidence on the distribution of global wealth,
life expectancy, and inequality with and between countries,
George paints a picture of an economic process starkly at odds
with the picture presented by globalization's defenders.
Indeed, for George, the term 'globalization' is itself misleading, conjuring up images of a world progressing together in
terms of living standards, rights, and access to markets. The
reality, however, is a systematic process of *de facto* exclusion
where numerous social and economic groups, as well as whole
countries, are ignored or left impoverished by the spread of
Western corporate capital. As Western neoliberalism shifted

to the world stage, the driving forces of globalization have little to do with respect for the principles embodied in the Universal Declaration of Human Rights (UDHR), and a great deal to do with capital's search for cheap and vulnerable labour markets. In his commentary on George's chapter, Michael Likosky extends the implications of George's argument by contrasting the dictates of neoliberal theory with the active role states play in intervening to advance the interests of capital.

Noam Chomsky, Institute Professor at the Massachusetts Institute of Technology, also emphasizes the role of state agency in his contribution to the volume, ' "Recovering Rights": A Crooked Path'. Locating globalization within the broader context of US foreign policy, Chomsky traces the evolution of the three major pillars of the post-Second World War international order: the UDHR, the Bretton Woods economic system, and the UN Charter. Of these pillars, Bretton Woods has, with the help of the US, given way to an unrestrained capitalism that has led to greater insecurity in the West and impoverishment outside it; the UN Charter, on the other hand, has been rendered redundant by the willingness of the US unilaterally to embark on forceful interventions in places like Kosovo. Finally, hostility to democratic movements when they threaten its strategic or economic interests has made US rhetoric on human rights hollow. In Chomsky's view, the future for the mixture of liberty, rights, and social justice outlined in the UDHR may not be unremittingly dim, but the struggle to make human rights a practical reality for most people will remain an onerous one. In his commentary, Alan Ryan questions the coherence of Chomsky's account of the relationship between the public, the media, and the state, and ponders the implications of Chomsky's worldview for the justification of humanitarian intervention to prevent human rights violations.

Both George and Chomsky challenge the globalization of rights thesis by showing how the logic of expanding corporate capitalism and the goals of US foreign policy create a disjuncture between the rhetoric and reality of human rights. For Vandana Shiva, by contrast, the gap between rhetoric and reality is diminishing, though in ways that are inimical to the security and welfare of poorer peoples. In 'Food Rights, Free Trade, and Fascism', the environmentalist, activist, and writer takes India as her point of departure and argues that the West is foisting on the South a truncated account of human rights that, while endorsing civil and political rights, dispenses with economic ones. Western corporations have used national and international law to undermine the right to food traditionally respected by non-Western cultures. Through a process of elevating themselves to the status of rights-holders under international law, and using technology to appropriate food patents, Western corporations have come close to cornering the world market in food production. The result, argues Shiva, has been devastating for the world's poor and marginalized. Not only are they steadily dispossessed of the rights and resources they need to survive, but the countries in which they are located, like India, experience growing ethnic and religious conflict as the violence done to the poor by international actors turns itself inwards. Yogi Sikand's commentary provides a different perspective on the current situation in India. He argues that the country's recent conflicts are rooted in divisions that long predate globalization and suggests that a proper understanding of current developments in Indian politics requires a fuller engagement with the implications of the caste system than Shiva provides.

The George, Chomsky, and Shiva troika offers an impressive set of rebuttals to the claim that the neoliberal economics associated with globalization harmonizes with increased security and freedom for much of the world's population. But the contemporary revolution in travel and destination does not only raise issues of economic rights. New challenges to how human rights are formulated, enforced, and articulated also result from the increasing influence of international organizations, NGOs, and social movements; new avenues for citizen scrutiny of government via novel information sources, such as the World Wide Web; growing immigration and refugee movements and the emergence of new diaspora communities that undercut traditional accounts of national identity and multiculturalism; and concerns about the adequacy of human rights as a cross-cultural standard. The remaining contributions to this volume by Joseph Stiglitz, Homi Bhabha, and Anthony Appiah, respectively, highlight the key human rights issues that arise from these challenges.

The web, video, cable and satellite television have transformed the sources through which people access information. Yet, according to Joseph Stiglitz, the former Senior Vice President and Chief Economist of the World Bank, governments still exercise too much control over the information to which their citizens have access. In 'On Liberty, the Right to Know, and Public Discourse', Stiglitz launches a resounding defence of an all-encompassing 'right to know', the respect of which would require major reforms to current state practices. Anticipating the criticism that governments need to keep a tight rein on certain sources of information for reasons of social and, particularly in the context of a global marketplace, economic stability, Stiglitz argues that the right to know is central to a real democratic politics. Moreover, as he points out, because it is acquired at the public expense, government information is owned by the citizens, and they should rightfully have access to it. As well as serving immediate democratic goals, greater openness would undermine the kind of government information monopolies that can create dependent and docile journalism. Stiglitz's target is both Northern and Southern governments, obsessed as both are by the need for secrecy to protect their own interests. But B. S. Chimni in his commentary takes Stiglitz's argument a step further. He argues that the standards of transparency that Stiglitz advocates should be extended to the new transnational institutions and organizations (e.g. the IMF and the World Bank) that have in recent times usurped many of the traditional powers of (particularly Southern) states.

While Stiglitz argues for the growing importance of a wide-ranging 'right to know', Professor Homi Bhabha of Harvard University defends the importance of the 'right to narrate'. In his contribution, Bhabha interprets this entitlement as the right of individuals and social groups to tell stories that create their own 'web of history', challenging and providing alternatives to those customs and conventions that currently dominate social discourse. Bhabha's articulation of this right is occasioned by a broader discussion of the implications of multiculturalism and its linked claims of cultural respect and recognition. Rejecting the dominant assumption that only the culture of 'whole societies' is worthy of respect, Bhabha defends the ethical importance and, in a globalized context, the increasing practical significance of what Charles Taylor has described as the 'partial milieux', partial or minority cultures. The right to narrate both recognizes and protects the vital role that minority cultures play in modern societies as 'moving signs of civic life'. In his response, Charles Taylor argues that Bhabha mischaracterizes his position on the respect due to partial cultures, but is at one with Bhabha in believing that the political identities recognized by states need to take more account of the complexity, ambiguity, and hybridity of our personal identities.

Homi Bhabha reminds us that a serious multiculturalism requires the recognition (even the celebration) of the role of minority or partial cultures. But as much as we need to acknowledge the importance and reality of social and cultural diversity, we need also to reach agreement on common standards to protect individuals and groups from exploitation, violence, and injustice. Must our growing acknowledgement of the need to respect diversity within and between cultures pull us further away from agreement on fundamental human rights? In the last contribution, Professor Anthony Appiah of Princeton University suggests that it need not. In 'Citizens of the World', Appiah develops an account of cosmopolitanism that is simultaneously respectful of cultural diversity, but can serve to encourage a moral dialogue across the boundaries of national societies. The key to reconciling diversity and commonality, according to Appiah, lies not in the search for rational agreement at the level of principle or the existence of true moral universals. It lies, rather, in considering more closely the contingent and 'enormously various' ways that people already reach agreement on particulars both within and between societies. This agreement is on display all around us in our shared ability to follow a narrative, or in the importance we attach to saving a drowning child. In the last section of his contribution, Appiah offers a picture of rights that attempts to do justice to both our commonality and our diversity. Rights, he argues, should be seen as tools for individual self-creation. In this view, social and cultural variety becomes 'an essential precondition' for a meaningful human life.

In his wide-ranging response, Richard Rorty finds himself sceptical about the philosophical bases of some of Appiah's conclusions, though less so about the conclusions themselves. Rorty differentiates himself more strongly when he suggests, *contra* Appiah, not only that there can be inspiring narratives that unify the human species as a whole, but that Appiah's vision will need them if it is to have any chance of coming to fruition.

Considered together, the essays that follow indicate a highly problematical relationship between globalization and human rights. And the reasons for this go beyond the traditional difficulty of translating the rhetoric of rights into effective institutional protections.[10] In an era of globalization, the spread of rights is haunted by two concerns. The first is that the current proliferation of rights across the globe may owe more to the inequalities in power, resources, and technology that epitomize international society than to the intrinsic appeal of the idea of rights itself. The second is that the spread of civil and political rights might collude in the expansion of global capitalism by reinforcing a view of human entitlements that greatly undervalues the importance of economic equality and security. These joint concerns suggest the possibility of a world where human rights are in the ascendancy, but where many people are becoming more insecure and exercising less power over their lives.

In the face of this paradox, all of the contributors to this series of Amnesty Lectures reaffirm the language of rights to express the legitimate claims and aspirations of the world's population. They are surely correct to do so. There is nothing dispensable about the language of rights, nor the compelling human interests it serves. But the contributors here go further, showing us the need to rethink human rights to ensure they remain relevant when the security and freedom of vulnerable people are at stake. In the essays that follow, the scope, legitimation, threats to, and limits of human rights are actively reconceived. The contributors propose understandings of rights that aspire to disentangle the empowering and inclusive elements of globalization from its other, less desirable effects. Whether the contributors are ultimately successful is for the reader to decide. But, at the very least, they provide compelling reasons why we should waive our own right to remain silent and make their aspirations our own.

1

Globalizing Rights?

Susan George

In this essay I shall try to explain why neoliberal globalization is incompatible with the globalization of human rights. This incompatibility is neither an aberration nor a temporary inconvenience which will improve with time but a built-in feature of the system.

Let me start by defining terms. What do I mean by globalization? Some people see it entirely in terms of technology. Globalization may have been given a decisive push by the information revolution, but computers and the internet didn't cause it. Similarly, purely economic definitions of globalization are inadequate even though it's quite true that cheap capital, information, and transport have been vital to its success.

If more intense international exchange of goods, services, and finance were all there is to it, one could argue that globalization has been with us since the Romans, the Italian Renaissance bankers, and the British Empire. Nor is globalization defined by the capacity of transnational corporations to produce, ship, and assemble anything anywhere or that of financial organizations to move money at the speed of light. We need a political definition as well and this in turn is linked to the end of the Cold War.

The Cold War had two major political consequences. First, no place in the world could be judged unimportant because even the most obscure and destitute country could become the scene of superpower rivalry. Second, the West had to maintain the postwar welfare state since it could not do less for its citizens than the Soviet Union did for its people. With the fall of the Wall, the situation has changed radically. Now that there is only one superpower, plenty of places in the Third World have sunk back into destitution and obscurity—think of Somalia! Similarly, the welfare state has come under permanent threat.

We all use the word 'globalization'; it figures in the titles of countless seminars, conferences, and lectures and has been repeated so often that we tend to accept it uncritically. Allow me to suggest that by doing so, we become victims of a particularly successful ideological hijacking of language because the word 'globalization' gives the impression that all people from all regions of the globe are somehow caught up in a single movement, an all-embracing phenomenon and are all marching together towards some future Promised Land.

I would argue that precisely the opposite is the case, that the term 'globalization' is a trap because it masks rather than reveals present reality and is convenient shorthand for *de facto* exclusion. It has nothing to do with the creation of a single, somehow integrated and unified world, nor with a process from which all earth's inhabitants will somehow benefit. Rather than encompassing everyone in a collective march towards a better life, globalization is a process that allows the world market economy to 'take the best and leave the rest'.

Now something about rights. Many people think of human rights exclusively in terms of torture, political prisoners, or massacres of civilians. All such horrors must be fought and Amnesty International has always stood courageously in the avant-garde of this battle. Let us not forget, however, that the framers of the 1948 Universal Declaration of Human Rights took a much broader view of the issue and devoted their attention to the choices of society with regard to the *just distribution of material and non-material advantages*. The notion of 'just distribution' includes inequalities both within and between nations; the shares allotted to different social classes in particular societies and also the disparities between rich and poor at the international level.

The Universal Declaration of Human Rights actually defined a collective ethics and laid down standards for a rights-based society which consciously chooses to respect the dignity of every human being so that no one is left out. An ethical, rights based society would be one in which Article 25 of the Universal Declaration of Human Rights would fully apply. Part of Article 25 reads as follows:

Everyone has the right to a standard of living adequate for the health and well-being of himself and of his family, including food, clothing, housing and medical care and necessary social services and the right to security in the event of unemployment, sickness, disability, widowhood, old age or other lack of livelihood.

Let me also remind you of John Rawls's classic work *A Theory of Justice*. Rawls says that before choosing the principles that should govern society, you should first imagine that society from the point of view of someone who is ignorant of his or her own place in it; someone who has no idea of his birthplace or status, nor of the talents and opportunities with which he or she will be gifted in life. You would then choose a world in which, according to Rawls, 'social and economic inequalities are arranged so that they are to the greatest benefit of the least advantaged'.

The Universal Declaration does not aim for complete equality and it certainly isn't compatible with a political system based on some form of coercive collectivism, or state socialism as it existed in Eastern Europe—quite the contrary. An ethical, rights-based society is one in which each person is guaranteed a decent and dignified material livelihood and opportunities for personal attainment, but is also guaranteed freedom of expression, of political association, of worship, and the like. So the realization of human rights clearly requires a democratic form of government as well.

If this is the case, then I hope to convince you that *globalization as I've defined it is directly opposed to human rights.* Why? Because globalization has inexorably transferred wealth from the poor to the rich. It has increased inequalities both within and between nations. It has remunerated capital to the detriment of labour. It has created far more losers than winners.

None of these statements is ideological and all are easy to prove. At the level of world wealth distribution, the United Nations Development Programme's annual Human Development Reports document the increase of rich–poor disparities, year after year. One of the most striking images is the well-known 'champagne-glass graph' which shows that the top 20 per cent of humanity now captures 86 per cent of all wealth (compared to 70 per cent 30 years ago), while the bottom 20 per cent has seen its already meagre portion of this wealth reduced to just 1.3 per cent.

Whole regions are being left out of the globalization process, including most of Africa, large parts of Asia and Latin America, and many regions within the supposedly rich countries themselves. Repeated financial crises exacerbate this trend towards radically unequal development.

Overall, the North–South differential was about 2 to 1 in the eighteenth century and 30 to 1 in 1965. It's now over 70 to 1 and rising. The comparison between the billionaires and the billions is also striking, even though it's not a scientific comparison. The top 225 fortunes in the world amount to a total of over 1,000 billion dollars (a trillion dollars). This sum is roughly equivalent to the annual revenues of the 2.5 billion poorest people in the world, about 42 per cent of the entire global population. The three richest people in the world have a collective fortune greater than the total Gross Domestic Product of the 48 poorest countries in the world.

Naturally, not everyone in poor countries is poor, nor is everyone in rich countries rich. If we look at wealth disparities within nations as opposed to global disparities between North and South, we discover the same tendencies towards greater inequality. Some 30 or 40 years ago, an American corporate Chief Executive Officer received salary and benefits roughly 40 to 60 times greater than his average employee. That was already a large spread. Today's CEO routinely receives 200–300 times as much as the average company employee.

If you were already among the haves—roughly the top 20 per cent of a given society—then you have benefited from globalization. If you were further down the social ladder, statistically you have lost. Twenty years of neoliberal policies—structural adjustment programmes in the South and in Eastern Europe; and Reaganite or Thatcherite policies in the North—have resulted in huge transfers of wealth from the bottom of society to the top. They have also caused a 'hollowing out' of the middle classes. Here are a few quotes from the *UNCTAD 1997 Trade and Development Report* to make this point:[1]

In the 1990s, income inequality has increased sharply from relatively low levels in the former socialist countries of Eastern Europe and also in China.

[This is also true in Latin America and in many OECD countries, particularly the US, Britain, Australia, and New Zealand.]

A recurrent pattern of distributional change in the 1980s was an increase in the income shares of the rich, which was almost invariably associated with a fall in the income shares of the middle class. For many countries, this was a reversal of trends before 1980 . . .

An important feature of these patterns is the degree of synchronization in the timing of distributional changes in countries with very different economic structures and cultures. *Synchronized shifts* can be taken as an indicator that income inequality trends are increasingly being influenced by forces common to all the countries, i.e. *forces which are global in character* . . . This phenomenon [of rising inequality despite, in some cases, growth] appears to be related to a sudden shift in policies giving a much greater role to market forces.

Hundreds of empirical studies document the huge increases in revenue shares at the top of society, the stagnation of wages and the growth of inequality—UNCTAD's data are based on 2,600 such studies.

Advocates of globalization point to the unprecedented creation of wealth in the past decade. Aside from the fact that much of this wealth is fictitious, mere poker chips in the casino economy, globalization has also created unprecedented numbers of losers. One reason is that the most powerful transnational corporations employ very few people relative to their size and are constantly downsizing their staffs. The top 100 corporations have over $4,000 billion ($4 trillion) in sales and account for over 15 per cent of world product yet they employ fewer than 12 million people worldwide. These companies, between 1993 and 1996, increased their sales by 24 per cent yet still managed to reduce their workforce by 0.5 per cent during the same period.[2]

It would be foolhardy to count on global corporations to provide jobs or job security. Even if one includes in the calculations the jobs they create indirectly, these companies employ less than 1 per cent of the world's available workforce. Most foreign investment doesn't lead to job creation either, quite the contrary. Depending on the year, between two-thirds and three-quarters of all so-called foreign direct investment is not devoted to new, so-called 'greenfield' investment but to mergers and acquisitions which almost invariably destroy jobs.

There are also loser nations. Raw material producers, including once powerful oil exporters, are pitted against each other, all exporting a fairly narrow range of products, yet are obliged to increase exports to pay off their debts. According to the most recent World Bank projections, downward pressure on prices will continue for all raw materials—affecting energy, minerals and metals, foods and beverages. This should hardly come as a surprise to the World Bank: with the IMF it has been the principal organizer of a world in which producers are forced to create gluts and can only watch as commodity prices drift lower and lower on world markets. The more they produce, the greater their poverty.

For a long time, many people believed that the Asian Tiger model could be generalized and would prove that globalization could work for everyone. Aside from the obvious fact that the four original tigers—Taiwan, Korea, Singapore, Hong Kong—have a population of only 65 million and the equally obvious fact that not everyone can win in the export markets, the financial crisis has shown how fragile the gains of the tigers really were. They too have learned what it is to become victims of competition.

What about losers at the individual level? What, exactly, does it mean for a person to be a loser in a globalized world economic system; to be among the 'rest' in a system that takes the best and leaves the rest?

Neoliberalism and the kind of globalization it has spawned are entirely based on competition. This means that ordinary people, even skilled people, have little or no protection. Anyone can be ejected from the system at any time—for reasons of illness, pregnancy, age, perceived failure, or for no particular reason at all. We could ask one of the victims of those *Newsweek* once labelled as 'Corporate Killers', like Mr Albert Dunlap, affectionately known as Chainsaw Al. This celebrated downsizer wrote a book titled *Mean Business* in which he explains how heartlessness pays off. It was very satisfying to me, and I'm sure to all other lovers of poetic justice, to learn that Chainsaw Al had himself been sacked last summer. But at least he was honest and made no bones about the fact that competition is brutal and violent.

To learn what it means to be a loser, we could also ask the homeless and the unemployed in Europe, or one of the 40 million Americans with no health insurance, or perhaps an ordinary Mexican. After the 1994–5 financial crisis and devaluation in Mexico, 28,000 small and medium sized businesses failed and half the Mexican population dropped below the poverty line. Sixty per cent of Mexicans are now reckoned as poor. A year or two ago, the Asian Tigers were the World Bank's poster children. Today, literal starvation has returned to Indonesia. A sharp increase in suicides has taken hold in Korea and Thailand where workers no longer see any hope. They kill themselves and their families: locally, these deaths are known as 'IMF suicides'. In Russia, life-expectancy rates for men have plummeted by seven years in less than a decade, an unheard-of occurrence in the twentieth century. Africa and its populations are virtually dropping off the map.

Unfortunately, no one responsible for the forward march of globalization has a clue what to do with the losers. But it's clear that the creation of untold numbers of unprotected, excluded people has profound implications for politics. It will necessarily shape all our lives and will pose stark choices. And it will naturally force organizations like Amnesty to step beyond their traditional boundaries.

For centuries, the central question of politics was who rules whom. Everything revolved around hierarchy and everyone knew exactly his or her place in that hierarchy. You sought favours from those above while dispensing them to those below you. This order began to break down in the eighteenth century and since then, particularly since the Second World War, the central question of politics has been who gets what share of the pie. Groups vie with other groups, petitioning governments more or less peacefully in order to increase their share.

But I would submit that politics in the twenty-first century will not be primarily about either of these questions, although naturally, aspects of both hierarchy and pie-sharing will remain. The really big, central question will be a quite different one.

If neoliberal globalization is allowed to endure, politics will concern primarily the deadly serious issue of survival. This is the bottom-line issue of human rights: who has a right to live and who does not? Do people who contribute nothing to the market economy either as producers or consumers—and one can easily foresee that there will be hundreds of millions of such people—do such people have the right to survive and to live decently or not? I am talking

23

about the kind of radical exclusion from the economic system which results in death.

My book *The Lugano Report*[3] is posited on a deep fear of the answer to that question—who has a right to survive? We are already witnessing in everyday life a radical separation between the 'best and the rest'. The people I call the fast castes, the transnational elites, are moving ever-upwards, leaving more and more slow, defenceless, rooted people behind.

How can we guarantee the human rights of those that globalization leaves behind? This is the same as asking what obligations, if any, have the fast castes to the slow ones, the best to the rest? This is the ethical question that needs to be tackled. The highly educated, highly skilled people of today will, on the whole, reap more material rewards from the world economy than any previous highly skilled and highly educated generation. This is because the system, so long as it continues on its present course, will necessarily continue to move money and power to the top. I believe that this power will, more and more, include power over life and death.

In other words, this advantaged young generation will have to decide how to deal with the losers or how to avoid having losers to begin with. Every ethical system has grappled with the fundamental problem of the nature of our obligations to other people. The Universal Declaration of Human Rights, now 50 years old, is merely the latest in a long series of answers to the solemn question, 'What do we owe to others?' Every world religion has replied with variations on a single theme. In Christianity it's called the Golden Rule: Do unto others as you would have others do unto you. Though good individuals of all religious persuasions have scrupulously observed this rule, I can think of no time in the entire history of humanity when it has been collectively practised, though some societies have obviously come closer than others and in modern times the welfare state has perhaps come closest of all.

One response of society to this question I personally find not only spurious but dangerous, although my view may well be considered controversial. As exclusion and loser-hood and collective disasters increase, they give rise to collective humanitarian impulses. In France, we have the Restaurants du Coeur, soup kitchens catering to indigents throughout the winter months. You all know about the action of Médecins sans Frontières—Doctors without Borders—in the Third World.

Far be it from me to criticize charitable volunteerism or donations, but it's still fair to say that charity for the system's losers will never cause them to be included in the social and economic system itself. The point is not charity for the excluded but the defence and the creation of an inclusive society in which people have rights, including the right to belong, as defined in Article 25 previously cited. The virtue required to create such a society is not charity but solidarity, which is not a one-way street but a two-lane highway; it is based on reciprocity. It also requires political choice, human organization, and hard work rather than following the lazy way, which is to allow markets to make all our social choices for us.

Another answer to the ethical question was given by the great Chinese sage Lao-tzu who concludes his timeless Tao-te Ching with these words: *'Above all, do not compete.'* Lao-tzu saw a great truth. Competition is at the root of many social ills, but his advice in the context of neoliberal globalization is about as welcome as saying 'Above all, do not breathe.'

We could also look to another source, the father of modern capitalism, Adam Smith. Not everyone remembers that Smith was a Professor not of Economics but of Moral Philosophy. He wrote a book called *The Theory of Moral Sentiments* which ought to be read in tandem with *The Wealth of Nations*. In this book, Smith develops the notion of what he calls 'fellow-feeling', which is basically the human instinct for fairness and justice. Adam Smith also believes we necessarily refrain from certain actions because we have great regard for the 'good opinion of others'; we respect those Smith calls the 'spectators' who observe, or could observe, our behaviour. Here is a short passage from *The Theory of Moral Sentiments*:

In the race for wealth, honours and preferment [a man] may run as hard as he can and strain every nerve and muscle in order to outstrip all of his competitors. But if he should jostle or throw down any of them, the indulgence of the spectators is entirely at an end. It is a violation of fair play which they cannot admit of.

Smith could thus not imagine that competition would lead to exclusion—in his words, we would not 'jostle and throw down' other people because natural, built-in, human ethical impulses and the desire for the good opinion of the 'spectators' would prevent such an outcome. Smith's ideas may have been valid in the eighteenth-century England of the Enlightenment, when capitalism was mostly local and people were rooted in their communities, but these ideas seem sadly outdated today.

Globalization as now conceived places in direct competition people who will never meet, so that, as Thomas Hobbes said, 'Every man is enemy to every man'. Such competition creates the well-known 'race to the bottom' with regard to labour rights and environmental standards as countries compete for foreign direct investment. Everyone is at the mercy of his neighbours who may be able to provide the same labour or product or service or raw material at a lower cost, regardless of the social and human consequences.

In neoliberal doctrine, however, competition is the central value and always seen as a virtue. It is good and necessary that all people, firms, regions, and nations compete because this is supposed to lead to optimum allocation of resources whether physical, natural, financial, or human.

Furthermore, in neoliberal doctrine, the problem of 'jostling and throwing down' other people and excluding them does not even arise because the goal and the obligation of industrial, service, or financial firms is to 'increase shareholder value'. Since this obligation is central, and by definition ethical, it follows that whatever increases shareholder value is good and whatever decreases it is bad. In such a scenario, there is no room for obligations to staff, to suppliers, to the community, or to the nation in which one happens to be located.

From these central principles of neoliberal virtue—competition and the obligation to increase shareholder value—one can derive secondary principles which characterize this ethical universe.

One such secondary principle is that *capital must have total freedom to cross borders*, whereas labour is rooted and cannot migrate freely. Capital can therefore seek out the best conditions for its employment, whereas people cannot.

Taxation should be avoided as far as possible because it reduces profits and shareholder value. *The Economist* says that in the past 20 years or so, taxes on capital and self-employment in Europe have dropped from 50 per cent of total receipts to under 35 per cent; in the United States, taxes on corporations are down from 27 per cent to 17 per cent of the total. According to the US Treasury, three-quarters of foreign businesses in the US pay no taxes at all. Transfer pricing or creative accounting, still according to the Treasury, results in losses estimated at anything from $12 to $50 billion annually in revenues.

Even the IMF is alarmed. Emerging market economy countries often give companies extraordinary tax concessions which the beneficiaries then use with their home countries to extract tax reductions there as well. The IMF calls this well-orchestrated process 'tax degradation, whereby some countries change their tax systems to raid the world tax base and export their tax burden'.[4]

In the political context, a system based on solidarity as opposed to charity, a rights-based system as opposed to an unregulated market free-for-all and competition, translates as taxation with redistribution to the less privileged. It requires the creation and maintenance of services including health care and education to which all citizens have access. When mobile international capital escapes taxation, as it increasingly does, it makes social protection much more difficult to pay for. It places heavy downward pressure on rights people thought they had won once and for all. Virtually all the gains of the past 50 years, if not the past century and a half, are suddenly up for grabs. Governments are trying to wind down their commitments and of course they also tax local salaries, wages, and consumption more heavily to make up for the loss caused by tax degradation.

Another principle of neoliberal doctrine is that *the private should always take precedence over the public and the state should stay out of business's way.* Government should confine its activities to creating a favourable climate for the proper operation of markets and to its judicial, police, and defence functions. This concept is sometimes referred to as the 'night watchman state'.

But this is a contradiction, since business invariably profits from state expenditure: public schools supply it with literate, productive personnel; road and rail transport brings that personnel to work; the health care system keeps employees in good shape, etc. However, as already noted, someone else is expected to pay for these conveniences. National taxpayers are also supposed to pay for the bailout of firms like Crédit Lyonnais, Chrysler, the Savings and Loans, the Japanese banks, etc. According to neoliberal doctrine, the welfare state is bad and wasteful when it provides allocations to citizens, but good when it provides them to businesses that have made disastrous mistakes.

A further principle derived from the principle of competition is that *one person's crisis is another person's opportunity for enrichment*. In competitive market terms, behaviour based on solidarity would be the height of foolishness. Rival firms and nations must, rather, seize their own advantage. The recent Asian crisis, arguably caused or at least worsened by the sudden withdrawal of volatile foreign capital, has resulted in windfalls for global business. *The International Herald Tribune* reported recently how foreign investors are 'snapping up' Thai and Korean companies and banks. Not surprisingly, these purchases are expected to result in 'heavy layoffs'.[5]

In other words, the result of years of work by thousands and thousands of Thais and Koreans is being transferred into foreign corporate hands. Many of those who laboured to create that wealth have already been, or soon will be, left on the pavement. This is clearly 'jostling and throwing down' on a huge scale, yet under the principles of competition and maximizing shareholder value, such behaviour is seen not merely as normal but as virtuous.

I could go on, and in particular would have liked to discuss environmental rights and obligations to the earth, but that is outside the scope of this essay. Let me sum up here: I see little hope for the losers, little hope for an ethics of solidarity and human rights so long as our economy is based exclusively on the values of competition, shareholder value, and profit maximization, and not on human needs, fulfilment, and inclusion.

But I don't want to end on such a depressing and pessimistic note. Let me at least try to recommend remedies that do not require the utter demise of world capitalism, an objective not even I am utopian enough to propose, or at least not yet. I don't even want capitalism to reach the terminal crisis it seems so bent on attaining because of the enormous human suffering it would create—I've already given a few examples of human costs from Asia, Mexico, and Russia. What rights-based rules would be in the longer-term interest of a stable society, without which markets—and indeed capitalism itself—can't work properly? Now I'm entering the realm not of what is, but of what ought to be.

The first rule is to *stop deifying the market*. The market can do many things well and should be allowed to do those things without hindrance. But it makes no sense to expect the market to make ethical choices for society. Only politics can do that. Democratic politics should decide what role the market should play, as a servant, not a master. The market is not God and it is not its job to dictate rules to society. Oscar Wilde reportedly said, 'Socialism is all very well but it takes too many evenings.' Well, democracy does too, and someone, preferably everyone, has to put in those evenings.

The second rule is *look to the well-being of the system as a whole, not simply that of the top 20 per cent or the profits of firm X, Y, or Z*. Cancer of the body occurs when certain cells want all the resources and space for themselves and multiply until they devour the whole body, which means that the cancerous cells die too because they have killed their host.

Marxists say it's not possible to change the rules, that capitalism will always engender its own crises, that its own avidity, greed, and iron laws will be its undoing. The daily papers seem to bear them out—look at the way the present unregulated system creates financial crisis; look at the way anarchic investment is creating huge overcapacity in production; look at the way the obsession with downsizing and reducing labour costs is getting rid of potential customers. Henry Ford said, 'I pay my workers so they can buy my cars' but his capitalist wisdom breaks down at the international level.

If the Marxists are right and the neoliberal, globalized system is incapable of policing itself, then we are on the road to the global accident. If such an accident occurs, human rights, including the right to survive, will be the first casualties. How does one avoid such a dire outcome? This is the test of neoliberal globalization. Can it recognize that the current model will necessarily produce and exacerbate poverty, crime, social exclusion, and conflict?

The Masters of the Universe, the leaders of globalization, have met in Davos in 2001 under the auspices of the World Economic Forum. Their self-declared objective is to 'shape the global agenda' and their themes at Davos, because they're getting more and more scared, were 'Responsible Globalization' and 'Governing Globalization'. So they may be pulling back from triumphalism, but they didn't get far. Let's write their governing charter for them.

They *should take the lead in designing equitable international taxation systems,* including a Tobin Tax on all monetary and financial market transactions and taxes on transnational corporation sales on a pro-rata basis. By that I mean that if you sell 15 per cent of your goods in France, you pay 15 per cent of your taxes, at a flat worldwide fee, in France, end of story. The first brokerage house that proposes to tax its own transactions will get the kind of public relations boost money can't buy. The receipts should be applied to reducing the North–South gap and to applying Article 25 of the Universal Declaration throughout the world.

Legitimate businesses and banks should be begging governments to get rid of tax havens and so-called fiscal paradises like the Caymans, Gibraltar, etc. Whatever helps criminals, particularly the drug economy, is harmful to the system as a whole and who knows better than business, their lawyers, and their consulting firms how to close the loopholes?

Business should accept that it has responsibilities not just to share-holders but to employees, suppliers, and the communities and nations where it is located, as well as to the environment.

Let me sum up now. The neoliberal model has been deliberately designed by mostly Western economists, Western politicians, international financial institutions, corporate and banking leaders—in other words, the sorts of people who met in Davos. Their claim that everyone will eventually benefit from their model is demonstrably false. Their system is a vast, planetary experiment which I deeply fear is going to blow up. That's the bad news.

The good news is that neoliberal globalization is not the natural and normal condition of mankind and it has not been put in place by God or by supernatural decree. What human beings have designed, human beings can reshape and reform. They can seek to restore power to communities and states while working to institute democratic rules and fair distribution at the international level. They can recognize that business and the market have their place, but it can't take up the entire space of human existence.

Further good news is that there is plenty of money sloshing around out there and a tiny fraction, a ridiculous, infinitesimal proportion of it would be enough to provide a decent life to every person on earth, to supply universal health and education, to clean up the environment and prevent further destruction to the planet, to close the North–South gap. In other words, it is well within the realm of human possibility, right now, to apply Article 25.

I suppose for me the basic philosophical issue is whether or not human systems, particularly the one we are living in now, are rational. Is this system capable of saving itself and the rest of us with it, or is it like a small child which, left alone with a box of matches, will set fire to the house? I can't answer this question, but what I do feel sure of is that this generation will be the last to get a shot at solving the problem, because if not the system will generate increasingly dramatic crises, collapse under its own weight, and take us all down with it.

So in a sense, it's the same old refrain that has to be brought up to date: 'We must love one another or die.'[6] That is, ultimately, the *raison d'être* of Amnesty and I am proud to have been a part of the Oxford Amnesty Lecture Series.

Response to George

Michael B. Likosky

It is popular to view the post-Second World War period as an era of growth and prosperity. Free enterprise has produced untold wealth and opportunity and, for those persons either permanently or temporarily unable to compete, the welfare state ensured that none would be left behind. With the end of the Cold War, so the narrative typically proceeds, the last impediment to state intervention in the market was overcome. Globalization and privatization thus represent a natural progression to a higher economic order. The free market system has at last come of age and the desirability and need for planned economies such as the welfare state have outworn their use and outstayed their welcome. Opportunity abounds and individual rather than structural impediments are all that stand in the way of creating one's own piece in the ever-expanding pie of global capitalism.

In the preceding essay 'Globalizing Human Rights', Susan George erodes the myths and ideologies of inclusion, unlimited opportunity, and progress underpinning the rhetoric of globalization. Instead, according to George, globalization 'is convenient shorthand for *de facto* exclusion'. The twin pillars of privatization and globalization are ensuring that the publicly financed and produced peace dividend is deposited into the bank accounts of the few. The virtual caste system in which we now live is in part the result of an ongoing looting of the public purse initiated shortly after the close of the Second World War and accelerated during the 1980s. By contrasting the rhetoric of globalization with 'actually existing globalization', George demonstrates the chasm between ideological representation and real-world practice. This comment will further elaborate upon one such incongruity raised in the article—the 'principle of neoliberal doctrine . . . that the private should always take precedence over the public and the state should stay out of business's way' and the reality of a state that regularly intervenes in the economy to support the commercial interests of businesses.

George refers to this principle as the 'night watchman state', in which government conduct is confined to 'creating a favourable climate for the proper operation of markets and to its judicial, police and defence functions'. Under this minimalist conception of the state, the role of law is to set forth neutral rules of the game, rather than to promote a specific set of private interests. This guise of neutrality, however, masks the extensive role of the state in favouring business interests. Identifying the incongruity, George explains,

But this is a contradiction, since business invariably profits from state expenditure: public schools supply it with literate, productive personnel; road and rail transport brings that personnel to work; the health care system keeps employees in good shape, etc. However, as already noted, someone is expected to pay for these conveniences. National taxpayers are also supposed to pay for the bailout of firms like Crédit Lyonnais, Chrysler, the Savings and Loans, the Japanese banks, etc. According to neoliberal doctrine, the welfare state is bad and wasteful when it provides allocations, but good and prudent when it provides them to businesses that have made disastrous mistakes.

Under this minimalist model, the state promotes and ensures corporate welfare by passing on the negative costs of business conduct to the general public. The state provides a social safety net for the rich, while disclaiming responsibility for the welfare of its owners—the public.

My response will discuss the genesis of the twentieth-century, business-friendly oligarchic state and its transnational circulation. First, the usurpation of state control in fully-industrialized countries by a small group of political and commercial actors will be highlighted. Second, the role of powerful governments, international organizations, and trans-national corporations (TNCs) in the transnational promoting of this oligarchic state model will be examined. Lastly, a specific project, Fibreoptic Link Around the Globe (FLAG), devoted to laying a fibre optic cable around the world, will be discussed to illustrate how private companies rely upon olig-archic states to carry out their global projects. Since the oligarchic state, by definition, represents a cartelizing of con-trol by the few over a popularly owned institution, the pro-jects themselves are subject to the possibility of a reassertion of popular control over the state. To demonstrate the significance of the fact that the political system authors the commercial order, the discussion of the FLAG project will highlight opportunities for strategic intervention to further public control over commercial decision-making.

Oligarchizing the State

Although discussions of the relationship between the state and private sectors in the second half of the twentieth century generally focus on the rise of the welfare state, an equally important synergetic phenomenon has characterized the period—the oligarchizing of the state by politicians and pri-vate commercial actors. In a frequently cited 1964 article,

Charles Reich argued that the marbelizing of the state was so extensive that a 'new property' had arisen, distinct from public and private property. Among other synergies, according to Reich, the Cold War period was characterized by a sharing of 'sovereign power . . . with large private interests'. Reich explained:

First, the impact of governmental power falls unequally on different components of the private sector, so that some gain while others lose. Second, the government largess often creates a partnership with some sectors of the private economy, which aids rather than limits the objectives of those private sectors. Third, the apparatus of government power may be utilized by private interests in their conflicts with other interests, and thus the tools of government become private rather than public instrumentalities.[1]

Concurring, in 1963, Michael D. Reagan spoke of the merging of public and private sectors, arguing,

While public attention has been largely directed at conflicts between government and business, a much more significant development has gone relatively unnoticed: the gradual erasure of long-standing distinctions between private and public economic activities, and, as a result, the increased amalgamation of the sectors.[2]

In the US, much of this amalgamation occurred in the defence sector. To wage the Cold War, the government made extensive use of federal contracts with private companies. High technology is a well-known product of this partnering, however, as Reagan explained, the public/private network was vast and irreducible to a single industry or product:

A kind of decentralization by contract ('federalism by contract' Don K. Price has called it) is involved here, with national policies carried out to local areas through contracting firms rather than through subordinate layers of government. Each prime contractor, for example, has been required in recent years to maintain a sub-contracting office whose public task is to seek out small business suppliers. This is done in order to counteract the main trend in defense contract awards, which concentrates prime contracts among a very small number of firms—for example, each year approximately two-thirds of such contracts go to 100 firms. Whether such a program can be very effective may be doubted, but that is irrelevant to the fact that private business firms are acting as *de facto* antitrust administrators under this system.[3]

This intermingling of the public and private sectors was accelerated in a number of ways. For instance, congressional committees charged with disbursing private sector contract awards were staffed by members of the private sector. Also, the government financed private sector lobbying for government defence contracts.[4]

With the institution of privatization programmes around the world in the 1980s and the end of the Cold War, the welfare state has been dismantled while the oligarchic state has emerged unscathed. Privatization has witnessed a dramatic extension of a federalism by contract into almost all walks of life. The welfare state has itself been transformed into this mode of governance as the pursuit of the public welfare has been ceded to private commercial companies. Despite the shift to a profiteering from public service model, the government has often maintained itself as the financier and licenser of these enterprises. For instance, in the United Kingdom, the government has established the Public Finance Initiative which determines which companies will be granted lucrative public service contracts.

Another synergetic relationship involving a proactive government partner is exampled by prison privatization in the

US. For example, in Washington State, the government has provided a private company—Microjet—with an opportunity to capitalize on incarceration. Microjet is a precision metal company, employing prisoners of the Washington State Penitentiary in Monroe. The use of prison labour has reduced company costs and bequeathed such a competitive advantage to the company that other companies in the sector have sued Microjet. The lawsuit alleges that the advantages of free rent and a disciplined, motivated, and captive labour force has provided Microjet with an unfair advantage. While the lawsuit has been brought against Microjet, the state also benefits financially from contracting out its inmates, receiving 20 per cent of worker salaries for prison operating costs.

The oligarchic state has not been limited to fully industrialized countries. In fact, these countries have actively exported this state model. In doing so, they have encouraged proactive foreign government support for the interests of Western businesses travelling abroad.

Exporting Oligarchic Institutions

During the postwar period, neoliberals have generally portrayed 'free market' countries as adhering to minimalist conceptions of the state. To the extent that the free market is constrained by public welfare concerns, it represents an outmoded approach. For instance, writing the introduction to the fiftieth anniversary of F. A. Hayek's *The Road to Serfdom*, the Chicago free market economist Milton Friedman remarks that 'it is only a little overstated to say that we preach individualism and competitive capitalism, and practice socialism'.[5] As Friedman makes clear through example, he is here concerned with the post-Cold War persistence of welfare states, rather than with the intransigence of the oligarchic state. Providing a transnational air to his discussion, Friedman cites approvingly those states devoted to the 'free market'—including Egypt, Formosa, Hong Kong, Israel, Japan, Malaysia, Singapore, and Thailand—as countries in which the free market is the primary vehicle for growth. While these countries were indeed US allies during the Cold War, all were oligarchic states whose 'business-friendly' approaches were promoted by the fully industrialized countries, international organizations, and TNCs.

Following the decolonization movements of the second half of the twentieth century, many newly formed states instituted planned economies. The Swedish sociologist Gunnar Myrdal provides the following definition of planned economies:

The basic principle in the ideology of economic planning is that the state shall take an active, indeed the decisive, role in the economy: by its own acts of investment and enterprise, and by its various controls—inducements and restrictions—over the private sector, the state shall be rationally coordinated, and the coordination be made explicit in an overall plan for a specified number of years ahead.[6]

The proliferation of planned economies outside the Soviet satellites was typically brushed under the carpet by free market ideologues who preferred to view these countries as free market economies. Just as they ignored the state intervention in their own economies, US and European governments similarly downplayed the role of the state in their overseas allies' commercial affairs. The leaders of the planned economies in developing countries, however, drew inspiration from 'Western' planners as well as the Soviet Union and China.[7]

Throughout the postwar period, developing countries have been actively encouraged by foreign actors to adopt the oligarchic state model. For instance, as Myrdal notes, the initial adoption of planned economies involved significant foreign intervention:

both private businesses and governments in the West . . . are interested in the existence of an overall plan into which the special projects are fitted and which can render it more likely that they will not fail. Quite apart from, and often contradicting, their ideological preferences at home, all Western governments as well as their business people are supporters of state planning . . . Where planning has lagged . . . the International Bank has been prepared to send experts to help formulate a plan. . . . the intergovernmental organizations, governments, private foundations, and universities have supplied personnel for planning.[8]

The international promotion of proactive business-friendly states has continued throughout the postwar period. For instance, foreign governmental and non-governmental actors systematically have promoted export processing zones, territorially delimited jurisdictions with a regulatory regime distinct from the rest of the country and devoted to catering to foreign businesses, creating a 'world factory system' for TNCs.[9] The World Bank (WB), the United Nations Conference on Trade and Development (UNCTAD), the United Nations Industrial Development Organization (UNIDO), the United Nations Centre on Transnational Corporations (UNCTC), TNCs, and foreign governments have widely advocated employing this oligarchic technology.

Oligarchic states have proliferated during the postwar period. As these states have entrenched themselves, a path dependency has ensued. The cartel of public and private actors in control of these states has increasingly relied upon the oligarchic model for legitimizing their commercial projects. In doing so, the interests of the owners of these public institutions have taken second place to the short-term desires of those dignitaries currently in control. So attenuated is control from ownership, that this transnational cartel has accorded a primacy to the commercial order to the detriment of the political order from which the commercial order's legitimacy derives.

Since the political system validates the commercial order, the oligarchy is vulnerable to a reassertion of control by the owners of public institutions. As the transnational commercial order is extensive and reliant at multiple junctures on a myriad of political systems, there are multiple opportunities for strategic intervention by owners.

'Let's Hope We Never Have to Find Out'

Although Susan George rightly identifies the wide-scale expulsion of the public from the transnational commercial order, she also makes clear that the commercially disenfranchised maintain political rights. If successfully mobilized and coordinated, these political actors may subvert commercial interests and reassert control over their states and lives. George thus argues that a latent narrative of empowerment coexists with the transnational commercial order. Political entrepreneurs, according to George,

can seek to restore power to communities and democratic States while working to institute democracy, the rule of law and fair distribution at the international level. They can recognize that business and the market have their place, but this place cannot occupy the entire sphere of human existence.

With this strategic-methodological aim in mind, opportunities for intervention existing within the FLAG project will be examined.

In 1995, US West finalized an agreement for the construction of FLAG. This 1.5 billion US dollar project would run a fibre optic cable from the United Kingdom to Japan. In the process, it would link up twenty-five political jurisdictions. While underwater telegraphic cables had been laid at the close of the previous century, this project represented the first ever privately initiated and financed transnational communications link of this size and scale. FLAG would form the hard infrastructure of the emerging global information economy. Although privately initiated, FLAG was only as strong as the public guarantees of the twenty-five licensing authorities involved in legitimizing the project.

While private actors would benefit commercially from this undertaking, governments were heavily involved in ensuring its success. Not only would each jurisdiction along the way have to grant valuable licences to run cable through their sovereign territories, but also insurance would be provided by the Export–Import Bank of the US. The licensing system would provide private companies with the right to sell their products to consumers. These licences thus represented a state cessation of public property to private actors. Unbeknownst to citizens of the constituent states, their governments had offered them up as consumers to private companies.

Regardless of whether FLAG was ultimately advantageous to citizens of the participant nations, its success depended upon the ongoing political acquiescence of each government and its population. To mitigate risk that a government would grant a licence and then repeal it, the private companies sought insurance from the US government through its

Export–Import Bank, which provides insurance against 'political risk'. As licensing approval by many states, under customary practice, involved not responding to faxed applications to licensing authorities, such risk was palpable. The feared volatility of this endeavour was acknowledged by A. Jay Baldwin, the Vice President and Chief Financial Officer of FLAG, who when asked about what the company would do if a constituent country revoked its licence, responded: 'Let's hope we never have to find out'.[10]

The fear expressed by Baldwin derived from the reliance upon popularly attenuated oligarchic states. The FLAG project has been chosen here to illustrate the volatility inherent in reliance on oligarchic states rather than because the project itself necessitated a disaster for the publics involved. Although these publics were not appropriately internalized into the decision-making process of the project, an evaluation of whether the project will produce public goods will have to wait for some time. In the meantime, however, it is clear that a number of private actors have benefited financially from the project. It is equally clear that the ongoing success of globalization and its fellow traveller, privatization, is not a foregone conclusion.

To the extent that the powers of the state have been cartelized and actively employed to promote an anti-democratic commercial order, we can agree with Susan George that the order itself remains volatile and subject to reassertion of public control. By juxtaposing the political rhetoric of globalization with its operation in practice, in non-quixotic fashion George identifies both the attenuation of the system and points to opportunities for strategic intervention.

2

'Recovering Rights': A Crooked Path

Noam Chomsky

The Confucian *Analects* describe the exemplary person—the master himself—as 'the one who keeps trying although he knows that it is in vain'. The thought is not easy to suppress at the 50th anniversary of the signing of the Universal Declaration of Human Rights (UD).

Regular human rights reports provide sufficient testimony to the dismal story, which continues to the present, as always including the major powers. To mention only one current example, the 'collateral damage' of the latest US–UK bombardment of Iraq merits little notice,[1] taking its place alongside the wanton destruction of a major African pharmaceutical plant a few months earlier, and other trivia.

And trivia they are, viewed against the background of other exploits: in Washington's 'backyard', for example, the liberal press was giving 'Reagan & Co. good marks' for their support for state terror in El Salvador as it peaked in the early 1980s, urging that more military aid be sent to 'Latin-style fascists . . . regardless of how many are murdered' because 'there are higher American priorities than Salvadoran human rights', and that Nicaragua be restored to the 'Central American mode' of El Salvador and Guatemala under a 'regional arrangement that would be enforced by Nicaragua's neighbours', the terror states then busy slaughtering their populations with US aid.[2] The comments are from left-liberal sectors; the rest take a harsher line.

Interpretations are different a step removed. A Jesuit-organized conference in San Salvador considered the state terrorist project that peaked in the 1980s and its continuation since then by the socioeconomic policies imposed by the victors. Its report noted the effect of the residual 'culture of terror' on 'domesticating the expectations of the majority vis-à-vis alternatives different to those of the powerful'.[3] The great achievement of the terror operations has been to destroy the hopes that had been raised in the 1970s, inspired by popular organizing throughout the region, the overthrow of the Somoza dictatorship, and the 'preferential option for the poor' adopted by the Church, which was severely punished for this deviation from good behaviour.

The Jesuit report generalizes to much of the Third World; and also to growing numbers at home, as the Third World model of sharply two-tiered societies is internationalized. The real world was captured in remarks by the Secretary-General of the United Nations Conference on Trade and Development (UNCTAD), which was established 'to create an international trading system consistent with the promotion of economic and social development'. Representing the UN at the 50th anniversary of the world trade system (GATT, WTO, etc.), he observed that 'no one should be fooled by the festive atmosphere of these celebrations. Outside there is anguish and fear, insecurity about jobs, and what Thoreau described as "a life of quiet desperation".'[4] The event received ample coverage, but the media preferred the festive atmosphere within.

The devastating consequences of Hurricane Mitch in October 1998 were graphically reported, but not their roots in the 'economic miracle' instituted by 'Latin-style fascists' guided by US experts—a development model geared towards a 'high level of poverty and [of] favouritism towards the minority while the majority has just the minimum to survive', a conservative Honduran bishop observed, condemning new programmes that will perpetuate the disaster. He was quoted in a rare discussion of its causes by a veteran Central America journalist who observes that hopes for change were terminated by the US-trained armies that 'caused the disappearance of the most vocal proponents of sharing the land', along with hundreds of thousands of others.[5] A fuller picture is far more grim, and instructive, but I will put it aside.

The direct impact of the hurricane is reviewed in the research journal of the Jesuit University in Managua. The analysts ask: 'Did Mitch have a class bias?' The hurricane had a devastating effect on poor farmers, who 'have been pushed into the most ecologically fragile zones, those least appropriate for agriculture': Posoltega, for example, the site of the murderous mudslide that horrified the world. A few miles away, the San Antonio refinery, 'one of Nicaragua's most emblematic economic emporiums', made out well, as did agro-export industries generally, benefiting from the rains on the fertile soil they monopolize. Basic crop production (corn and beans) was ruined, a disaster for the farmers and the general population. Reconstruction is directed to magnifying the same distinctions in a 'New Nicaragua', highly regarded for its impressive economic growth, while the population sinks to Haitian levels. That includes funds from abroad as well as the domestic institutions, redesigned to satisfy the requirements of the international financial institutions. Credit, research, and policy generally are being directed even more than before to provide 'services exclusively to those who can pay for them', undermining what is left of agrarian reform. 'The class bias' of the hurricane and the aftermath is not 'divine will or [a] mythical curse against the poor' but 'the result of very concrete social, economic, and environmental factors'.[6] The story again generalizes to much of the world.

A side effect of the hurricane was to scatter tens of thousands of land mines that are a relic of the Nicaraguan component of Washington's terrorist wars of the 1980s. Fortunately, a team of de-mining experts was sent to help—from France. The facts were reported in the pacifist press.[7] The lack of concern in a more obvious place is not surprising in view of the reaction to far more extreme human rights violations of a similar sort, proceeding as I write. Perhaps the most striking example is the human toll of the anti-personnel weapons littering the Plain of Jars in Laos, the scene of the heaviest bombing of civilian targets in history, it appears, and arguably the most cruel: this furious assault on a poor peasant society had little to do with Washington's wars in the region.

The episode is called a 'secret war'—secret by choice; information was readily available.[8] The choice of silence extends to the aftermath. Estimates of current casualties range from hundreds a year to 'an annual nationwide casualty rate of 20,000', more than half of them deaths, a veteran Asia correspondent of the *Wall Street Journal* reports, in its Asia edition. Unlike landmines, these tiny bomblets, components of cluster bombs, are designed specifically to kill and maim. The victims are mostly children who pick up the colourful 'bombies' or farmers who dislodge them while attempting to clear the remnants of hundreds of millions of these devices. The bomblets have an estimated 'failure to explode' rate of 20–30 per cent and were only a fraction of the technology deployed, which included advanced missiles to penetrate caves where families sought shelter.

Efforts to publicize and deal with the continuing atrocities have been led by a US Green Beret veteran and an English businessman/journalist who has worked in Asia. The Mennonite Central Committee has been active there since 1977, joined later by the British-based Mine Advisory Group (MAG), Nobel Peace prize co-laureate in 1997. The US is 'conspicuously missing from the handful of Western organizations that have followed MAG', the British press reports, though it has finally agreed to train some Laotian civilians. MAG specialists report that the US refuses to provide them with 'render harmless procedures' that would make their work 'a lot quicker and a lot safer'. These remain a state secret, as does the whole affair in the United States. Citing the primary agency responsible for de-mining in Cambodia, the Bangkok press reports similar problems with 'bombies', particularly in the Eastern region where US bombardment from early 1969 was most intense.[9]

The earliest and always prime target of the US wars in Indochina were South Vietnamese civilians. There too children continue to be killed by unexploded US bombs, arousing little interest or even report.[10] But there is occasional mention of the chemical warfare programme initiated by the Kennedy Administration, destroying crops and forests and leaving hundreds of thousands dead or suffering cancer and hideous birth deformities. A prominent Israeli correspondent reporting from Vietnam was reminded of 'what we heard during the trials of Eichmann and Demjanjuk'. We should pay more attention to the matter, the quality press occasionally recommends, noting that Vietnam provides an 'ideal laboratory' and 'controlled environment' to study the effects of chemical warfare. 'South Vietnam was sprayed, North Vietnam was not', hence Vietnam provides an 'ideal location for more research into potential links between dioxin and cancer, reproductive dysfunction, hormone problems, immune deficiencies, disorders of the central nervous system, liver damage, diabetes and altered lipid metabolism', particularly among the 'many women and children' affected. Much could be learned of potential benefit to Americans from this experiment. But the research opportunity is being lost. European and Japanese aid efforts have gained no US support, because 'The US, emotionally spent after losing the war, paid no heed'.[11]

The last comment is not entirely accurate. Washington achieved its primary war aims, and its absence from aid efforts cannot be attributed solely to emotional distress. The error was corrected by the *New York Times* correspondent just quoted on the possible usefulness to us of an inquiry into the effects of chemical warfare in Vietnam. She pointed out that interactions with Vietnam have been hampered by lack of progress on resolving the issue of Americans missing in action. There might have been progress under President Carter, but his 'efforts to open links to Hanoi were thwarted by Vietnam's invasion of Cambodia in 1978', terminating Khmer Rouge slaughter. That outrage required still harsher punishment, duly administered with the cooperation and support of those who now demand the right of 'humanitarian intervention'. When Vietnamese withdrawal could no longer be concealed, the MAI (Multilateral Agreement on Investments) problem resumed its place as the sole moral issue remaining from a war that left millions of corpses in Indochina and three countries devastated. Expectations for diplomatic relations between the US and Vietnam 'may be set back by a resurgence of interest in one piece of unfinished business that will not go away: the fate of missing Americans'.[12]

Two years ago, however, the Clinton Administration

announced that 'the dialogue between the United States and Vietnam has moved beyond the single issue of identifying the remains of prisoners of war', a lead story reported.[13] The occasion was the agreement by the Vietnamese government 'to repay' $140 million of debts owed to the US by its client state in the South, 'many of those debts . . . incurred to bolster the South's war effort'—the war effort of the client state established by Washington as part of its war against the South, later all of Indochina. Though Vietnam has still not agreed to repay the 'vast sums . . . in direct military assistance' that the US provided to its Saigon client, Washington is willing to drop trade sanctions, a forthcoming step towards 'the end of a raw chapter in American history'. Vietnam is at last beginning to acknowledge its crimes against the United States, recognizing—as President Bush admonished—that we do not seek 'retribution for the past', merely an honest accounting. The adjacent front-page story reports Japan's puzzling failure to 'unambiguously' accept the blame 'for its wartime aggression'.[14]

President Bush might, perhaps, have felt that President Carter moved too far towards 'moral equivalence' when he stated that we owe Vietnam no debt and have no responsibility to render it any assistance because 'the destruction was mutual', eliciting no comment.[15] As the 50th anniversary of the UD approached, the national press once again reported Japan's inexplicable failure to acknowledge fully its war guilt, unlike the US, where 'some of the key architects of the American involvement in Vietnam . . . now admit that it was a colossal mistake for the US to commit its young men and funds to that effort'. For accuracy, it should be added that in dramatic opposition to elite opinion across the spectrum, a large majority of the population continue to regard the war *not* as a 'mistake', but 'fundamentally wrong and immoral'—a remarkable phenomenon for almost 30 years, since public attitudes receive virtually no support from articulate opinion.[16]

New Rights?

Let us move on to the general setting in which the rights that have been sought gain their life and substance.

The UD broke new ground in significant respects. It enriched the realm of enunciated rights, and extended them to all persons. In a major law review essay on the 50th anniversary, Harvard Law Professor Mary Ann Glendon observes that the Declaration 'is not just a "universalization" of the traditional 18th-century "rights of man", but part of a new "moment" in the history of human rights . . . belong[ing] to the family of post-World War II rights instruments that attempted to graft social justice onto the trunk of the tree of liberty', specifically Articles 22–7, a 'pillar' of the Declaration 'which elevates to fundamental rights status several "new" economic, social, and cultural rights'. It is fair to regard the UD as another step towards 'recovering rights' that had been lost to 'conquest and tyranny', promising 'a new era to the human race', to recall the hopes of Thomas Paine two centuries ago.[17]

Glendon stresses further that the UD is a closely integrated document: there is no place for the 'relativist' demand that certain rights be relegated to secondary status in light of 'Asian values' or some other pretext.

The same conclusions are emphasized in the review of the human rights order issued by the United Nations on the 50th anniversary of the Charter, and in its contribution to the first World Conference on Human Rights at Vienna in June 1993.

In his statement opening the conference, the Secretary-General 'stressed the importance of the question of inter-dependence of all human rights'. Introducing the 50th-anniversary volume, he reports that the Vienna conference 'emphasized that action for the promotion and protection of economic and social and cultural rights is as important as action for civil and political rights'.[18]

The Vatican took a similar stand in commemorating the 50th anniversary of the UD. In his 1999 New Year's Day message, Pope John Paul II denounced Marxism, Nazism, fascism, and, 'no less pernicious', the ideology of 'materialist consumption' in which 'the negative aspects on others are considered completely irrelevant' and 'nations and peoples' lose 'the right to share in the decisions which often profoundly modify their way of life'. Their hopes are 'cruelly dashed' under market arrangements in which 'political and financial power is concentrated', while financial markets fluctuate erratically and 'elections can be manipulated'. Guarantees for 'the global common good and the exercise of economic and social rights' and 'sustainable development of society' must be the core element of 'a new vision of global progress in solidarity'.[19]

A tepid version of the Vatican's 'post-liberation theology', as it is called, is admissible into the free market of ideas, unlike the liberation theology it replaces. The latter heresy 'is almost, if not quite, extinct',[20] commentators inform us. The modalities of extinction have been consigned to their proper place in history, along with the archbishop whose assassination opened the grim decade of Washington's war against the Church and other miscreants, and the leading Jesuit intellectuals whose assassination by the same US-backed 'Latin-style fascists' marked its close. The two theologies differ in one particularly critical respect. The 'preferential option for the poor' that somehow became extinct encouraged the poor to participate in shaping their own social world, while the tolerable version of the replacement asks them only to plead with the rich and powerful to share some crumbs. In the tolerable version, the Church is to 'rattle the conscience' of the rich and powerful, instructing them in 'Catholic values of generosity and self-sacrifice' instead of organizing Christian based communities that might offer people a way to exercise the 'right to share in the decisions which often profoundly modify their way of life' that has been transmuted to a plea for more benevolent rule as it passed through the doctrinal filters.

Glendon observes that recent discussion is mistaken in supposing that socioeconomic and cultural rights were included in the UD 'as a concession to the Soviets': on the contrary, support was 'very broad-based'. We may recall that such ideals were deeply entrenched in antifascist popular forces in Europe and in the colonial world, and among the population of the United States as well. These facts were profoundly disturbing to US political and economic elites, who had a different vision of the world they intended to create. They expressed their concerns about 'the hazard facing industrialists' at home in 'the newly realized political power of the masses', and about the 'new aspirations' among populations abroad who were 'convinced that the first beneficiaries of the development of a country's resources should be the people of that country' rather than US investors. The steps taken to overcome these hazards constitute major themes of postwar history, matters that I have to put aside here, despite their evident relevance.

There were some, of course, who dismissed the UD with contempt as just a 'collection of pious phrases', the oft-quoted remark of Soviet delegate Andrei Vyshinsky, whose own record need not detain us; or as 'a letter to Santa Claus. . . . Neither nature, experience, nor probability informs these lists of "entitlements", which are subject to no constraints except those of the mind and appetite of their authors'—in this case, Reagan's UN Ambassador, Jeane Kirkpatrick, deriding the socioeconomic and cultural provisions of the UD. A few years later, Ambassador Morris B. Abram described such ideas as 'little more than an empty vessel into which vague hopes and inchoate expectations can be poured', a 'dangerous incite-ment', and even 'preposterous'. Abram was speaking at the UN Commission on Human Rights, explaining Washing-ton's rejection of the right to development, which sought to guarantee 'the right of individuals, groups, and peoples to participate in, contribute to, and enjoy continuous economic, social, cultural and political development, in which all human rights and fundamental freedoms can be fully realized'. The US alone vetoed the Declaration, thus implicitly vetoing the Articles of the UD that it closely paraphrased.[21]

Despite the relativist onslaught, the UD is surely worth defending. But without illusions: the world's most powerful state has been a leader of the relativist camp, and even within the subcategory of human rights it professes to uphold, 'there is a persistent and widespread pattern' of abuses, Amnesty International concludes in a recent review.[22]

The call for the 1999 Amnesty International lectures asks whether the rights articulated in the UD are indeed 'a uni-versal good', or does 'the spread of the idea of human rights across the globe symbolize the West's success in universalizing its own moral code', as critics often allege? It is a fair question, but we should not overlook the assumptions that underlie it. About these, three questions arise: (1) What ideals does the

West profess? (2) How do these relate to practice? (3) How does the practice conform to the UD—or to some higher standard, since that is surely not the end of the road?

The West is heterogeneous and diverse. I will keep here largely to the world-dominant power, an appropriate choice because of its influence, its stable and long-lasting democratic institutions, the accolades it commonly receives as leader in the crusade for human rights, and its substantial achievements in some central areas, notably protection of freedom of speech from state interference—a real achievement, though a recent one, it is well to recall, one of the many advances of the 1960s. These considerations aside, neither history nor logic suggests that some different distribution of state power would have led to more favourable outcomes.

Naturally practice is far more significant than ideals proclaimed. No one is impressed by the uplifting words of Stalin's Constitution, or the condemnation of Western crimes by Taliban leaders. It is the merest moral truism that the prime concern should be the predictable consequences of one's own actions, or inaction. That simple truth holds whatever the relative scale of crimes may be, more forcefully when those that fall to one's own account are by no means slight.

The terrible atrocities of official enemies elicit justifiable horror—at appropriate moments at least, as we have recently observed once again. Saddam Hussein's crimes are now familiar to everyone, particularly the ultimate horror for which he is rightly denounced, most passionately in the US and UK as they unilaterally bombed Iraq once again in December 1998: the use of chemical weapons in warfare and even against his own population. Clearly such a creature must be destroyed. Commonly ignored—and in the US virtually banned from discussion—is the fact that these crimes cannot possibly be the reason for the current outrage, given the reaction when they occurred. Those who now profess great indignation continued to welcome the monster as a privileged friend and ally. The discovery of Saddam's biological warfare facilities shortly after his gassing of Kurds elicited instant official denials; the same sites are now offered as proof of his ultimate evil. The US eagerly offered subsidized food supplies that the regime needed after its destruction of Kurdish agricultural production, along with advanced technology adaptable to military production, some specifically designated 'for protection of the head of state'. A delegation of prominent US Senators, including Republican leader Robert Dole, visited Saddam in Kurdish Mosul in April 1990, bringing President Bush's greetings and assuring him that his problems do not lie with the US government, but with some journalists, whom he should invite 'to come here and see for themselves' to overcome their misconceptions, Senator Simpson advised. The performance reminded an Israeli Mideast historian of the Munich encounter. There is no need to review Britain's role.[23]

After the Gulf War, Saddam received a tacit grant of authority to slaughter Shi'ites and Kurds—a necessity, to maintain 'stability', the leaders of the free world proclaimed, also reiterating their official ban against contacts with opposition leaders. US allies Israel and Turkey opposed efforts to save the Kurds, Turkey with ambivalence because of its own repression of Kurds (just then escalating to extremes of brutality), Israel out of concern over the 'territorial, military, contiguity between Teheran and Damascus' if Kurds gain independence, views extending from the departing Chief of Staff to leading doves.[24]

Washington's preference for a military dictatorship that would rule Iraq with an 'iron fist', just as Saddam had done, was endorsed by respected commentators. Tacitly acknowledging past policy, Secretary of State Albright announced in December 1998 that 'we have come to the determination that the Iraqi people would benefit if they had a government that really represented them'.[25] We need not tarry on the plausibility of the delayed conversion; the fact that the words can be articulated, eliciting no comment, is informative enough.

Conversions with regard to the suffering of the Kurds have occurred with some frequency and with delicate specificity, closely tracking power interests.[26] The story continued when Saddam shifted from favoured friend to reincarnation of Attila the Hun after committing the crime of disobedience, apparently the first one that mattered. High policy required toleration of his renewed assault on Iraqi Kurds, later an intricate record of support and betrayal by their alleged protectors. By the mid-1990s attacks on Kurds by Washington's Turkish ally reached new levels of violence; one index is the flight of over a million Kurds from the devastated countryside to the unofficial Kurdish capital Diyarbakir from 1990 to 1994, many more later. 1994 marked two records: it was 'the year of the worst repression in the Kurdish provinces' of Turkey, Jonathan Randal reported from the scene, and the year when Turkey became 'the biggest single importer of American military hardware and thus the world's largest arms purchaser', using the gifts in ways that Saddam doubtless appreciated. The mounting terror, still underway, made an impressive contribution to the ethnic cleansing of the 1990s, leaving about 3,500 villages destroyed, tens of thousands killed, some 2 to 3 million refugees, right within NATO and under the jurisdiction of the Council of Europe and the European Court of Human Rights, which regularly hands down sentences. When human rights groups exposed Turkey's use of US jets to bomb villages, the Clinton Administration found ways to evade laws requiring suspension of arms deliveries, much as it was doing in Indonesia and elsewhere. Most military aid is in direct violation of US law, from the lead recipients on down, as human rights organizations have been protesting for years; in vain, and with only the rarest mention.[27]

Policy goals are revealed most clearly in nearby regions, where there are few impediments apart from the domestic population. The outcome of US intervention, intensified in the 1980s, has plausibly been described as 'guardian democracy', 'truncated and militarized forms of democracy' that retain the links with US military and intelligence that helped establish and sustain the national security states of the past 30 years, but now with 'the procedural trappings of democracy such as formal elections as long as the regimes in question welcome US investment and political guidance'. In a scholarly review of the political outcome of the recent version, Thomas Carothers—who writes with an 'insider's perspective', having taken part in 'democracy enhancement' programmes in Reagan's State Department—concludes that Washington sought to maintain 'the basic order of . . . quite undemocratic societies' and to avoid 'populist-based change', 'inevitably [seeking] only limited, top-down forms of democratic change that did not risk upsetting the traditional structures of power with which the United States has long been allied'.[28]

Nonetheless, Carothers regards the 'liberal critique' as fundamentally flawed, leaving 'the old debate unresolved'.[29] The 'perennial weak spot' of the 'liberal critique' is that it offers no alternative to the policy of establishing and sustaining terror states and 'traditional structures of power'. A theoretical alternative comes to mind: according the people of the region, the right to make 'the decisions which often profoundly modify their way of life'. But that option is not part of 'the debate', hence need not be rejected.

The guiding principle has distinguished origins, among them the thoughts of the eminent eighteenth-century moral philosopher Frances Hutcheson, who held that the principle of 'consent of the governed' is not violated when the rulers impose plans that are rejected by the public, if later on these 'stupid' and 'prejudiced' objects 'will heartily consent' to what has been done in their name. The doctrine was labelled 'consent without consent' by an American sociologist justifying the slaughter of hundreds of thousands of Filipinos by their liberators. 'We have the consent of our own consciences', President McKinley explained, and in 'obeying a higher obligation' the 'liberator' should not 'submit important questions . . . to the liberated while they are engaged in shooting down their rescuers', failing to comprehend God's will. It is enough that in time, survivors may come to accept the humanitarian intervention.[30]

The assumptions have rarely been challenged, or even recognized. The implications for the promise of the UD need no comment.

Current policy has new guises, but otherwise has changed little with the end of the Cold War. The Center for International Policy in Washington recently observed that 'the closeness and significance of the US military relationship' with Latin America has scarcely changed, apart from 'rationale'. Much the same holds for the Middle East, where the fall of the Berlin Wall brought the official concession that the significant 'threats to our interests' that required military engagement 'could not be laid at the Kremlin's door'. The same is true of weapons sales and giveaways worldwide, in sharp conflict with announced policy, including some of the most 'repressive or warring governments'.[31] And much more. Simple questions arise about the actual roots of policy, but I will again put the topic aside, despite its evident bearing on Western ideals and practice, and the Universal Declaration.

The Economic Order and Human Rights

I mentioned the internal linkage of the components of the human rights regime, but the integration extends beyond. The human rights regime was one of three related pillars of the New World Order established by the victors in the aftermath of the Second World War. A second was the political order articulated in the UN Charter; the third the economic order formulated at Bretton Woods. Let us take a brief look at these components of the projected international system, focusing on the human rights dimension.

The Bretton Woods system functioned into the early 1970s, a period sometimes called the 'Golden Age' of postwar industrial capitalism, marked by high growth of the economy and progress in realizing the socioeconomic rights of the UD. These rights were a prominent concern of the framers of Bretton Woods, and their extension during the Golden Age was a contribution to translating the UD from 'pious phrases' and a 'letter to Santa Claus' to at least a partial reality.

One basic principle of the Bretton Woods system was regulation of finance, motivated in large part by the understanding that liberalization could serve as a powerful weapon against democracy and the welfare state, allowing financial capital to become a 'virtual Senate' that can impose its own social policies and punish those who deviate by capital flight. The system was dismantled by the Nixon Administration with the cooperation of Britain and other financial centres. The results would not have surprised its designers.

For the major industrial powers, the period since has been marked by slower growth and the dismantling of the social contract, notably in the US and Britain. In the US, the recovery of the 1990s was one of the weakest since the Second World War and unique in American history in that the majority of the population has barely recovered even the level of the last business cycle peak in 1989, let alone that of a decade earlier. The typical family puts in 16 weeks of work a year beyond the level of 20 years ago, while income and wealth have stagnated or declined. The top 1 per cent has gained enormously, and the top 10 per cent have registered gains, while for the second decile, net worth—assets minus debt—declined during the recovery of the 1990s. Inequality, which steadily reduced during the Golden Age, is returning to pre–New Deal levels. Inequality correlates with hours of work. In 1970, the US was similar to Europe in both categories, but it now leads the industrial world in both, mostly by wide margins. It is alone in lacking legally mandated paid vacation. Open government complicity in corporate crime during the Reagan years, sometimes accurately reported in the business press, and continuing since, has severely undermined labour rights. All this proceeds in direct conflict with the UD—that is, with the parts that are denied status under the prevailing relativism.[32]

A concomitant of current social policy is the need to deal with the superfluous population. One mechanism has been the 'drug war'.[33] When the latest phase was proclaimed by the President ten years ago, one of the few Senators to pay attention to social statistics, Daniel Patrick Moynihan, observed that the timing and design amounted to a decision 'to have an intense crime problem concentrated among minorities'. 'The war's planners knew exactly what they were doing', criminologist Michael Tonry comments, spelling out the details. The cynicism was highlighted by the coincidence of the presidential declaration of war, generating media furor, with simultaneous proceedings that were virtually ignored: Washington's resort to the threat of severe trade sanctions to force Asian countries to accept US-produced lethal drugs and advertising directed to vulnerable sectors—another opium war, the ultra-conservative Surgeon-General charged, to no effect.[34]

Thanks primarily to carefully contrived 'drug wars', the prison population has risen sharply. Twenty years ago, US incarceration rates were similar to those of other industrial societies. Today they are 5–10 times as high, a world record among countries with meaningful data. It is generally recognized that the 'war on drugs' has no significant effect on use of drugs or street price, and is far less effective than educational and remedial programmes. But it makes sense as a device to remove 'disposable people', as they are called in US client states, and to frighten the rest. 'Under the rhetoric of equality', an eminent jurist observed, Congress 'envisions the criminal process as a vast engine of social control' (former Chief Judge Bazelon).

The Amnesty International report I mentioned earlier is one of many that document the abuse of fundamental human rights associated with this engine of social control. There is ample evidence to support the conclusion of the human rights organizations and many criminologists that these processes undermine even the most traditional rights incorporated in the UD, including Articles 5, 7, and 9.

The press regularly reports 'an age of almost unparalleled prosperity' in the US that Europe should aspire to emulate, and a 'remarkably successful US economy'.[35] The reports are based primarily on 'the return on capital achieved by American companies'—which has indeed been 'spectacular', as the business press has been exulting through the Clinton years—and the vast increase in stock prices, which has conferred remarkable prosperity upon the 1 per cent of families who own almost half the stock and the top 10 per cent who hold most of the rest, and who jointly are the beneficiaries of 85 per cent of the gains of asset values in the 'fairy tale economy'. Good deeds do not pass unnoticed. President Clinton was 'likened to Martin Luther King, Jr and generally celebrated at a Wall Street conference' in mid-January 1999, the press reported, citing the president of the New York Stock Exchange, who 'told Mr Clinton that Dr King was surely smiling down on the gathering' at the annual King memorial, recognizing how Clinton had benefited 'my little corner of southern Manhattan'.[36] Other little corners fared somewhat differently.

The fairy tale was attributed in part to 'greater worker insecurity' by Federal Reserve Chair Alan Greenspan, citing a near-doubling of the proportion of workers fearing layoffs in large industries from 1991 to 1996. Other studies reveal that 90 per cent of workers are concerned about job security. In a 1994 survey of working people, 79 per cent of respondents said efforts to seek union representation are likely to lead to firing, and 41 per cent of non-union workers said they think they might lose their own jobs if they tried to organize. Decline in unionization is generally taken by labour economists to be a significant factor in the stagnation or decline of wages and the deterioration of working conditions.[37]

Polls also report 'consumer confidence'; it is tempered,

however, by the observation that 'expectations have dimin-ished'. The Director of the University of Michigan's Survey Research Center comments that 'it is a little like people are saying, "I am not earning enough to get by, but it is not as bad as it could be", while in the '60s they thought, "How good can it get?" '[38]

For the 'developing world', the post–Bretton Woods era has been largely a disaster, though some escaped, temporarily at least, by rejecting the 'religion' that markets know best, to borrow the words of the Chief Economist of the World Bank. He points out that the 'East Asian miracle', which is 'historic-ally unprecedented', was achieved by a significant departure from the prescribed formulas, though its rising star, South Korea, was badly damaged after agreeing to liberalization of finance in the early 1990s, a significant factor in its current crisis, he and many other analysts believe, and a step towards 'Latin Americanization'. Latin American elites experience far greater inequality and a 'weaker sense of community than found among nationalistic East Asian counterparts', and are 'connected more with foreign high finance'—factors that enter into their 'avid pursuit of European and US high-style consumption and high culture', international economist David Felix points out. 'Mobile wealth has also enabled Latin America's wealthy to veto progressive taxes and limit outlays on basic and secondary education while extracting generous state bailouts when suffering financial stress', a typical feature of free market doctrine for centuries.[39]

In his highly regarded history of the international monet-ary system, Barry Eichengreen brings out a crucial difference between the current phase of 'globalization' and the pre-First World War era that it partially resembles.[40] At that time, gov-ernment policy had not yet been 'politicized by universal

male suffrage and the rise of trade unionism and parliamentary labour parties'. Hence the severe costs of financial
rectitude imposed by the 'virtual Senate' could be transferred
to the general population. But that luxury was no longer
available in the more democratic Bretton Woods era, so that
'limits on capital mobility substituted for limits on democracy
as a source of insulation from market pressures'. It is therefore
natural that the dismantling of the postwar economic order
should be accompanied by a sharp attack on substantive democracy and the principles of the UD, primarily by the US and
Britain.

There is a great deal to say about these topics, but with
regard to the human rights aspect, the facts seem reasonably
clear and in conformity with the expectations of the founders
of the Bretton Woods system.

The Political Order and Human Rights

The third pillar of post–Second World War world order,
standing alongside the Bretton Woods international economic system and the UD, is the UN Charter. Its fundamental principle is that the threat or use of force is barred,
with two exceptions: when specifically authorized by the
Security Council, or in self-defence against armed attack
until the Security Council acts (according to Article 51).
There is no enforcement mechanism apart from the great
powers, decisively the US. But Washington flatly rejects the
principles of the Charter, both in practice and official
doctrine.

The practice we need not review. With regard to the doctrine, in the early years it was generally confined to internal
documents, as in 1947, when the first memorandum of the

newly formed National Security Council (NSC 1/3) called for military intervention in Italy and national mobilization at home 'in the event the Communists obtain domination of the Italian government by legal means'—a danger thwarted by control of food supplies and other modes of subversion. Or in 1954, after the 'disaster' of a diplomatic settlement of the first Indochina war, when the National Security Council called for a broad range of covert actions throughout the region, and even possible attack on China, in the event of 'local Communist subversion or rebellion *not constituting armed attack*'— (my emphasis); the phrase articulates with intended clarity the rejection of the UN Charter. The decisions are repeated verbatim annually through the 1950s, and have yet to enter history. The same fate has befallen the official definition of 'aggression' to include unwelcome internal political development; not only 'overt armed attack from within the area of each of the sovereign states' but 'aggression other than armed, i.e., political warfare, or subversion'.[41]

Guiding principles gained some public expression in the early 1960s, as when UN Ambassador Adlai Stevenson declared that in Vietnam the US is defending a free people from 'internal aggression'—what President Kennedy called the 'assault from the inside' as he escalated from state terror to assault from the outside. The essential point was expressed by Dean Acheson in 1962, when he justified the blockade of Cuba by informing the American Society of International Law that the 'propriety' of a US response to a 'challenge . . . [to the] . . . power, position, and prestige of the United States . . . is not a legal issue'. 'The real purpose of talking about international law was, for Acheson, simply "to gild our positions with an ethos derived from very general moral principles which have affected legal doctrines".'[42]

The main innovation of the past 20 years is that contempt for the principles of world order has become completely open. Thus the Reagan Administration justified its bombing of Libya as 'self-defense against future attack', hence permissible under Article 51. Israel's bombing of Tunis in 1988, killing 75 people, was carried out with US cooperation, though Secretary of State Shultz drew back from his public approbation when the UN Security Council unanimously denounced the bombing as an 'act of armed aggression' (the US abstaining). The World Court was dismissed on the official grounds that many members of the UN 'cannot be counted on to share our view of the original constitutional conception of the UN Charter.' and 'this same majority often opposes the United States on important international questions'; hence we must 'reserve to ourselves' the right to decide when Court rulings apply, and will not 'accept compulsory jurisdiction over any dispute involving matters essentially within the domestic jurisdiction of the United States, as determined by the United States'—in this case, the US actions against Nicaragua that were condemned by the Court as 'unlawful use of force'. Meanwhile Secretary of State George Shultz declared that 'negotiations are a euphemism for capitulation if the shadow of power is not cast across the bargaining table', condemning those who advocate 'utopian, legalistic means like outside mediation, the United Nations, and the World Court, while ignoring the power element of the equation'. His remarks, not without precedent in modern history, were timed to coincide with the bombing of Tripoli and Benghazi, killing many civilians, the first bombings in history planned for prime time TV.[43]

In the Clinton years, all pretences have been dropped. UN Ambassador Albright, now Secretary of State, informed the

Security Council that Washington will resort to force 'multilaterally when we can, unilaterally when we must', to secure its interests, unconstrained by solemn treaty obligations. In the December 1998 Iraq crisis, the official stand was that 'we prefer to act through our allies', but will resort to force alone if we so choose. We do not even 'prefer' to act through the United Nations, as required by international law, for the evident reason that it does not endorse our actions; not even regional allies do.[44]

The principles were further illustrated during debates about deployment of OSCE monitors in Kosovo in October 1998. European powers wanted to ask the Security Council to authorize the deployment. Washington, however, refused to allow the 'neuralgic word "authorize"', the *New York Times* reported, though it did finally permit 'endorse'. The Clinton Administration 'was sticking to its stand that NATO should be able to act independently of the United Nations'. A leading strategic analyst explains that 'to require the Security Council's blessing would essentially hand them a veto over our policy', as articulated in the UN Charter.[45]

Similar conclusions had been drawn by British counterparts. Foreign Secretary Douglas Hurd instructed Parliament that Article 51 entitles a state to use force 'in self-defence against threats to one's nationals'. He was speaking in support of Clinton's 'justified and proportionate exercise of the right of self-defence' when he launched missiles against Iraq, on grounds that Iraqis might—or might not—have been involved in a failed assassination attempt against an ex-President two months earlier. There would be a 'dangerous state of paralysis' in the world, Hurd continued, if the US were required to gain Security Council approval before undertaking such actions.[46]

'The basic US view', one senior-level European diplomat commented, 'is that the era of the UN is over', and the US will rely on NATO and the World Trade Organization. At least when they are reliable; not, for example, when the US rejected WTO authority in response to EU charges concerning Washington's Cuba embargo, the harshest of any, barring even food and (effectively) medicine, and declared a violation of international law even by the judicial organ of the normally compliant Organization of American States.[47]

The framework of world order has long ceased to exist, even in words, as the rhetoric has become too inconvenient to sustain. The approved principle is the rule of force. The sophisticated understand that an appeal to legal obligations and moral principle is legitimate as a weapon against selected enemies, or 'to gild our positions with an ethos derived from very general moral principles', in Dean Acheson's words. But nothing more than that. The level of support for this stand among educated sectors should not be taken lightly. The human rights implications require no comment.

Increasingly, the 'legal basis' in international law for the unilateral resort to force is held to be the principle of 'humanitarian intervention'. The legal basis would be hard to find, but the issue does reflect an inconsistency of spirit, at least, in the postwar international order: the UN Charter guarantees state sovereignty, but the UD implicitly rejects it. One might argue, then, that international law should be modified to provide a legal basis for humanitarian intervention.

The matter is of great human significance. I will have to put it aside here, noting only that in the years ahead there is likely to be regular appeal to highly selective versions of the doctrine of 'humanitarian intervention'. The right to undertake it, in practice, is restricted to the states powerful enough to exert their will without concern for international law, treaty obligations, world opinion, or institutions of world order, a virtual truism recognized 50 years ago by the World Court, which determined in the Corfu Channel case that 'The Court can only regard the alleged right of intervention as the manifestation of a policy of force, such as has, in the past, given rise to most serious abuses and such as cannot, whatever be the defects in international organization, find a place in international law . . . From the nature of things, [intervention] would be reserved for the most powerful states . . .' The operative choices are a regime of international organization, 'whatever be its defects', or the use of force by the powerful as they choose. They must also be assured a compliant intellectual class to interpret what they do as right and just, possibly a 'mistake' if 'benign intentions' go awry. The historical record suggests that these conditions will not be hard to satisfy, and also provides substantial evidence concerning the likely consequences.

It should come as no surprise that 'emerging norms of humanitarian intervention' became a major topic immediately after the Cold War ended. With the deterrent gone and nonalignment a fading memory, the concerns of most of the world's population can be disregarded, and the self-identified 'enlightened' and 'civilized' states can return to their historic mission, under guises that are hardly novel.

In brief, of the three pillars of the post–Second World War international order, two—the Bretton Woods system and the Charter—have largely collapsed. And the third, the UD, remains to a large extent 'a letter to Santa Claus', as the leaders of the relativist crusade contend.

Rights for Whom?

As widely noted, a major innovation of the UD was the extension of rights to all persons, meaning persons of flesh and
blood. The real world is crucially different. In the US, the
term 'person' is officially defined 'to include any individual,
branch, partnership, associated group, association, estate, trust,
corporation or other organization (whether or not organized
under the laws of any State), or any government entity'.[48] That
concept of 'person' would have shocked James Madison,
Adam Smith, or others with intellectual roots in the
Enlightenment and classical liberalism. But it prevails, giving a
cast to the UD that is far from the intent of those who formulated and defend it.

Through radical judicial activism, the rights of persons have
been granted to 'collectivist legal entities', as some legal his-
torians call them; and more narrowly, to their boards of directors, 'a new "absolutism"' bestowed by the courts.[49] These
newly created immortal persons, protected from scrutiny by
the grant of personal rights, administer domestic and international markets through their internal operations, 'strategic
alliances' with alleged competitors, and other linkages. They
demand and receive critical support from the powerful states
over which they cast the 'shadow' called 'politics', to borrow
John Dewey's aphorism, giving no little substance to the fears
of James Madison 200 years ago that private powers might
demolish the experiment in democratic government by
becoming 'at once its tools and its tyrants'. While insisting on
powerful states to serve as their tools, they naturally seek to
restrict the public arena for others, the main tenet of 'neoliberalism'. The basic thesis was expressed well by David
Rockefeller, commenting on the trend towards 'lessen[ing]

the role of government'. This is 'something business people tend to be in favour of', he remarked, 'but the other side of that coin is that somebody has to take government's place, and business seems to me to be a logical entity to do it. I think that too many business-people simply haven't faced up to that, or they have said, "It's somebody else's responsibility; it's not mine." '[50]

Crucially, it is not the responsibility of the public. The great flaw of government is that it is to some degree accountable to the public, and offers some avenues for public participation. That defect is overcome when responsibility is transferred to the hands of immortal entities of enormous power, granted the rights of persons and able to plan and decide in insulation from the annoying public.

Current policy initiatives seek to extend the rights of 'collectivist legal persons' far beyond those of persons of flesh and blood. These are central features of such trade treaties as NAFTA and the MAI, the latter temporarily derailed by public pressure, but sure to be reconstituted in some less visible form.[51] These agreements grant corporate tyrannies the rights of 'national treatment' not enjoyed by persons in the traditional sense. General Motors can demand 'national treatment' in Mexico, but Mexicans of flesh and blood will know better than to demand 'national treatment' north of the border. Corporations can also (effectively) sue national states for 'expropriation'—interpreted as failure to meet their demands for free access to resources and markets—and are doing so, with some success, setting precedents for more imaginative procedures.

Even without such a formal grant of extraordinary rights in radical violation of classical liberal principles, something similar follows from the role of these collectivist entities as 'tools and tyrants' of government and masters of doctrinal systems. One illustration is Article 17 of the UD, which states that 'no one shall be arbitrarily deprived of his property'. In the real world, the 'persons' whose rights are most prominently secured are the collectivist entities, under a doctrine, formulated in the same years as the UD, which affirms the right to 'adequate, effective, and prompt compensation' for expropriated property at 'fair market value', as determined by those in a position to enforce their will. The formula, attributed to Roosevelt's Secretary of State, Cordell Hull, has been termed the 'international minimum standard of civilization' in respected treatises of international law.[52]

Criteria for application of the formula may appear inconsistent on the surface, but not when real–world factors are taken into account. The formula is the basis for US economic warfare against Cuba for 40 years, justified by the charge that Cuba has not met this 'minimum standard of civilization'. The formula does not, however, apply to US investors and the US government, who took the properties at the turn of the century when Cuba was under US military occupation. Nor does it apply to the US government and private powers who stole Spanish and British possessions in Cuba and the Philippines at the same time—for example, the Spanish-owned Manila Railway Company. After the bloody conquest of the Philippines, the US threw out the Spanish concession because it 'had been inspired by Spanish imperialistic motives'— unlike the US possessions that Cuba nationalized when it was at last taken over by Cubans in 1959.

The formula also does not apply to the founding of the United States, which benefited from expropriation of British possessions and those of loyalists, who were probably as

numerous as the rebels in the civil war with outside intervention known now as the American Revolution. New York
State alone gained close to $4 million by taking loyalist prop-
erty, a considerable sum in those days. In contrast, the formula
does apply to Nicaragua. The US compelled Nicaragua to
withdraw the claims for reparations awarded by the World
Court, and, after Nicaragua capitulated on all fronts, the
Senate voted 94 to 4 to ban any aid until Nicaragua meets the
international minimum standard of civilization: returning or
giving what Washington determines to be adequate compensation for properties of US citizens seized when Somoza fell,
assets of participants in the crimes of the tyrant who had long
been a US favourite, including wealthy Nicaraguan exiles
who are retroactively US citizens.

Laws and other instruments are 'spider webs', a popular
seventeenth-century poet wrote: 'Lesser flies are quickly ta'en
/ While the great break out again.'[53] Some things change,
others persist.

The Right to Information

The immortal collectivist persons are easily able to dominate
information and doctrinal systems. Their wealth and power
allow them to set the framework within which the political
system functions, but these controls have become still more
direct under recent Supreme Court rulings defining money as
a form of speech. The 1998 election is an illustration. About
95 per cent of winning candidates outspent their competitors.
Business contributions exceeded those of labour by 12 to 1;
individual contributions are sharply skewed.[54] By such means,
a tiny fraction of the population effectively selects candidates.
These developments are surely not unrelated to the increasing

cynicism about government and unwillingness even to vote. It should be noted that these consequences are fostered and welcomed by the immortal persons, their media, and their other agents, who have dedicated enormous efforts to instill the belief that the government is an enemy to be hated and feared, not a potential instrument of popular sovereignty.

The realization of the UD depends crucially on the rights articulated in Articles 19 and 21: to 'receive and impart information and ideas through any media' and to take part in 'genuine elections' that ensure that 'the will of the people shall be the basis of the authority of government'. The importance of restricting the rights of free speech and democratic participation has been well understood by the powerful. There is a rich history, but the problems gained heightened significance in this century as 'the masses promised to become king', a dangerous tendency that could be reversed, it was argued, by new methods of propaganda that enable the 'intelligent minorities . . . to mold the mind of the masses, . . . regimenting the public mind every bit as much as an army regiments the bodies of its soldiers'. I happen to be quoting a founder of the modern public relations industry, the respected New Deal liberal Edward Bernays, but the perception is standard, and clearly articulated by leading progressive public intellectuals and academics, along with business leaders.[55]

For such reasons, the media and educational systems are a constant terrain of struggle. It has long been recognized that state power is not the only form of interference with the fundamental right to 'receive and impart information and ideas', and in the industrial democracies, it is far from the most important one—matters discussed by John Dewey and George Orwell, to mention two notable examples. In 1946, the prestigious Hutchins Commission on Freedom of the

Press warned that 'private agencies controlling the great mass media' constitute a fundamental threat to freedom of the press with their ability to impose 'an environment of vested beliefs' and 'bias as a commercial enterprise' under the influence of advertisers and owners. The European Commission of Human Rights has recognized 'excessive concentration of the press' as an infringement of the rights guaranteed by Article 19, calling on states to prevent these abuses, a position recently endorsed by Human Rights Watch.[56]

For the same reasons, the business world has sought to ensure that private agencies *will* control the media and thus be able to restrict thought to 'vested beliefs'. They seek further to 'nullify the customs of ages' by creating 'new conceptions of individual attainment and community desire', business leaders explain, 'civilizing' people to perceive their needs in terms of consumption of goods rather than quality of life and work, and to abandon any thought of a 'share in the decisions which often profoundly modify their way of life', as called for by Vatican extremists. Control of media by a few megacorporations is a contribution to this end. Concentration has accelerated, thanks in part to recent deregulation that also eliminates even residual protection of public interest. In the latest edition of his standard review of the topic, Ben Bagdikian reports a decline in controlling firms from 50 in 1984 to 10 today—huge empires such as Disney and General Electric, though the spectrum has broadened with Rupert Murdoch's entry.[57]

Bagdikian also reviews the ever more blatant 'manipulation of news to pursue the owners' other financial goals', along with those of advertisers, to ensure 'the promotion of conservatism and corporate values', crucially including 'materialist consumption' in which 'the negative aspects on others are considered completely irrelevant'. That process too has been accelerated by the merger/acquisition boom, which has 'consolidated advertising dollars in the hands of a shrinking number of marketers', the *Wall Street Journal* reports in a lead story, describing how 'Advertisers Flex Muscles' to assure that editors 'get the message' about permissible content—but without 'trying to impinge on their editorial integrity', the chief executive of a major ad agency assured the *Journal*.[58]

Young children are a particular focus of the massive onslaught, which extends to regimenting the minds and attitudes of the rest. The controls are to be extended worldwide, and must include the new media created in large measure within the huge state sector of the industrial economy. As a developing country, the US took 'far-reaching precautions . . . to insure that the telecommunications industry remained in US hands', a recent academic study points out; but having achieved global dominance thanks to crucial state intervention, the industry now demands that all others open themselves to 'free competition', so that Article 19 will be effectively nullified worldwide.[59]

The dedication to this principle was revealed with unusual clarity when UNESCO considered proposals to democratize the international media system to permit some access on the part of the vast majority of the world. The US government, together with the media, bitterly condemned UNESCO with a most impressive flood of deceit and lies—uncorrectable, and reiterated without change after refutation, which was rarely permitted expression. 'The stunning irony of this achievement', an academic historian of US–UNESCO relations observes, 'was that the United States, having proved that the free market in ideas did not exist, attacked UNESCO for planning to destroy it'. A detailed review of media and government deceit was published by a university press, but was also ignored. That history provides a revealing measure of the attitudes towards the basic principles of freedom and democracy.[60]

Control of the internet is currently the 'hot issue'. Developed primarily in the state sector for almost 30 years and commercialized against the will of two-thirds of the population, the internet and the web are regarded by the business world as 'the primary platform for the essential business activities of computing, communications, and commerce', as 'the world's largest, deepest, fastest, and most secure marketplace', not only for goods but also for 'selling' ideas and attitudes. They are expected to provide enormous profits, as well as new means to carry forward the mission of civilizing attitudes and belief, if they can be brought under corporate control and commercial sponsorship—that is, if they can be taken from the public, the owner of the airwaves and cyberspace by law, and transferred to a handful of immortal and unaccountable collective 'persons' with extraordinary global power. A primary goal, one trade journalist observes, is 'to turn the once-eclectic Web into the ultimate 24-hour marketing machine'.[61]

New software and technologies are being devised to direct this public creation to marketing, diversion, and other safe activities, undermining the 'once-eclectic' character that has provided a way to escape doctrinal constraints and construct a public counterforce to concentrated power, sometimes to considerable effect. In Indonesia, a visiting Australian academic specialist writes, the internet 'proved a godsend' for communication and 'mobilizing cultural and political activism', with results that are as unwelcome to domestic elites as to the foreign beneficiaries and supporters of the threatened regime, unusual in its corruption and brutality. Another notable recent example is the success of grassroots and public interest organizations in deflecting the state-corporate attempt to institute the MAI in secrecy, an achievement that elicited near-panic, and even the fear that it may become 'harder to do deals behind closed doors and submit them for rubber-stamping by parliaments', as trade diplomats warned. Overcoming these hazards is a high priority for business leaders.[62]

It is only to be expected that private power and its 'tools and tyrants' should seek to ensure that others can do no more than 'keep trying although they know that it is in vain'. But the Confucian judgement is surely too grim. The words are hard to utter after this terrible century, but there has been substantial improvement in many aspects of human life and consciousness, extending an earlier history of progress—agonizingly slow, often reversed, but nonetheless real. Particularly in the societies that are more privileged and that have won a significant measure of freedom, many choices are available, including fundamental institutional change if that is the right way to proceed. We need not quietly accept the suffering and injustice that are all around us, and the prospects, which are not slight, of severe catastrophes if human society continues on its present course.

Response to Chomsky

Alan Ryan

Professor Chomsky's essay provides, as always, an invigorating blast of fresh air that will blow away any complacency about the world's progress towards implementing a serious human rights regime. Much that he says about the violence and brutality either directly employed by the United States in Indochina and elsewhere or employed by those whom the United States had armed, encouraged, and assisted, is well taken. It is also very hard to resist a good deal of what he says about the failure of the US economy to extend the benefits of prosperity to anything more than the top 10 per cent or so of its own population.

But mere acquiescence in Professor Chomsky's views is no service to the reader. I want, therefore, to nag away at two or three issues on which I am at odds with him. None of these affects an assessment of US policy in Latin America, the Vietnam War, and the inadequacies of the American—and British—welfare state. It is perfectly possible to think US policy criminal without having any very deep views about just why that policy is the way it is; one might, and I in fact do, think that its cruelties in Vietnam served no rational purpose, not even the purposes of those who proposed and implemented them. It is also possible to think that the Universal Declaration of Human Rights is something of an intellectual muddle, without thinking that the aspirations it espouses, such as the demand for universal literacy and for paid holidays for working people, are anything other than ones we should endorse. One may simply believe that the idea of a *right* to be literate is confused.

Chomsky's fundamental principle is that American and British foreign policy—their domestic policy too—is driven by the needs of corporate capitalism. This often emerges in the form of what one might call left-functionalism. Right-functionalism was the view, canonical in American sociology in the 1950s, that societies tend to maintain a stable equilibrium in which the psychic, material, and organizational needs of their citizenry are met in the ways that at that place and time are generally felt to be adequate. Left-wing students used to hate it, not least because of the implicit suggestion that anyone who was radically opposed to the political and economic order of modern society was simply deranged— 'maladjusted'.

Chomsky, however, comes perilously close to endorsing what many students of the time who were opposed to these blandly conservative ideas came up with in their place: the thought that capitalist societies function so as to protect the interests of corporate capitalism, otherwise known as 'the system'. Now nobody doubts that rich people will try to hang onto their wealth, that the powerful will try to hang onto their power, and that they will often use disgusting means to do so. But the notion that *everything* that the USA either does or aids others in doing is to be laid at the door of the interests of corporate capitalism seems implausible. Even the critic of American imperialism ought to allow room for some non-instrumental forms of nastiness—Christian arrogance about the supposed benightedness of non-Christians, simple racial prejudice, class prejudice of a non-economic, status-driven kind. Genghis Khan was a mass murderer who, so far as one can see, was driven by a pure lust for power and a desire to see others terrified of him.

It may be that Chomsky does not hold quite the version of left-functionalism that I describe here. Sometimes he seems to hold the sort of simple conspiracy theory that Bertrand Russell held in his later years. At the back of all the atrocities are nameable individuals who decide to perpetrate them—generally, in order to preserve their own wealth and power or at one remove the wealth of their masters. As to why a democracy should endorse—when it does endorse—this sort of wickedness, Chomsky finds the explanation in the manipulation of the mass media, in the hiding of information, and in the subversion of the public's capacity for independent thought. I do not wish to suggest that the persons Chomsky so detests are in fact saintly egalitarians; they manifestly are not. I do want to say that they have very often done evil by mistake and inadvertence. Typically, they have thought that their victims will be moved to cooperate by the threat of coercion, and then find themselves unable to draw back as the stakes are raised, and finally find themselves like Macbeth implicated in a bloodbath they had not expected.

I also want to say that the picture of the manipulation of the public is not wholly coherent. Sometimes the public appears to be an unlikely candidate for deception, as when they are given credit for being quite clear about what has happened and why it is wrong. They are said to be sure that the Vietnam War was immoral, not merely a mistake. Sometimes the information the public lacks is said to be perfectly visible, as it must be when so many of Chomsky's references are to articles from the *New York Times*. But then it is not obvious quite what Chomsky supposes it is that has happened to the public's grip on American (or the British public's grip on British) policy. Have they swallowed lies, had the facts withheld, or merely found their everyday lives too preoccupying to allow them much time for careful examination of these things?

In short, it is much easier to agree that a world in which thousands of children are exposed to the dangers of unexploded ordinance of the ghastliest kind is a world in a very bad way than it is to agree that the entire blame for that state of affairs is to be laid at the door of American foreign policy operating in the interests of capital behind the back of a deceived general public. But this is a lecture provoked by the anniversary of the United Nations Universal Declaration of Human Rights, and I want to say two further things about rights, universalism, and critics of the Declaration.

There is a familiar view that many of the 'positive' rights that the Declaration asserts cannot be rights at all. This is not because the Declaration is a letter to Santa Claus, nor because what they assert that we have a right to is intrinsically absurd or not worth having—a right to jump 30 feet in the air unaided fits both categories. It is because the assertion of a right is the assertion of a right *against* somebody with the correlative duty. When I promise to take my daughter to the movies, she has a right to have me take her, and I have a duty to take her. Because I can easily do it, there is no question about the plausibility of saying she has that right and I have that duty.

Universal rights are trickier. They do not spring from some originating act such as a promise. For this reason, many people have thought that all universal rights should be negative ones, rights to forbearance, or immunities. My right not to be tortured does not require that my government, the country's armed forces, or the local police force should do anything whatever; it only requires that they should *not* do something—that they leave me alone in the crucial respect. Certainly, to make use of this right, we may need institutions whose members have positive duties towards me as well; senior officers in the military have a duty to stop their troops if they start torturing me, and courts have a duty to punish policemen who torment me, and so on. Negative rights may be of very little use—'parchment barriers' as Madison said— without enforcement mechanisms behind them. But in principle, we can meet the obligations that they impose by doing nothing whatever. I can avoid committing murder everywhere on earth without lifting a finger, and in that way I can respect the universal right to life at no cost. But neither I nor anyone else can provide literacy or paid holidays at no cost.

It is not an ignoble view that much of what we need from governments and individuals is covered by these negative duties, and that a lot more is covered by their enforcing the observance of these rights when they are threatened. Governments must control their police and military, but the purpose is not so that they do good things to me, rather that so long as I do not threaten others they leave me alone. But this raises the other point on which I have some anxieties.

It is to me unclear what Professor Chomsky thinks about humanitarian intervention; or rather, it is clear that he thinks that the US will pretend to be moved by humanitarian considerations when it is moved by something else entirely, but unclear whether he thinks that states are entitled to be left alone under all conditions save when they actively invade or attack other states. There is nothing suspect about the rights that wicked governments violate; they are the familiar negative rights not to be tortured, imprisoned, or murdered. The difficult question is who is to enforce those rights when their government violates them. John Rawls and Michael Walzer have grappled with the problem, much as John Stuart Mill did in the nineteenth century. In essence, we are pulled in one direction by the thought that if states are violating the rights of their own subjects we should get in there and stop them doing so, and pulled in the other direction by the difficulties of setting priorities—shall we save the Kurds from the Turks before or after we have saved the Albanians from the Serbs?—and the impossibility of knowing whether the damage we do in effecting the rescue is greater than the damage done to the innocent by their rulers.

To such questions there are no easy answers, and Professor Chomsky does his readers a disservice by sweeping past the arguments in his indignation. Certainly we should feel outrage at the horrors he describes, but if we are to do better than we have, we have also to think our way to some partial solutions. But I shall not end on that note. Years ago I wrote a little book on Bertrand Russell's politics, defending his decision to put aside (what he counted as) philosophy and write not as a philosopher but as an outraged human being, denouncing the political horrors inflicted by business as usual. Professor Chomsky needs no defence, but I intend the comparison to convey both respect and admiration.

3

Food Rights, Free Trade, and Fascism

Vandana Shiva

Free Trade vs. People's Freedom

Free trade has hijacked our most powerful aspiration—the will to be free. It has substituted corporate for personal freedom, and passed off increased freedom for corporations as the expansion of democracy and human rights.

The West has been considered one of the sources of the notion of human rights, but brutality was integral to the Western project of colonialism and imperialism. The North has dominated the South by systematically denying full human status to the Southern peoples. This was first done through the West's 'civilizing mission'—the *white man's burden*; now it is done through globalization and free trade. Globalization is today rewriting the human rights agenda by redefining what being human means.

Naturalizing Domination

The first means used to dehumanize human communities and impose globalization is to 'naturalize' its anti-democratic and coercive structures. Naturalization is a mode traditionally used by colonial powers and patriarchal structures. There is nothing natural or inevitable about globalization—globalization is a project of domination by the North over the South, by corporations over citizens, by patriarchal structures over women, by humans over other species.

Nor is there anything free about free trade; it is the most coercive system imaginable. But it is made to appear 'natural' and inevitable. Bill Clinton's policy was, while President, to promote free trade. Despite the US Congress's rejection of his fast-track proposal, at the 1988 meeting of the WTO in Geneva, he stated, 'globalization is not a policy choice—it is a fact.' The British Prime Minister, Tony Blair, has said, 'whether there should be free trade is not the question now'; free trade is 'an irreversible and irresistible trend'. While these statements were being made, globalization was being reversed in South East Asia.

The statements come from leaders of the G-7 countries, who have bulldozed the South and their own citizens into accepting the rules of globalization. Peter Fitzpatrick has pointed out the contradiction between the 'inevitability' of globalization and the political push for globalization by global powers. 'It may seem a little puzzling why these oracles of the globe go to such extraordinary lengths to bring about something that exists already or is inexorable.'[1]

Fragmenting Freedom: Neither Bread nor Freedom

The second means by which people's freedoms are dismantled under globalization is the dissociation of civil and economic rights. Human rights are indivisible. Freedom from hunger is no less a human right than freedom of speech. Without the former, the latter does not exist.

The Universal Declaration of Human Rights treated the right to social security, the right to work and protection against unemployment, the right to health, food, clothing, and housing as core human rights (Articles 22–5). But over the

50 years since the Universal Declaration of Human Rights was drafted, the human rights agenda has been fragmented. Socioeconomic rights and freedoms have been separated from civil liberties, and then deleted. Human rights have been reduced to civil liberties alone. As a result, both socio-economic rights and civil liberties are being destroyed. A divided notion of human rights has left people without either food or freedom.

The primary human right is the right to life. First and foremost this is the right to be free of hunger. But it includes the freedom to exercise a livelihood so that one's entitlement to food is ensured. The most basic of human rights is today under threat as the right to food is sacrificed to the right to trade.

Once human rights are divided, the erosion of socio-economic rights is no longer perceived as a human rights violation. It then becomes possible to assume that globalization is the globalization of human rights. It is falsely assumed that globalization leads to the higher civil and political rights necessary for articulating dissent, and that these in turn will correct economic injustice and ensure economic rights.

But globalization does not globalize human rights. It globalizes inhuman rights and human wrongs.

Economic Globalization as the Globalization of Inhuman Rights

The globalization of inhuman rights places the rights of corporations above the rights of states and citizens. But the corporation is not a person at all; it is a legal fiction. Treaties like the Uruguay Round of GATT, and institutions such as the WTO, protect and defend the rights of corporations. A system in which the rights of a non-human construction are given higher status than those of people is a system of inhuman rights. Globalization 'humanizes' two fictions: the corporation and money. Money, a construct developed to reflect access to resources, has been personified.

Globalization is in fact the establishment of the rule of corporations over governments and people. People and their rights have been reduced to 'protectionist' forces that interfere in free trade and economic growth. A minority uses the corporate form to dominate the majority. Corporate entities were first equated with privileged human persons, and have now been elevated above people.

Globalization has made the citizen disappear and reduced the state to an instrument of global capital. The fictional persona has displaced the humans on which it was modelled. Their only role is as consumers; the role of human beings as members of productive, cultural communities is being erased. On the one hand this renders human beings dispensable to the process of providing for our needs. On the other, it erodes cultural diversity: the way in which people are shaped by and have interacted with nature to meet their needs.

Rights and Absolute Irresponsibility

Further, while people have rights and responsibilities, the corporation only has rights. The proposed Multilateral Agreement on Investment (MAI), which has been put on hold due to citizen mobilization, is the ultimate statement of rights being vested exclusively in corporations; governments and people are stripped of theirs.

The MAI prevents governments from interfering in foreign investments. The rules of the MAI apply to all levels of government: federal, state, county, and city. Under the MAI, no country could prevent entry by foreign companies. The 'free flow of capital' will be sanctified by MAI. To further empower corporate dominion over nation-states, the MAI gives private corporations and investors 'legal standing' to sue sovereign governments. The former Director-General of the World Trade Organization, Renato Ruggiero, saw the MAI as designed to become the 'Constitution for a single global economy'.

In this new global constitution, the institutions and values that have protected us are being dismantled and criminalized. Food provision, health care, education, and social security are transformed into corporate monopolies under the guise of 'competitiveness' and 'efficiency'. Safety and health regulations are stigmatized as 'protectionism'. The protection of the environment is treated as a form of non-tariff trade barrier that needs to be dismantled. Corporations thus acquire absolute rights without responsibility, and citizens and the state carry all the responsibilities without the corresponding rights.

Free trade rules also globalize inhuman rights in the sense that they force each person to become inhuman; they make greed and competitiveness the organizing principles of society. One of the highest expressions of our humanity is the creation and sharing of knowledge. Intellectual Property Right (IPR) regimes globalized through Trade Related Intellectual Property Rights (TRIPs) make knowledge-sharing a crime.[2] By redefining knowledge as private property, even in areas where knowledge is socially created, they redefine the exchange of knowledge as theft.

In Third World peasant societies, saving seed and exchanging seed is not just a right, it is the highest duty: it is our *dharma*.[3] Seed patents make seed the 'creation' and 'property' of corporations, converting our highest dharmic acts into crimes of piracy and theft. Corporations are reported to have hired detectives to spy on farmers and fined farmers for saving seed.

What is still more ironic is that these patents are claimed on knowledge and resources that have themselves been pirated from the Third World. Examples of such biopiracy include patents on neem, turmeric, ginger, pepper, and basmati, to name just a few.

Patents on life are another example of inhuman rights. They remove us still further from our ecological kinship with other species, and convert life forms and living systems into human 'inventions' and 'property'.

The most significant lesson of the ecology movement is that our humanity is predicated on our being earth citizens. By introducing ownership of life's processes of renewal and regeneration, and by claiming that species are 'inventions' and therefore patenting them as property, we are degraded as humans.

The globalizing of these inhuman rights is the globalization of the values of one part of one culture—the patriarchal, capitalist structures of the West. It violates all other cultures, in the West and elsewhere.

The Right to Food vs. the Right to Trade

When the World Food Summit took place in Rome in 1996, the Food and Agriculture Organization (FAO) estimated that malnutrition affected 800 million people, compared with 450 million at the time of the first Food Day in 1981. Enshrining the right to food should therefore be the highest priority of all national and international policies. Instead, at the World Food Summit, the US Secretary of Agriculture, Dan Glickman, announced that the US could not recognize the right to food, since it infringes the right to trade.[4] Since then, the right to food has been dismantled in favour of the right to trade.

In 1992, Mexico imported 20% of its food. In 1996, it was importing 43%. Two years of NAFTA reduced food consumption by 30%; 2.2 million Mexicans lost their jobs and 40 million were pushed to extreme poverty.[5] In Indonesia, under the Suharto regime, there was a human rights deficit but sufficient food. According to the ILO, after the financial collapse caused by IMF conditionalities, 97 million people lacked food.

Globalization is threatening the most fundamental of human rights—the right to life—by treating food security and food rights as a trade barrier. In his State of the Union Address, given during the impeachment procedure, President Clinton stated that increasing farm exports from the US would be the national priority.[6] To create markets for US corporations, the US has pushed the Agriculture Agreement in the WTO, and now intends to push the free trade agenda of corporations even further. But freedom for corporations denies people their rights both as producers and consumers of food.

Hunger for the Consumers; Suicides for Farmers

More and more people in the Third World are being denied their right to food by a combination of processes. These include destruction of livelihoods, diversion of land to luxury products such as flowers and shrimps, rising food prices, and the dismantling of public distribution systems. Women and children are the worst hit by this erosion of food rights. Free trade might more appropriately be called forced trade.

One form of forced trade is the imposition of unnecessary

technology, which eliminates small producers. An example is the law that imposes industrial packaging for edible oils in India. Since 80% of edible oil is produced by tiny village units, this law, introduced on grounds of food safety, has created a monopoly for large-scale industry and, particularly, the global soya trade. It has destroyed millions of livelihoods in production and taken an essential food item beyond the reach of the poor.[7]

Forced trade causes the corporatization of agriculture, thus displacing millions of peasants from their livelihoods and destroying their food security. Forced imports through free trade make dumping possible, and dumping can destroy local markets for Third World producers.

Global market integration is pushing up the prices of basic foods, even as currencies are devalued and livelihoods destroyed. Rising prices and declining purchasing power mean lower entitlements and hence a denial of food rights. In India, on 27 January 1999, the government announced an increase in food prices by withdrawing Rs. 50 billion of food subsidies.[8] During 1998, it was widely reported that thousands of Indian peasants had committed suicide because of high debt linked to the marketing efforts of seed and agrichemical corporations under the new free market environment. The suicides went unnoticed by the human rights movement.

Destruction of the Cultural Diversity of Food

People are being denied their right to culturally appropriate and safe foods as the Macdonaldization and Cocacolonization of the world food system squeezes diverse and healthy food cultures into a monoculture of Americanized fast food and processed food cultures. Instead of eating different cereals, pulses, and oilseeds cooked in culturally diverse ways, Indians are being forced to eat soya beans as cereal, soya oil, soya beans for *dal*. This is why the women's food rights alliance dumped soya beans during protests in Delhi related to World Food Day, which in 1998 had the theme 'Women Feed the World'.

While water rights are being undermined and drinking water is becoming more scarce, Coca-Cola has managed to make inroads into new markets. The CEO of Coca-Cola stated when Coke re-entered India after 20 years, 'our market is guaranteed because if people cannot have water, they will drink Coke.'

As the Annual Report of the Coca-Cola Corporation stated in 1993,

All of us in the Coca-Cola family wake up each morning knowing that every single one of the world's 5.6 billion people will get thirsty that day . . . If we make it impossible for these 5.6 billion people to escape Coca-Cola . . . then we assure our future success for many years to come. Doing anything else is not an option.[9]

While Europeans were resisting genetically engineered foods, the then US Secretary of Agriculture, Dan Glickman stated,

We've got to make sure that sound science prevails, not what I call historic culture, which is not based on sound science. Europe has a much greater sensitivity to the culture of food as opposed to the science of food. But in the modern world, we just have to keep the pressure on the science. Good science must prevail in these decisions.[10]

Monopoly Control over Food Production and Distribution

The concentration of control over the food system is a major threat to food security and food democracy. Five corporations control the bulk of world grain trade. The top two, Cargill and Continental, have merged and Cargill now reportedly controls over 70% of the world's trade in cereals, including 85% of US wheat exports, 95% of US corn, 90% of Canada's barley exports, 80% of Argentina's wheat exports, and 90% of Australia's sorghum exports. Cargill's annual sales in 1989 were said to register US$ 44 billion, 60% higher than that of the next corporation and 300 times higher than that of the third.[11]

In addition, large chemical companies are buying up seed companies and small biotechnology companies. Chemical companies also head the list of those applying to field-test genetically engineered crops. Between 1987 and 1993, they contributed 46% of applications in the US.

Control over Seed: the First Link in the Food Chain

Hugely powerful private corporations have the biggest stake in pushing genetic engineering in agriculture. By aggressively marketing their own products (such as genetically engineered bovine growth hormones, and genetically engineered soyabeans resistant to herbicides), the Transnational Chemical Industry has made total control of seed a realistic prospect. Moreover, by controlling seed, the first link in the food chain, they control the food system. If farmers—the original seed-developers—could all be forced into the market every year, the seed industry would have a $7.5 billion market. The industry gaining total control over seed supply is, as we have seen, increasingly concentrated. As one corporate executive stated, 'What you're seeing is not just a consolidation of seed companies, it's really a consolidation of the entire food chain.'[12]

Many companies with a major seed market and companies

holding significant patents have recently been bought out, leading to the emergence of new corporate giants.

Thus seed is falling into the hands of a handful of corporations with little accountability and non-transparent functioning, but which control the entire food and agricultural system. As Bill Frieberg, editor of *Biotech Reporter* said: 'Big agricultural company profits will need to be squeezed out of farmers, one way or the other. And there's only so much blood that can be squeezed out of the proverbial turnip.'[13]

The stronger the rights of TNCs, the weaker the rights of farmers, since it is the erosion of farmers' rights that creates TNC monopolies. Patents on seed are a direct undermining of the human rights of farmers to save, exchange, and multiply seed. Patents allow corporations to prevent farmers from saving seed. When these patents are broad species patents, it is not just the human rights of farmers but everyone's right to food security that is threatened.

There are two ways in which farmers' rights are being eroded. First, seed legislation forces farmers to use only 'registered' varieties. Second, farmers are forced to give up their right to save, exchange, and improve seed through 'intellectual property rights'. Farmers' varieties are not registered and individual small farmers cannot afford the costs of registration, so they are slowly pushed into dependence on industry.

Seed legislation pushes out farmers' varieties and makes farmers' own seed-development an illegal activity. The case of farmer Josef Albrecht in Germany and potato-seed farmers in Scotland are examples of this. Josef Albrecht is an organic farmer in the village of Oberding in Bavaria. Not satisfied with commercially available seed, he developed his own ecological varieties of wheat. Ten other organic farmers from neighbouring villages took his wheat seeds. He was fined by the government of Upper Bavaria for trading in uncertified seed. He has challenged the penalty and Seed Act because the law restricts him in the exercise of his occupation as an organic farmer.

Agreements between farmers and corporations often lead to punitive fines on farmers for violation of seed arrangements and bind the heirs and personal representatives of successors of growers. Such agreements are the latest step by the seed industry in its attempt to claim far-reaching monopoly rights over seeds and farmers, while avoiding the ecological or social responsibility associated with the introduction of herbicide-resistant or pest-resistant genes into crops. This one-sided system can protect neither biodiversity nor food security. It is a system of bio-totalitarianism.

Farmers in the US have reportedly been sued for saving seed. Detectives have been hired by firms to generate 475 cases against farmers in 20 states. In one absurd case a Canadian farmer whose fields were invaded by a corporation's seed was charged with theft. The farmer in return challenged the corporation to 'charge bees and wind' for putting its genetically engineered product all over his farm.

Industry concentration and plant patents thus create a form of high-tech enslavement. Farmers can no longer exercise their role as plant-developers, or as producers freely saving and exchanging plant material. And since women are the seed savers and seed selectors, their rights too are violated.

The Terminator Logic

The latest attempt at total control is the 'terminator technology', developed jointly by the US Department of Agriculture and Mississippi-based Delta and Pine Land Seed Company. It switches a plant's reproductive processes off so that the harvested seed will be sterile if farmers attempt to replant it. Farmers are thus forced to buy seed every year and hence create a permanent market for the biotechnology industry. Genetically engineered sterility may be a good mechanism for total control, but it is a bad idea for feeding the world. Feeding the world requires enhancing the fertility of soils and seeds, not killing off the fertility of soils and killing off the fertility of seeds with 'terminator technology'.[14]

Food Fascism

Consumers' food rights are also denied by treating labelling as interference in free trade. In the absence of labelling, the consumer cannot know how the food was produced and is thus denied the right to choose.

In June 1997, US Trade Representative Charlene Barshefsky warned the European Union Agriculture Commissioner Franz Fischler not to go through with proposals to require the labelling of genetically modified organisms (GMOs) or their segregation from regular products. The Trade Representative told the Senate Agriculture Committee that the US could not tolerate a step that would cause major disruption to US exports to the EU.

The EU Commissioner was under pressure from European Consumers to label GMO foods in accordance with their democratic right to information and choice. However, consumer rights were defined by the US trade representative as 'arbitary, politicized, and scientifically unjustified' rules. If consumers insisted on pursuing 'non-science based restrictions', this would lead to a 'trade war of major dimensions'.[15]

In a letter to the US Secretary of State on 12 June, US agribusiness corporations stated that the segregation of crops for labelling is both scientifically unjustified and commercially unfeasible.[16] According to US industry, food labelling violates the GATT agreement on free trade. The Sanitary and Phyto Sanitary Measures in GATT are thus viewed by industry as protecting their interests. The right to information should not be curtailed by arbitrary technocratic and corporate decision-making about what is 'sound science' and what is not. An attempt was made in the US to treat genetically engineered foods as organic and to treat any labelling that differentiated between the two as illegal. In George Monbiot's words, this is the ultimate in Food Fascism.[17]

Onions and Democracy

The result of free trade policies is the rise of food prices in the Third World. This is, in fact, part of the policy of globalization. The World Bank has stated that India should:

allow agricultural as well as farmgate prices to increase by linking them more closely with world prices by eliminating controls on international trade including canalisation (import restrictions will be phased out by 2003), and phasing out controls on domestic trade, such as movement and storage controls, and pan-territorial and pan-seasonal pricing for rice and wheat distributed through the Targeted Public Distribution System.[18]

When prices rise and incomes go down, food insecurity is inevitable. During 1998, when prices of essential commodities rose in India, protests started. Onion prices shot up from Rs. 2/kg to Rs. 100/kg. The Congress Party, currently in opposition, took the onion as a symbol for the regional elections. It won in three states, and the elections were dubbed the 'onion' elections.

Despite the loss of these states, on 30 November 1998, the

Prime Minister of India, Atal Behari Vajpayee, addressed the World Economic Forum's 'India Economic Summit'. He reassured the global business leaders that their interests would be protected. As he put it, 'the democratic drama of the day will not derail reforms'. Democracy is thus reduced to a local 'drama' in the process of globalization.

The rise of the Bharatiya Janata Party (BJP) has coincided with the new trade liberalization policies of the 1990s. Prior to that, it was an insignificant party in the Indian Parliament. Globalization or 'economic reforms' were first introduced by the Congress Party government of P. V. Narasimha Rao in 1991. The people rejected the globalization agenda by throwing out the Congress Party. The United Front came into power in 1996 on the basis of a critique of the reform process, but immediately accelerated it. When the coalition government fell, the BJP's manifesto included a commitment to protect people's livelihoods; the BJP with its coalition partners was voted into Parliament on an anti-globalization mandate.

However, every anti-people policy that the Congress Party had tried but failed to introduce has been rushed through by the BJP coalition. The Insurance Bill, the Patent Amendment Bill, free trade in agriculture, free investment in the anti-social sectors of tobacco and liquor have been some of the landmark anti-national decisions our nationalist party has made. Since trade liberalization was introduced in 1991 through the New Economic Policies, the people of India have voted consistently against these economic reforms, which are destroying livelihoods and denying Indian people their basic needs.

Atal Behari Vajpayee's statement that 'our party has depoliticized the economic agenda' is nothing less than an admission that democracy is dead. In a democracy, the economic agenda is the political agenda. People vote for parties on the basis of their commitment to economic policies promoting the people's well-being. The Congress Party won three states from the BJP because it promised to bring down food prices. But the economic reforms have raised food prices, and unless the Congress Party in opposition challenges the free trade paradigm, it too will fail the people, and we will have another round of musical chairs.

Decisions on economic affairs are moving out of the national sovereign space. They are controlled by global structures, such as the WTO, World Bank, and IMF; these in turn act to promote and protect the interests of TNCs. National democracy is thus emptied of its economic content and reduced to an empty shell. Elections become rituals. Politics emptied of its economic core increasingly shifts from basic needs and economic justice to caste, religion, and ethnic conflict. When politicians cannot influence economic processes, they shift their popular power base to the policy of 'divide and rule'. The politics of communal strife is the ultimate logic of policies without economic content.

As Indian citizens, we can either sink deeper into despair and disintegration, or we can reconnect politics with the economy. This is the real meaning of Gandhi's *Swadeshi*.[19] Gandhi dreamed of an economic freedom in which everyone had a livelihood and could be free of want. Globalization is forcing the government to undermine economic democracy and the economic security of the majority of Indians. The protection of people's economic rights means trimming back the absolute rights and monopolies that the TNCs are seeking. It also means changing the rules of WTO, which is dismantling the Indian economy to create opportunities for foreign investors.

Fundamentalism: the Underside of Globalization

Immediately after the BJP lost the regional elections, the party held a national convention to take stock. It passed a resolution against the free trade policies of the BJP government and called for a debate on the Patent Bill and the Insurance Bill. The Prime Minister forced the party President to delete the anti-globalization resolutions. While the economic issues were thus removed from the political agenda, suddenly and mysteriously the attacks on Christians started, first in Gujrat and later in other parts of the country. Since onion and food prices could not be determined by public intervention but were left to global free markets, the popularity of the Congress Party could not be contested on the basis of regulation of food prices. When elected governments are no longer free to ensure food rights to their citizens, they can only stay relevant by raising issues beyond basic economic rights. Fundamentalism is thus born of the death of economic democracy.

The Congress Party had to be opposed on the basis of religion. The fact that it is headed by Sonia Gandhi, a Christian, has triggered the attacks on Christians. The Prime Minister silenced a national debate on patents, and called for a national debate on conversions by Christian missionaries. The electoral slogan that is emerging is 'Rome Rajya' vs. 'Ram Rajya'.[20] Since they can no longer influence economic policy, political parties look to other agendas: racism and religious and ethnic hatred. When economic decision-making is taken out of the hands of the people and their elected representatives, democracy becomes not merely a drama, but a fascist drama. We are witnessing this in India today.

Politics emptied of economic rights exploits fear and insecurity, and builds hate as political capital. India is not alone in seeing the rise of fascist and fundamentalist forces as globalization denies people the means to defend their lives and livelihoods through democratic means. In Indonesia, the IMF further reduced the scope for economic democracy after the financial collapse. Since then, ethnic and religious riots have been on the increase. In Ambon, Malaysia, forty Christian villagers including women and children were killed by a Muslim mob in January 1999. As Mark Todd reported for the *New York Times*:

Not much was left of the village of Nama, formerly a harmonious bayside community where Muslims and Christians were neighbours. Almost the entire village, with a population of more than 1,000, had been torched.[21]

It is time that the human rights community awoke to this worldwide pattern: diverse communities living in harmony are transformed into warring neighbours divided by ethnicity or religions, and the context for this is the socioeconomic-political changes induced by globalization.

Fundamentalism and fascism have always emerged when societies are driven into a state of deep insecurity. This is what occurred in Germany during the Nazi era. Imperialism created communalization in the Indian subcontinent 60 years ago with its policy of 'divide and rule'. With the rise of communalism, the Indian Independence movement was diverted, and could not focus its political energy on combating colonial rule. Thousands died in the massacres that led to the partition of India and the formation of West and East Pakistan (now Bangladesh). Women were the principal victims of communalism then and this is still true today.

Fundamentalism is once again on the rise around the world. The pulling down of the Babri Masjid,[22] the recent attacks on churches in Gujrat, the digging up of the cricket pitch where the Indo–Pakistan match was to take place,[23] the burning of cinema halls where the film *Fire*[24] was being screened—all these things bear witness to the transformation of India from a tolerant, inclusive, and diverse society into a society burdened with cultural, religious, and caste conflict.

This is no accident. In *The Violence of the Green Revolution* (1985), I attempted to show how the Green Revolution resulted not just in a non-sustainable agriculture, but in the rise of violent Sikh nationalism. Angry, unemployed youths took up guns exported by the very global powers that had destroyed Indian agriculture. Later, in my *Bertrand Russell Peace Lectures* (1994), I tried to show how economic globalization sows the seeds of communal politics and religious fundamentalism. Globalization fuels fundamentalism at multiple levels.

- Fundamentalism is a cultural backlash to globalization; the alienated and angry young men of colonized societies and cultures react to the erosion of their identity and security.
- Dispossessed people robbed of economic security by globalization cling to politicized religious identities and narrow nationalisms for security.
- Politicians robbed of economic decision-making organize their vote banks along lines of religious and cultural difference, promoting fear and hatred.
- Imperialist forces, using the divide-and-rule strategy, exploit religious conflicts to fragment the opposition to globalization.

The globalization process must be resisted. In India, this means (i) fighting the WTO and World Bank policies of 'free trade' and (ii) fighting the rule of TNCs. We must also fight the forces of fascism and fundamentalism. For women it means fighting both religious and capitalist patriarchy. (Hinduism is one of the most inclusive, pluralistic, and tolerant of all religions. Hindutva,[25] on the other hand, is a political ideology. It has little to do with the spiritual and philosophical roots of Hinduism, which are peace, compassion, and tolerance. Hinduism's strength has always been in its inherently pluralistic nature, its respect for other religions and its freedom to worship different gods and goddesses, or none at all. By contrast, Hindutva ideology is based on hatred, not love, promotes exclusion rather than inclusion, and divides our diverse society.)

Towards an Inclusive Agenda for Human Rights

The response to the violence of globalization, and the related violence of fundamentalism, must take non-violent forms, in particular a human rights agenda that does not exclude the right to economic security. Globalization is a political project and needs a political response.

All liberation movements in recent history have been partial and exclusionary. They excluded other species and other cultures. And they neglected women's politics: the politics of making change through everyday life. Now, for the first time, we have an opportunity to seek freedom in inclusive ways; to seek freedom for humans in partnership with other species and without violence. This is the alternative to globalization.

Third World people, and women in particular, have frequently had to organize to define and defend our personhood. We know what it is like to be excluded. We need to remember how we built democratic institutions and cultures.

An inclusive agenda for human rights must make human

rights the basis of economic systems. Human rights cannot be residual, they must be foundational. They cannot be fragmented, they are indivisible. The human rights movement must address globalization as the most basic and universal threat to human rights in our times.

Third World women's movements have constantly emphasized the interconnection of rights; without food and water, no other rights can be exercised. They have also repeatedly stressed that globalization is undermining women's human rights. Third World women organized protests against globalization at the Women's Conference at Beijing. In Leipzig, at the Plant Genetic Resources Conference, we launched the Leipzig Appeal to keep food security in women's hands (17–23 June 1996). And we are now building a worldwide movement of Diverse Women for Diversity in the defence of food rights and biological cultural diversity.

Women produce 60% of the world's food with next to no resources. They produce more with less. They produce nutrition for the soil and their families and sell real surpluses to the market. They work with other species rather than annihilating them. Their model of food security is based on biodiversity and decentralized production. The patriarchal model of corporate control of agriculture is based on monocultures and monopolies. In the first, the needs of the weakest are looked after first. In the patriarchal model, the rights of the strong to trample on the weak are globalized through free trade.

The human rights community needs to stop finding easy market-friendly, corporate-friendly ways of articulating human rights. It needs to make a choice: will it back the rights of the non-person, the corporation, by default, through silence, or will it defend the rights of ordinary people to have food, water, shelter, and economic and social security?

Globalization has made this choice stark. The defenders of human rights can no longer ignore economic security. Corporate profit through globalization now directly threatens the ecology of the planet and the economic security of its inhabitants.

Response to Shiva

Yogi Sikand

The mantra of globalization, Vandana Shiva tells us in her essay entitled 'Food Rights, Free Trade, and Fascism', spells doom and destruction for millions of people in the so-called 'Third World'. Contrary to what the global media insist on our hearing, she argues that, far from helping to usher in more freedom and democracy for people who need them most, viz. the poor and the marginalized, the globalization project is actually calculated to further enrich ruling elites and Western corporations. Economic liberalization, she says, is further adding to the misery of peasants and workers in 'Third World' countries, and, this being the case, it is imperative for human rights advocates to take a strong stand against it.

Shiva's thesis, put simply, is that globalization and free trade substitute uncontrolled freedom for Western corporations for personal freedoms, this being Western colonialism in a new garb. The free play granted to Western corporations means that they take the place of human beings as the locus of economic rights. Control over food by corporations leads to what Shiva calls 'food fascism', which in turn, she argues, has resulted in the emergence of ethnic and religious chauvinism in many 'Third World' countries, as comprador elites stoke the flames of hatred between communities in order to 'divide and rule', de-politicizing the economic agenda so as to serve their own interests as well as those of Western corporations. This, then, is the link between free trade, food, and fascism.

While there certainly is merit in her argument, it would be misleading to assume, as she indeed seems to, that ethnic strife in countries like India today can be reduced simply or even largely to 'food fascism'. In the case of India, with which Shiva deals at length, Hindutva fascism, as represented by the ruling Bharatiya Janata Party and allied organizations, is a much more complex phenomenon, and considerably predates all talk of globalization and free trade. In India, Hindu chauvinism as an organized political force directed principally at the country's large Muslim minority, can be traced back to the mid-nineteenth-century colonial period, which eventually led to Muslim demands for a separate homeland, Pakistan. In 1947 India was partitioned amidst the killing of almost two million people, Hindus, Sikhs, Muslims, and Dalits (lower castes), in what was until then the most bloody ethnic war in the known history of all humankind. Can it be anyone's case that all this had even the most remote connection with 'food fascism'?

Given the fact that the seemingly ever-increasing scale of ethnic violence in India today is rooted in the events leading to the Partition in 1947, can 'food fascism' unleashed by the forces of globalization be deemed the major factor behind ethnic strife in contemporary India?

The case of Indian fascism, with which Shiva deals at length, is unique in its own right. Shiva locates the origins of Hindutva fascism as a mass phenomenon to recent times, particularly to the onset of the globalization project. This is easily contestable. If fascism is all about dictatorial rule, denial of democratic rights, particularly of the working class and other marginalized sections of society, ethnic or religious chauvinism, and whipping up hatred against ethnic minorities, who are made the scape goat of all the ills of the 'nation', then all the ingredients of fascism seem to have existed in Hindu India long before the arrival of the first European adventurers. The key to understanding this lies in the institution of caste, about which Shiva, curiously, nowhere makes any mention.

Hinduism, or, to be more precise, Brahminism, lacks a standard set of religious beliefs or rites, and the only qualification in order to be considered a Hindu is membership in a particular caste. Caste is determined by birth, and the various castes, of which there now exist several thousands, are grouped in a steeply hierarchical order, at one end of which are the Brahmins, the priests, considered to be 'gods on earth' (*bhu-devata*), and, in some Brahminical texts, as even superior to the gods. At the other end of the Hindu hierarchy are the so-called untouchables and unseeables, who are considered so 'impure' and 'polluting' as to rank among Satan's children. Indeed, the principal devils and demons in classical Hindu mythology are believed to be untouchable heroes who dared to challenge the might of the Brahmins.

Brahminism exhibits in its clearest form the features of fascism mentioned above, and it is no surprise, therefore, that German Nazi scholars acknowledged a debt of deep gratitude to the authors of the Brahminical texts. ('Brahminism, the Mother of Nazism' is the title of an immensely popular booklet penned recently by a well-known 'untouchable' intellectual and social activist.) Little wonder, too, that the 'lower' castes have, over the centuries, flocked in droves to convert to Buddhism, Islam, Sikhism, and Christianity in order to escape from the shackles of the Brahminical system. It is interesting to remember that the unchallenged leaders of the 'lower' castes in twentieth-century India, Mahatma Jyotiba Phule, Bhimrao Ambedkar, and Periyar Naicker, all saw British imperialism as having played a crucial and positive role in the process of 'lower' caste emancipation, whatever else British rule might have meant for the country as a whole. Indeed, they went so far as to argue that British rule was, from the point of view of the 'lower' caste majority, far preferable to the Brahmin Raj. Continuing in that tradition, the largest-selling English Dalit periodical in India today, *Dalit Voice* insists that globalization, if undertaken selectively and judiciously, might actually prove to be a boon rather than a bane for the 'lower' castes if it means an undermining of the power of the Brahminical state.

Shiva mentions the term *dharma* at several points, employing it to suggest a harmonious village community based on cooperative exchange, hinting that a revival of *dharma* can be a potent weapon in order to fight wicked Western corporations. Although she seeks to distinguish between the 'true' *dharma* of classical Hinduism and what she sees as its corrupted and much abused form in contemporary Hindu chauvinist discourse, they are, from the point of view of the 'lower' castes, actually two sides of the same coin, with little to choose between them. *Dharma* in the classical Brahminism that Shiva seems to extol before modern-day Hindu militants came along to 'pollute' it, did not correspond in any sense to the word 'religion' as it is understood in the Christian West. *Dharma* actually implied a bundle of duties and rights that differed according to a person's caste, age, and sex.

Thus, the *dharma* of a Brahmin was to learn the scriptures and expect to be worshipped as the representative of the gods on earth. The *dharma* of the untouchable was to slave for the Brahmins and the other 'upper' castes, with no expectation of any reward. The *dharma* of a woman was to adore her husband as her god, and, according to some *dharmic* texts, when widowed, to leap onto his funeral pyre. The Bible of Brahminism, the *Manu Smriti*, records these and more such details at considerable length in addition to bone-chilling punishments that are to be meted out to those who dare to violate these *dharmic* laws. Of this, Shiva makes no mention at all.

Nothing less than a radical critique of the notion of *dharma* is called for, a task that Shiva clearly seems unwilling to undertake. Shiva's glorification of Hinduism as 'tolerant' and 'peaceful', a marked contrast to 'food fascism'-inspired Hindutva, too, is, from the 'lower' caste point of view, questionable and represents, in essence, a Brahminical perspective. Is it at all surprising that all Hindu gods and goddesses appear in images and icons as heavily armed? The modern Hindu apologist argument that this represents the victory of good over evil may be quickly dismissed, for, as we pointed out earlier, the devils of Brahminical mythology are, for the most part, believed to be none other than the ancestors of today's 'lower' castes, who dared to challenge the hegemony of the Brahmins. Lacking a common, well-defined set of beliefs, Hinduism's 'tolerance' of difference seems calculated to ensure Brahminical supremacy in any situation. Thus, a wide variety of belief systems are indeed tolerated as long as they do not challenge Brahmin supremacy. If they transgress this law, they are to be mercilessly attacked, branded as devils, and punished as enemies of the gods. An anthropological history of devils and demons in Hinduism still awaits to be written.

Is it at all surprising then, that even today if the 'lower' castes so much as dare to enter a temple in large parts of India or draw water from a village well, Brahminical tolerance suddenly vanishes, as the hapless Dalits are mown down in a barbaric frenzy? Such gory incidents date back to classical *dharmic* times that Shiva hankers after, and can, in no way, be said to be a modern invention of Western corporations, Hindutva militants and 'food fascists'.

For the 'lower'-caste victims of the Hindu caste order, the most oppressive and hierarchical social system that man has ever devised (a fact which easily escapes Shiva's attention), Hinduism offers no respite from the terrors of 'food fascism', Shiva so graphically portrays. It is hardly surprising that conversion to egalitarian religions has long been seen by the Dalits as an integral part of their quest for social liberation. An effective response to fascism in India today, would, then, require not just an interrogation of free trade, globalization, and the politics of Hindutva, as Shiva seems to suggest, but also of local forms of oppression, particularly Brahminism and the caste system, which are shared by classical Hinduism and modern Hindutva. There seems to be considerable merit in the argument of Dalit ideologues in India today that most well-known and articulate Indian human rights activists, being from the 'upper' castes, have shown considerable hesitation and reluctance to take up this task, one that Shiva, in her glorification of Hinduism, completely ignores.

4

On Liberty, the Right to Know, and Public Discourse: The Role of Transparency in Public Life

Joseph E. Stiglitz

Introduction

The East Asia crisis has brought to the fore an issue with which I have been concerned for years: transparency. Amnesty International has long been an effective champion of free speech and a free press, two of the basic human rights. Free speech is both an end in itself—an inalienable right that governments cannot strip away from the citizenry—and a means to other equally fundamental goals. Free speech provides a necessary check on government: a free press not only makes abuses of governmental powers less likely, it also augments the likelihood that basic social needs will be met. Amartya Sen, the winner of the 1999 Nobel Prize in economics, has argued forcefully that famines do not occur in societies in which there is a free press.[1] It is not the lack of food in the aggregate that gives rise to famines, but the lack of access to food by the poor in famine regions. A free press exposes these problems; once exposed, the failure to act is absolutely intolerable.

I want to push the argument one step further, and argue that there is in democratic societies a basic right to know, to be informed about what the government is doing and why.

To put it baldly, I shall argue that there should be a strong presumption in favour of transparency and openness in government. The scourges of secrecy during the past 70 years are well known in country after country: it is the secret police that has engaged in the most egregious violations of human rights. I want to write about the kind of secrecy that is pervasive today in many democratic societies. Let me be clear: this secrecy is a far cry from that pursued by the totalitarian states that have marred the twentieth century. Yet this secrecy is corrosive: it is antithetical to democratic values, and it undermines democratic processes. It is based on a mistrust between those governing and those governed; at the same time, it exacerbates that mistrust.

Francis Bacon pointed out long ago that 'Knowledge itself is power.' Secrecy gives those in government exclusive control over certain areas of knowledge, and thereby increases their power, making it more difficult for even a free press to check that power. In short, a free press is necessary for a democratic society to work effectively, but without access to information, its ability to perform its central role is eviscerated.

The consequences of secrecy can be grave. Consider one example that loomed over much of this century. In his recent book, Senator Moynihan has argued powerfully that the Cold War and many of its manifestations, such as the arms race, were greatly exacerbated by the secrecy imposed by the military establishment.[2] A more open discussion of the evidence would have shown what is now all too apparent—Russia was not the formidable opponent, the industrial giant, that it was depicted as for almost half a century. In this essay, I want to set forth the case for greater openness and transparency in government. It may seem ironic that I, an American, should have delivered a lecture on this theme in the United Kingdom: after all, the United States and the United Kingdom are two of the most open and transparent societies in the world. And indeed, they set an example for much of the rest of the world. Yet we should not take comfort in that relative virtue: our countries are still bedevilled by far too much secrecy, far too little transparency. If we are truly to set an example for the rest of the world, we must confront our own difficulties with transparency and openness head on.

Secrecy and Transparency in Recent Public Policy Debates

Before turning to the analytics of the subject—to the causes and consequences of secrecy—I want to begin with a few more personal words. The immediate impetus for this paper was the East Asia crisis, which put the issue of transparency at the top of the international public policy agenda. Lack of transparency, it is argued, gave rise to crony capitalism; crony capitalism gave rise to weak financial and corporate institutions, which made these countries vulnerable to the financial and economic crisis. That crisis has thus given rise to a greater recognition of the importance of transparency in general and in our public institutions in particular. I have tried, for instance, to argue for a more open discussion of every aspect of the crisis, from the factors that led up to the crises—including the extent to which transparency was at the root of the problem—to the appropriate design of the policy responses, the nature of the openness and participation in arriving at those policy responses, and the consequences of both the structure of the decision-making and the policies pursued. But there have been attempts to stifle the international dialogue on these issues arising both from within the international institutions, which were responsible for addressing the crisis, and the US Treasury.

My interest in openness has been long-standing. As with so many others of my generation, the Vietnam War brought home to me forcefully this and other fundamental questions facing our society. I remember vividly conversations we had back in Cambridge, Massachusetts, in the mid-1960s concerning the dilemma before the members of the Council of Economic Advisers, which advises the US President. One of the Council's duties was to make economic forecasts. It was apparent to many of us that the government was spending far more on the Vietnam War than it was admitting. One of the problems was that not only did we not know for sure *how much* it was spending, but we did not even know *who knew*, and so we did not know the true extent of culpability of President Johnson's economic advisers. You will recall the context. Johnson was trying to avoid the proverbial guns vs. butter trade off; he wanted both his War on Poverty and his War on Vietnam. The major consequence of his attempt to deceive the American people through secrecy was inflation—the inflationary episode that was subsequently reinforced by the oil shock, and that wreaked such havoc during the subsequent decade. We young assistant professors at Harvard and MIT debated among ourselves the responsibility of the President's economic advisers. How open should they have been about the situation? Should they have resigned in protest if the Administration refused to put forward an honest forecast? How would we act in a similar situation?

During my tenure as Chairman of the Council of Economic Advisers, I would repeatedly confront similar—though fortunately, far less dramatic—quandaries and find myself reflecting back on those conversations of three decades ago. A few years later, while I was the Drummond Professor of Political Economy at Oxford, I was approached to do some consulting for the British government. In that capacity, I was asked to sign the Official Secrets Act. This troubled me. I viewed this as a direct affront on an open democratic society. Britain was not at war, and nothing that I might do would even remotely touch upon matters of national security. What rationale could there be for such secrecy? It was, in my case, mainly a formality, but a formality that raised important questions that I promised myself I would revisit someday. It is thus fitting that I use this opportunity to return to the broader concerns of openness.

As an economist of the public sector, I have long argued for the virtues of transparency and openness. In one of my earlier textbooks, I contrasted two views of taxation: one view described the art of taxation as akin to plucking a goose in a manner that ensures that it does not squawk.[3] The value-added tax is consistent with this mindset; one of its alleged virtues is that individuals pay the tax in dribs and drabs, so that they are never fully conscious of how much they pay for public services. I had taken the contrasting view of taxation, arguing that one of the major attributes of a *good* tax system was transparency.[4] One of my major criticisms of the corporate tax, for example, was that the burden of that tax was not transparent.

Later, when I turned my attention to monetary economics in the aftermath of the US savings and loan crisis, I was one of the many who argued for more transparent accounting systems in the United States.[5] Specifically, I argued for moving to mark-to-market accounting—that is, requiring banks to record all assets at their current market value.[6] I had pointed out the huge distortions associated with current practices.[7] To be sure, since it will be difficult to mark to market non-marketed assets, not all assets will be treated the same; the realization of this may affect how we use the more accurate information that marking-to-market provides. But how could one really argue that it is better to have an accounting system that is less accurate? Similar issues of transparency arose in establishing risk-based capital-adequacy standards. The question was how to gauge the risk of long-term bonds. What is relevant is the risk of a change in market value; given their substantial market volatility, long-term bonds can hardly be considered perfectly safe. And yet the Federal Reserve decided to recognize only credit risk, and not market risk, a decision that clearly had the effect of reducing transparency.

After I joined the White House, I was confronted by a number of issues that tested my commitment to openness. Later I will have occasion to refer to several of the lessons that I have drawn from that experience. For now, I want to mention only two that bring home forcefully the issue of transparency, and raise serious questions about the depth of commitment to it. The first relates to another accounting issue. The Financial Accounting Standards Board (FASB), the independent body that sets accounting standards in the US, in 1993 proposed a new rule for treating stock options. Outstanding stock options represent an important source of dilution of shareholder value, and transparency clearly dictates that the value of those options—a major form of compensation for executives in high-technology companies—be fully disclosed on a firm's balance sheet. The high-tech companies had strong incentives to resist such transparency, and they waged a quiet campaign to persuade the Clinton Administration to intervene, even though FASB was supposed to be independent precisely to avoid this kind of pressure. Two of the agencies most susceptible to such influence, Treasury (Secretary Rubin) and Commerce (Secretary Brown), weighed in, expressing their opposition to the change in accounting standards. They argued that there were difficulties in valuing the options, which there were; but surely the status quo, which implicitly valued the options at zero, was wrong. At the Council, we developed a methodology for constructing a (fairly accurate) lower-bound estimate to the value of the option, a value that would have been far better than the value of zero currently used. Yet there was no debate on the substance of the issue, and virtually no public debate about the propriety of Cabinet officials taking a public stance on this matter, especially a stance against transparency.[8] Not surprisingly, FASB knuckled under the political pressure, agreeing to a far inferior solution of disclosure of the existing options, thus leaving the complicated problem of valuing those options to potential shareholders.

A far more troubling episode concerned the most important privatization initiative in the United States. I jokingly suggested that peer pressure from Europe may have been partly to blame for this episode. In the excitement of the privatization initiatives of the 1980s, the United States felt left out. After all, the United States had not nationalized enterprises, in the way that many European countries had, and so there was really little to privatize—a little $2 million helium plant in Texas could hardly compare with the billion-dollar privatizations going on in Europe. But then, in a stroke of genius, someone conceived of an idea that few other countries would have even dreamed of: privatizing the making of atomic bombs. (Indeed, since relatively few countries had the capacity to make such bombs, there were few countries that could have contemplated this bold initiative.) To be more precise, privatization focused not on the entire atomic bomb, but the central ingredient, the highly enriched uranium.[9]

A slight complication with the uranium privatization plans arose in the aftermath of the Cold War. To prevent nuclear proliferation, the US agreed to buy the nuclear fuel from Russia's decommissioned atomic warheads, converting it from highly enriched uranium to low enriched uranium suitable for nuclear power plants. The American agency responsible for enriching uranium, the US Enrichment Corporation (USEC), was given the sole right to import the material into the United States. The Council of Economic Advisers pointed out that, once privatized, USEC would have a strong profit incentive not to import the material (the imports would compete against its own production, and lower the market price)—even though it was of first-order importance for the entire world that as little of this material be left behind in Russia as possible and that the Russian agencies responsible for guarding the material be given the resources to do their job adequately.

The conflict between social and private interests was palpable, and even before the privatization occurred, USEC entered into a secret agreement with the Russians. The Russians had proposed increasing sales by 50 per cent, which would clearly have adversely affected USEC's market prospects; USEC, in their secret agreement, paid the Russians a large sum to agree not to increase shipments and to keep their silence on their offer. So a US government agency was entering into a secret agreement that it did not disclose even to others in the White House, who were presumably engaged in making key decisions concerning the future course of privatization. The very same week that they asserted that no such agreements would ever be undertaken—claiming they were as committed as we all were to having as much of the nuclear material brought to the US as possible—USEC signed the secret agreement attempting to suppress shipments.[10] I cannot reveal how we uncovered the secret agreement. But remarkably, while the discovery delayed the privatization process, it did not stop it. News stories published after the privatization confirmed our forecasts over the dire consequences. But the point I want to highlight is that this decision, one of potentially great public importance, was never subject to widespread public scrutiny. There were a few editorials in the *New York Times*. But those who know most about this issue, those who could have provided the information that would have sparked a meaningful public debate, were under a gag order not to discuss the matter: it was a matter of secrecy.[11]

The Rationale for Openness

With these remarks as prelude, let me turn now to the case for openness. I shall divide my remarks into seven sections. In the first, I shall give the most basic rationale for openness. In the second, I shall describe the incentives *of those within government* for secrecy. In the third, I shall trace through some of the adverse consequences of secrecy, as it is often pursued by public officials. In the fourth, I shall comment on how it is that secrecy is enforced. In the fifth, I shall discuss the variety of circumstances that represent the exceptions to the presumption for openness, reviewing the arguments put forward for secrecy by the advocates of secrecy. In the sixth, I shall discuss some of the elements required for implementing a regime of greater openness in public discourse. In the final section, I shall try to pull together the arguments, summarizing my case for greater openness in democratic societies.

It is perhaps worth noting that the issue of secrecy in matters of public affairs has been long a source of public concern.[12] The arguments against secrecy intermingle with the arguments against censorship and in favour of free speech.[13] The classic case was made in John Milton's *Areopagitica* (1644),[14] but James Madison, the architect of the First Amendment of the US Constitution guaranteeing the right of free speech, captured the crux of the argument:

A people who mean to be their own governors must arm themselves with the power that knowledge gives. A popular government without popular information or the means of acquiring it is but a prologue to a farce or a tragedy or perhaps both.[15]

Jeremy Bentham based his constitutional system on the motive of 'personal interest corrected by the widest publicity' and took publicity as the principal check against misrule.[16] John Stuart Mill, in his famous essay *On Liberty* (1859), held that subjecting arguments to public scrutiny was unconditionally beneficial and provided the most assured way of sorting out good from bad arguments.[17] In *Considerations on Representative Government* (1861), Mill extended the argument for 'publicity and liberty of discussion' to emphasize the virtues of popular participation.[18]

Walter Bagehot developed a strong case for 'government by discussion' and played an important role in fostering those ideas during his editorship of *The Economist*. The modern economics of information emphasizes that once knowledge is made public, then it becomes a public good that cannot be made private again. Bagehot makes the same point in his inimitable way pointing out at the same time the role of information in free choice.

'Democracy', it has been said in modern times, 'is like the grave: it takes, but it does not give.' The same is true of 'discussion.' Once effectually submit a subject to that ordeal and you can never withdraw it again; you can never again clothe it with mystery, or fence it by consecration; it remains for ever open to free choice, and exposed to profane deliberation. (Walter Bagehof, 1948 [1969], *Physics and Politics*, New York: Knopf.)

To me, the most compelling argument for openness is the positive Madisonian one: meaningful participation in democratic processes requires informed participants. Secrecy reduces the information available to the citizenry, hobbling their ability to participate *meaningfully*. Any of us who has participated in a board of directors knows that the power of a board to exercise direction and discipline is limited by the information at its disposal. Management knows this, and often attempts to control the flow of information. We often speak of government being accountable, accountable to the people. But if effective democratic oversight is to be achieved, then the voters have to be informed: they have to know what alternative actions were available, and what the results might have been. Those in government typically have far more information relevant to the decisions being made than do those outside government, just as management of a firm typically has far more information about the firm's markets, prospects, and technology than do shareholders, let alone other outsiders. Indeed, managers are paid to gather this information.

The question is, given that the public has paid for the gathering of government information, who *owns* the information?

Is it the private province of the government official, or does it belong to the public at large? I would argue that information gathered by public officials at public expense is owned by the public—just as the chairs and buildings and other physical assets used by government belong to the public. We have come to emphasize the importance of intellectual property. The information produced, gathered, and processed by public officials is intellectual property, no less than a patentable innovation would be. To use that intellectual property for private purposes—or not to share that information with the public—is just as serious an offence against the public as any other appropriation of public property for private purposes. There are, to be sure, circumstances in which fully sharing that information may not be appropriate—the important 'exceptions' to the presumption for openness that I will discuss later.

The issue can be put in a slightly different way. As an American public servant, whom do I work for: the President or the American people? As an international civil servant, do I work for the Treasuries and central banks who serve on the governing board, or do I work for the citizens of the world? To be sure, if there were no *agency* problems (in the jargon of the modern economics of information), then those to whom one was directly accountable would perfectly reflect the interests of the citizenry: there would be no discrepancy. But there are agency problems, both at the domestic and international levels.[19] Central banks, for instance, do not fully represent the interests of all citizenry: the interests of certain groups are almost always over-represented, and the interests of some groups may not be represented at all.

If public servants do really work for the public, shouldn't they report directly to the public? Should they really keep secrets from their true employers? One might argue that, in a society with a free press and free institutions, little is lost by having secrecy in government; after all, there are other sources of relevant information. Indeed, modern democratic societies, recognizing the importance of information for effective governance, try to protect the freedom and independence of the press and endeavour to promote independent think-tanks and universities—all to provide an effective check on government in many areas. The problem is that often, government officials represent the only or major source of relevant and *timely* information. If officials are subjected to a gag order, then the public has no real effective substitute.

To reiterate, openness is an essential part of public governance. Albert Hirschman[20] described exit and voice as instruments for discipline in organizations. In the private marketplace, how a firm organizes itself—whether it keeps secrets or not—makes little difference. Customers care about the products and prices; regardless of how the firm organizes production, if it produces good products at low prices it will succeed. There are transparency issues, of course: firms often lack the incentive to disclose fully the attributes of their products, and government, accordingly, enforces a variety of disclosure requirements,[21] including truth in advertising, disclosure requirements on loans, disclosure requirements on firms seeking to raise capital publicly and fraud laws. But by and large, market mechanisms (including reputation) provide essential governance to firms.

But public organizations are not subjected to the same kind of discipline. It is only through voice, through informed discussion of the policies being pursued, that effective governance can be exercised. Because in many of the areas in which public agencies operate, they have an effective monopoly, exit is not an option. And because for public organizations, exit is typically not an option, there must be greater reliance on voice. Consider the difference between a doctor in a community in which there are many physicians and a doctor who is the only source of advice in the community. A doctor might be tempted to blame the patient when his prescription fails to work: the patient did not do exactly what was asked. But if *there is competition*, when the prescriptions of the doctor do not work—possibly because no patient can follow them precisely—the doctor will eventually lose his practice, his reputation will be tarnished, and his patients will exercise 'exit'. If there is monopoly, however—if there were a single doctor dispensing treatment—the doctor might well try to control information. He might well argue that doing so is necessary to maintain confidence in his cures (and, because of the placebo effect, there may even be a grain of truth in the argument). And he knows that there is no competitive pressure to force him to disclose information or allow exit as an effective option.

In all organizations, imperfections of information give rise to what economists call *agency* problems. As a result, there may be important disparities between, say, the actions of managers and the interests of shareholders. Similarly, in the public sector agency problems may give rise to a disparity between, say, the actions of those governing and the interests of those that they are supposed to serve. In modern parlance, the lack of an exit option may exacerbate the consequences of these agency problems. Quite obviously, improvements in information—decreases in secrecy—can reduce the magnitude and consequences of these agency problems. While public organizations in general thus must rely more on voice—implying that the information required for meaningful exercise of voice is all the more important—the problems of governance may be even greater for international organizations, which are not directly accountable to voters.

There is, to refer again to the technical jargon of information economics, a pyramiding of agency problems. In those organizations, governance is typically exercised by one ministry or another from each of the various member governments. Thus, the views of the governing board may not be fully reflective of the national governments as a whole. Even with the best of information *revelation*, these agencies will play a predominant role, simply because they are in a position to be better informed. But if the flow of relevant public information is suppressed, their information advantage is increased even more, thus impairing even further the effective exercise of discipline reflecting broad societal values.

The Incentives for Secrecy

The arguments presented in the preceding section provide, I think, a compelling case for openness. Yet even seemingly public-spirited public servants often engage in secrecy. In some cases, it is because they really do not believe in democratic processes: they worry about demagoguery, fearing that openness allows demagogues to enter the fray and to sway innocent voters. Anyone who has ever lost a public debate is convinced of the importance of demagoguery, especially as used by special interest groups to advance their own interests. Yet this is the fundamental quandary of democracy: although we recognize its pitfalls, there is no real alternative to public debate.[22] In the end, we are committed to having voters make decisions at least about the decision-makers. Shouldn't we prefer that they be better informed—that is, in a better position to evaluate the quality of decision-making?

Compelling as these public interest arguments for openness may be, they run up against powerful private incentives, the private incentives of government bureaucrats, elected officials, and the special interest groups that try to influence them. Public choice theory has emphasized the importance of these incentives.[23] In this section, I shall take a closer look at these private incentives.

Two such incentives have received extensive attention. The first is that secrecy provides some insulation against being accused of making a mistake. If a policy fails to produce desired results, government officials can always claim that matters would have been even worse but for the government policy. While we all recognize human fallibility, government officials seem particularly loath to own up to it, and for good reason: the public judges mistakes harshly. But there is a vicious circle: given that so little information is disclosed, the public must rely on results in judging government officials. Officials receive credit for good results, whether they deserve the credit or not, and they are condemned for bad results, whether government action or inaction was responsible or not. With more information, the public might be able to discern more accurately the *value added* of public action.

Conversely, secrecy breeds more of itself.[24] Given that so little information is disclosed, any disclosure of a policy failure is taken as a far more important piece of news. There are thus even greater pressures not to disclose. If more information were disclosed, then the adverse consequences of disclosing a failure would be smaller, and the adverse consequences of not disclosing (of hiding) a failure might be far greater. Given that secrecy is the norm, however, the public does not attach great opprobrium to those who engage in the practice. It is what they have come to expect of public officials, whom, after all, they suspect of not really serving in the public interest.

Worry about being accused of making a mistake has, I think, been a major reason for the suppression of discussion on the appropriateness of contractionary monetary and fiscal policies in the response to the East Asian crisis. (Other reasons will be dealt with in the following section.) Only a few outside governments and international organizations have been able to follow what is going on in a timely way.

There are key analytic issues under debate, that are relevant not only to these crises, but to future crises. For instance, if the best forecast for an economy absent a change in policy is a recession, should monetary and fiscal policy be adjusted to exacerbate the recession? Will that restore confidence? If the underlying source of the problem relates to the refusal of banks to roll over private debt, under what circumstances will the increased likelihood of non-repayment more than offset the higher interest rates, so that the exchange rate is weakened, not strengthened, by these policies? These are analytic and empirical issues. Should debate on these issues be suppressed, simply because such a debate might lead to a consensus that the policy that had been pursued was mistaken?

I would go further. There was a lack of transparency in the way that the US Treasury focused attention on transparency in the context of the East Asian crisis: an attempt to cover up the real source of the problem, the financial and capital market liberalization that had occurred shortly before. Korea was previously subjected to enormous pressure from the US Treasury to open up its financial market and capital account. Some within the Clinton Administration warned that financial market deregulation, without accompanying improvements in the regulatory infrastructure and lowering of the debt equity ratios of the firms, was an invitation to a financial disaster. As it turned out, those who urged caution were correct; though to be sure, the extent of vulnerability might have been reduced if the form of deregulation had taken a different course. If these issues had been the subject of public debate—with the risks and consequences fully argued—would different decisions have been made? Was the rapid financial deregulation more in the narrow interests of those who might directly benefit from the opening than in the broad interests of the United States? At least that issue should have been publicly vetted.

Indeed, the early days of the Clinton Administration saw an attempt to set forth a set of priorities and principles for market-opening measures. The Council of Economic Advisers, for instance, argued that some of these measures were more likely to create jobs and increase incomes of a broad array of Americans, while others might be far more narrowly targeted. Remarkably, even this discussion of priorities was suppressed, with the US Treasury playing a key role: it knew that in any objective set of priorities, its efforts at increasing market access, e.g. for destabilizing derivatives, would not rate high. Not only did it not want any public discussion of these issues of prioritization, it did not want the President to get a chance to weigh in on these issues.

While those engaged in making the policy may well have an incentive to suppress such a discussion, the question is, in the framework of the architecture of public policy, shouldn't there be a presumption in favour of, and an insistence on, openness?

The second incentive that public officials have for pursuing secrecy is that secrecy provides the opportunity for special interests to have greater sway. In some societies, this takes the naked form of corruption and bribery. But even in societies where this is viewed as unacceptable, politicians need campaign funds to get elected and re-elected. The special interest groups who provide the funds do not do so for the greater public good, but because they believe that by doing so they can influence policy in ways that enhance their profits and profitability. But if these actions in support of special interest groups are subject to public scrutiny, the scope for favouritism is greatly circumscribed. It is in the midnight meetings of the tax committees that the special provisions benefiting one firm or another are introduced. In the words of Justice Brandeis: 'Sunlight is the most powerful of all disinfectants.' Secrecy is the bedrock of this persistent form of corruption, which undermines confidence in democratic governments in so much of the world.

During my time in the White House, I always suspected that when the policy wonks were cut out from the discussions, and decision-making reverted to a small inner circle, that special interests were at play. The most notable example was the treatment of ethanol, where the environmental, scientific, and economic policy offices were all in agreement—against the policies that were eventually pursued. To be sure, politics—the indirect influence of special interests—may have played as important a role as direct influence of special interests. Still, the fact that the environmental, scientific, and economic experts all concluded that the special treatment of ethanol (and ETBs) was not in the national, environmental, and economic interest should have been aired publicly.

These, as I have said, are the traditional main 'explanations' of governments' desire for secrecy. There are four others that I want to discuss. The first is that lack of information, like any form of artificially created scarcity, gives rise to rents. The adverse consequences of rent-seeking have long been of concern. There is an unhealthy dynamic: public officials have an incentive to create secrets, which earns them rents. The existence of secrets give rise to a press determined to ferret out the secrets. One of the ways in which public officials reap the rents is to disclose 'secrets' to those members of the press that treat them well.[25] Thus, not only is the public deprived of timely information—which I have argued is theirs by right—but government officials use their control of information to distort information in their favour. It is not just the puff pieces of which public officials are so fond. Rather, it is the very characterization of events and circumstances. Woe to the reporter who breaks the implicit contract! Ostracism—being cut off from the source of news—is the consequence; and even a liberal-minded editor has no choice but to reassign the reporter. One reporter from a reputable newspaper, having offended the powers that be, whom he depended upon for his stories, went from covering prominent national issues out of Washington to reporting from and on Detroit. This symbiotic relationship between the press and officialdom undermines confidence in both, and interferes with the ability of a free press to carry on its essential functions. Can a reporter be an effective critic, if his access to the information he requires can be curtailed upon the submission of an excessively critical article?

There is another, perhaps even more corrosive effect of and an incentive for secrecy by public officials. I referred earlier to management's attempt to control information as limiting the ability of shareholders and their elected directors to exercise discipline. Elsewhere, I have also shown how by *creating* information asymmetries, managers can create barriers to the entry of outside managers—to takeovers—and by doing so, they can increase their managerial rents (at the expense of shareholders).[26] The same is true of public managers—elected officials. If outsiders have less information, voters may feel less confident that they will be able to take over management effectively. Indeed, the lack of information of outsiders does increase the costs of transition, and make it more expensive (for society) to change management teams. That the alternative management teams have less information means that there is a higher probability that any proposals that they put forward will be ill-suited to the situation. By increasing the mean cost of transition and increasing the subjective variance, secrecy puts incumbents at a distinct advantage over rivals.[27]

By the same token, secrecy undermines participation in democratic processes even by voters. Voters are more likely to exercise independent judgements—both to vote, and to vote independently of party—if they feel confident about their views. And this in turn requires that they be informed. There is a cost to becoming informed. Now, most voters are not perfectly selfish; if they were, it would be hard to rationalize participation in the political process at all (after all, the public good is a public good). But they have a threshold, a limit to the amount of time and energy they are willing to invest in the pursuit of the public interest. Secrecy raises the price of information; in effect, it induces more voters who lack special interests to avoid active participation, leaving the field more to those with special interests. Thus, not only do special interests exercise their nefarious activities under the cloak of secrecy, but the secrecy itself discourages others from providing an effective check on the special interests through informed voting. This highlights the importance of 'public information institutions' designed to ferret out information for the benefit of the public: a free and, if need be, adversarial press (as opposed to a captive or lapdog press), the legitimate opposition always playing a probing and possibly devil's advocate role (buttressed by practices like the opposition's questioning of government in Parliament), and a myriad of public interest organizations (such as Amnesty International) to blow the whistle on the cloaked activities of special interest groups.

A third incentive for public officials to engage in secrecy is that it may discourage potential competitors, not only because their prospects of success in the voting process are (rationally) reduced, but because it increases their own subjective uncertainty about whether they can improve matters. How often have officials been elected on a platform, only to discover that the budgetary situation is far worse than had been envisioned, forcing them to abandon all their previously designed plans and engage in a budget balancing act (for which they may have neither comparative advantage nor passion)?

One last—and in some sense more general—incentive for secrecy is that it extends the scope of discretion of the public official. It removes an important check on behaviour. Earlier, I emphasized some of the more nefarious aspects: their ability to respond to special interests, cover up mistakes, garner rents. But some public officials simply like to exercise power, unchecked as far as possible by other disciplines. In the late 1980s the Fed argued strongly (and successfully) for using a less than fully transparent accounting system for banks—not marking assets to market and not adjusting capital adequacy standards for market risk. One of the arguments put forward was that this gave them more regulatory discretion!

The Adverse Effects of Secrecy

In the previous section, I set forth some of the reasons why public officials so ardently pursue secrecy, even when openness is apparently an essential part of democratic processes. One of the reasons for devoting so much time to understanding the incentives for secrecy is that unless we understand the drive for it, we cannot succeed in uprooting it. But another reason is that it provides deeper insights into the adverse effects of secrecy.

I have already called attention to several of these adverse effects: Secrecy provides the fertile ground on which special interests work, serves to entrench incumbents, discourages public participation in democratic processes, and undermines the ability of the press to provide an effective check against the abuses of government. But the adverse effects are even more pervasive. To maintain secrecy, often the circle of those involved in decision-making is greatly circumscribed; those who are able to provide valuable insights are cut out of the discussion. The quality of decision-making is thereby weakened. There is, again, a vicious circle. With more mistakes, public officials become more defensive; to protect themselves, they seek even more secrecy, narrowing the circle further and eroding still further the quality of decision-making. Public programmes may be designed not on the basis of the impact that they have, but on (government officials' beliefs about) the perceptions of those impacts. Those perceptions will be affected by the information that is publicly available; programme design may be as sensitive to those perceptions (and the extent to which they can be controlled) as it is to real impacts.

There is still one more, related effect: as the space of

informed discourse about a host of important issues becomes circumscribed, attention focuses more and more on *value* issues. It takes an enormous amount of information to make judgements concerning complex economic questions. It takes far less (or a far different kind of) information to come to a view concerning abortion or family values. Thus, secrecy has distorted the arena of politics. The adverse effects of secrecy are multiple: not only are important areas of public policy not dealt with effectively, but also debate focuses disproportionately on issues that are often far more divisive.

Adverse Economic Effects

While most of this paper is concerned with the adverse effects of secrecy on the political process, I should also note the adverse *economic* effects. The most obvious concern the economic consequences of political decisions: a large fraction of the decisions made in the political arena have economic consequences, not only for aggregate output, but also for its distribution. Openness affects decisions, including that of who will bear the costs of the risks inevitably associated with the uncertainties of public policy-making.

It is now generally recognized that better, and more timely, information results in better, more efficient, resource allocations. The increasingly large fraction of the workforce involved in gathering, processing, and disseminating information bears testimony to its importance. Ironically, many of these workers are engaged in ferreting out information from the public sector—information that, one might argue, ought to be public. Businesses have legitimate reasons for maintaining secrecy in some of their activities (after all, the fact that information is valuable means that disclosing information is giving away something of value to rivals), but the same reasoning leads to the conclusion that information paid for by the public should be publicly disclosed. Does it make sense, if better information leads to better resource allocations, for the government to conceal information deliberately, rather than letting the market itself decide what is or is not relevant?

But the most adverse economic consequences are associated with the corruption that so often follows from excessive secrecy. It is not an accident that the leading international non-governmental organization fighting corruption is called Transparency International. Research at the World Bank, reported in the *1997 World Development Report*, has shown that corruption has strong adverse effects on investment and economic growth.

Public officials do have strong incentives for secrecy. If we are to avoid the myriad adverse political and economic consequences of secrecy in the design of the architecture of public institutions, we need to take this into account. We need to force more openness than public officials might willingly offer.

The Implementation of Secrecy

Given the strong interests of public officials in secrecy, it is not surprising that so many governments have engaged in such extensive secrecy, going well beyond the requirements of national security. But while it may be in the interest of the government as a whole to maintain secrecy, it may not be in the interests of particular individuals. Indeed, that is what gives rise to the whole problem of leaks. As in the case of other forms of collusive behaviour, there are incentives for individuals to deviate. If a secret is shared among a number of individuals, any one of the individuals can reap the scarcity rents for himself by disclosing the information to the press.

Here again reputation mechanisms become important: the press must be relied upon to conceal the source of their leak. If they disclose their source, it dries up. Indeed, if the source of the leak becomes public knowledge, others within the government are likely to 'sanction' the individual, denying him access to information or ostracizing him in some other way.

The press and officials have an incentive to engage in symbiotic activity. But as in any reputation model, there is always a danger of unravelling in any finite game. From the point of view of the government official, what matters is the reputation of the reporter: can he be discreet in keeping his sources confidential? Since new government officials will quickly become apprised of each reporter's reputation, he has a strong incentive to maintain this confidentiality.

Still, the nature of the bilateral relationship is such as to give an advantage to some public officials over others: it pays to develop a good relationship with someone who leaks more regularly and more *exclusively* (non-exclusive leaking diminishes the value of the information being leaked) and who is likely to be a source for a long time. (If a reporter has a limited supply of puff pieces to give out, it is better to use them on those for whom the present discounted value of the information disclosed is high.)

Secrecy serves another sociological function. Many clubs, not to mention secret societies,[28] have secret rituals. Secrets serve to set apart those 'with' the secret from those 'without' the secret. It provides a form of bonding. I described earlier the 'sanctions' that make each member hostage to the bond, but the sanctions are only part of the story. Ethical values, subscribing to group norms, affect most members of the group. If the group norm is to keep a secret, they feel an individual responsibility to conform to that norm.

In recent years, however, there has been weakening of these norms. This is partly because of the increasing recognition of the undemocratic and corrosive effects of secrecy. While many directly involved with government condemned the leaking of the *Pentagon Papers*, many outside thought this an act of moral courage.[29] But there is another reason. As norms more generally have broken down, there are more instances of individuals who do not feel or at least react to 'peer pressure', who put their own interests above that of the group, who recognize the nature of the secrecy game, recognize that even if it comes to be widely believed that they are a source of leaks, it is sufficiently hard to prove that they may be immune from sanctions. Worse still, their special relationship with the press gives them a kind of immunity: they can use this special relationship to fend off any attacks. (Individuals who establish this special relationship may, in an almost hypocritical way, be the strongest advocates of secrecy; for their rents depend on *their* controlling the flow of information. Their position is undermined if there are independent sources of information.) It would thus appear that the 'complete' secrecy equilibrium may be somewhat fragile. But the partial secrecy equilibrium is just as distortive of democratic processes. Indeed, because not all government officials are equal players in the 'leaking game', the information flow may be particularly distorted.

The Exceptions

In their quest to maintain secrecy, public officials do not, of course, appeal to the effects that I have just described. They do not argue that secrecy is important because it gives incumbents an advantage over outsiders. They point to a number of problems to which *excessive* openness gives rise. (In today's world, no one argues against openness, only against *excessive openness*.) In this section, I try to provide a taxonomy of the arguments against secrecy that I have heard. I conclude that while there are indeed limits to openness, governments today—even the most open governments in the West—are far too secretive. Many, if not most of the arguments are simply self-serving rationalizations.

The Privacy Exception

The most important and convincing exception concerns privacy matters affecting individuals (and organizations). The government, in the exercise of its duties, gathers enormous amounts of information concerning individuals (such as income and health statistics). But few if any of the issues with which I am concerned here fall within the privacy exception.

Confidentiality Exception

A closely related exception concerns certain information the receipt of which would be impaired by the knowledge that it would be subsequently disclosed. For instance, the World Bank is sometimes asked by a country to help it restructure its banking system. In the process of doing so, certain weaknesses in the banking system may be uncovered. If it were known that the World Bank would disclose those weaknesses—at least, before they were repaired—the countries would have a strong incentive not to come to us for advice. There has been a worry that more extensive disclosure of letters of recommendation may have resulted in less informative letters. The importance of confidential doctor–patient and lawyer–client relationships has long been recognized. There are a limited number of interactions within the public sector that should fall within the confidentiality exception.

The National Security Exception

The importance of secrecy in times of war has long been recognized. When a nation's survival is at stake, it must do everything in its power to increase its chance of winning. The success of a military attack may well depend on surprise—on the enemy not being able to take the necessary precautions. The problem is that the national security exception has been extended to areas where clearly national security is not at issue. What is often at issue is covering up mistakes. This was brought home forcefully by the *Pentagon Papers* that looked not at how the country was currently engaged in the Vietnam War, but how it got into the war in the first place.

There will remain hard choices; one of the hardest questions the US faced in the late 1960s and early 1970s was whether to continue the war in Vietnam. Critical to that decision was information about how the war was faring. Yet that information itself might have been of value to the perceived enemy.

The worry is that much of government secrecy extends well beyond issues of national defence. Even in the area of the privatization of the corporation which enriches uranium, secrecy was pursued not because of national defence, but because of a fear of criticism, perhaps embarrassment, should the policy become a matter of public discussion. The secrecy with which the discussions on health care or welfare reform proceeded had to do not with national security, but with politics.

Crying 'Fire' in a Crowded Theatre

Occasionally, the disclosure of information can have life-threatening effects. Typically, the issue is not *whether* to disclose the information, but *how*. Justice Holmes's famous exception to the right of free speech was based on *causing a panic* by crying 'Fire' in a crowded theatre.

In matters economic, this particular exception takes on a special form; open discussion of certain issues (such as monetary policy) might upset the market, leading to instability. Curiously, those who take this position are typically those who are strong advocates of markets: while they have a great deal of confidence in the market, they evidently believe that market allocations are affected by irrelevant 'noise'. If, of course, the information being discussed or disclosed is of relevance, that is, if it affects economic fundamentals, then disclosing the information as soon as possible allows the more efficient allocation of resources.

A particular variant of this focuses on monetary policy. There has been extensive discussion of the extent to which central banks should act in secret; should they disclose their proceedings, and if so, with what lag and with what fullness of detail? Again, there is a certain irony in these discussions: while market advocates praise the price 'discovery' function of markets, much of the price discovery function in the bond market is directed at figuring out what the central bankers believe and are likely to do. Rather than having this indirect 'dance', would it not make far more sense to have the central bank directly disclose the information? If the market believes that that information is of value—as evidenced by the huge number of individuals who watch the actions of central banks throughout the world—then shouldn't government make that information available? And in a timely way? Evidently, central banks (and their governments) are less than committed to transparency when it comes to their own operations!

Neither theory nor evidence provides much support for

the hypothesis that fuller and more timely disclosure and discussion would have adverse effects. Indeed, since information eventually comes out, the current procedures, which attempt to bottle up information, result in periodic disclosures of large amounts of information. Just as the economy is likely to be more stable with frequent small adjustments in exchange rates than with few, large ones, so too is the economy more likely to be stable with a steady flow of information. With a flow of information, less attention would be paid to any single piece, and there would be smaller revisions in posterior distributions.

Similarly, there seems to be no evidence of increased instability following the UK decision to have greater transparency on the part of its central bank. Secrecy in matters economic may not only contribute to overall instability, but in many countries can be a major source of corruption, undermining confidence in government more generally.

At best, however, the argument that fuller disclosure and discussion might upset markets is only an argument concerning the timing and manner of disclosure; it is not an argument for an indefinite postponement of public discussion. To return to the metaphor of 'crying fire in a crowded theatre': no one would argue that, if one knew that there was a fire in the theatre, the patrons should not be informed in a way that allows an orderly evacuation. No one would contest that after the fire is over, a thorough investigation of the fire should be carried out, to determine what caused it and, if there were deaths or severe injury, to see what might be done (both in the construction of the theatre and in the design of the response) to avoid similar disasters in the future. And no one would argue that, because it might 'disturb' theatre-goers, one shouldn't have lighted exit signs, to indicate how to evacuate the theatre, since we know that no matter how well theatres are constructed, there is still a danger of fire.

In the case of information that, it is feared, might disturb markets, there is another point: shouldn't we have enough confidence in democratic processes and in the market to believe that the market can see through the cacophony of voices, assess the fundamental arguments, and weigh the evidence? I am not convinced that there is any real trade-off between the pursuit of democratic transparency, on one hand, and the stability and growth of the economy on the other. But in the event that there is a conflict, I put my voice solidly behind the importance of democratic processes of openness.

To be sure, democratic societies must find and have found ways of engaging expertise in complicated and technical decision-making in a manner that reflects both shared values and expertise. But the decisions cannot reflect just the interests of the industry groups that are likely to have a disproportionate share of expertise. They should be forged in ways that leave open both the decisions and the framework within which those decisions should be made to democratic processes. Indeed, to the extent that there has been greater delegation of responsibilities, e.g. to independent agencies, to engage greater expertise and to isolate the decision-making from the vicissitudes of the political process, there appears an even greater need for openness and transparency.

Open Covenants not Openly Arrived at[30]

A part of the American credo that every schoolchild learns is Woodrow Wilson's dictum in the aftermath of the First World War: open covenants openly arrived at. Eighty years ago, transparency was at the top of the international public agenda. It was widely perceived that secret treaties secretly arrived at were a major problem prior to and during the First World War. But both before and after, there has been little enthusiasm for *excessively* open deliberations. The worry is that open discussions will inhibit free expression of ideas, and special interests will take advantage of the situation to weigh in, before the delicate compromises and complex coalitions that are at the heart of successful democratic processes have a chance to work themselves out. Secrecy is needed for the successful completion of delicate negotiations.

There is, I think, some validity to this argument. The question is, how much weight should we give it? After all, the proposals will have to be put forward to public debate eventually. Special interests will still have time to undermine any coalitions that have been formed. And indeed, if there were more public disclosure of the debate as it proceeded, the news that a particular idea was being explored would carry far less weight than today, when the very fact that an idea becomes public leads to the belief that it is being very seriously considered, bringing down the full force of close scrutiny. The thrust of this exception is again one of timing: there may be a period of secrecy, while deliberations proceed, but eventually positions—and the arguments that went into them—should be fully disclosed.

As a practical matter, I have observed two dangers with this position. First, the time is never ripe for public discussion. One 'delicate' moment is followed by another. And second, the public is all too often treated disparagingly: it is entitled to know the arguments for the proposal, but not all the pros and cons that went into it—like a child who should not witness disagreements between the parents. But the public knows that few matters are black and white. Issues of public policy involve judgements, often about matters where there is considerable complexity and uncertainty.

Consider the discussion concerning the degree of openness in the debates about the best policies in response to the East Asian crisis. I do not want here to enter into the debate about the policies themselves; my concern is with the role of public discourse. At first, the argument was that such debates would upset markets that were clearly fragile. When the markets settled down, the argument switched: now the concern was that open discussion might undermine support for new funding. When the funding was received, the argument switched again: there were delicate negotiations underway concerning the new global financial architecture.

Positions are asserted with a confidence that the available evidence simply does not warrant. At the very least, public agencies should be honest and more transparent in describing their uncertainties. One of the arguments for not doing so is that confidence in these institutions would be undermined. I would argue to the contrary: doctrines of institutional infallibility actually undermine confidence in the institutions simply because they are not credible—and are so transparently false.

Undermining Authority, or Don't Air Your Dirty Linen in Public

The argument that public discussions—including discussions of uncertainties and mistakes—will undermine the authority of public institutions is one of the most corrosive of democratic processes. It is akin to the kinds of arguments that authoritarian regimes conventionally use. I would argue, on the contrary, that were governments to deal honestly with their citizenry, then confidence in government and public institutions would increase, not decrease. We all know, in the immortal words of Alexander Pope, that 'to err is human'. Human fallibility is a cornerstone of the design of our political institutions. It is why we have systems of checks and balances. We all know that there is imperfect information and that these imperfections of information play out in some of the most important decisions we have to make.

Thus, to pretend that any institution is infallible, or that there is perfect confidence in the actions being undertaken, is to fly in the face of reality. Only those who want to be fooled will be. Admission of fallibility and demonstration that one can learn from one's mistakes should enhance public confidence in an institution, at least by demonstrating that the institution has enough confidence in itself and in democratic processes to engage in open discussions.

Those of us who are committed to democratic processes see one of our objectives as the strengthening of democratic institutions and the democratic system. This may, to be sure, occasionally entail weakening the authority of a particular individual. But we are paid and empowered by the public, and it is ultimately to the public that we owe our loyalty.

Yet organizations cannot function without a certain degree of loyalty and structure.[31] Democratic processes cannot work without well-functioning organizations within it. It is here that the most delicate issues arise. Making the democratic system work in its entirety may indeed necessitate working to increase the credibility of the institutions within it (though to repeat, this does not mean trying to persuade anyone either of an infallibility or a degree of certitude that is simply not there), and this may entail circumscribing full disclosure.

Again, what is most at stake is the question of timing. Once a decision has been made, any government must convince others of the correctness of its views. This may not be effectively accomplished if the disagreements that existed prior to a decision being made continue to be aired in public. More broadly, one can view any government as a *team*. Before decisions are made, there must be open discussions, at least within the team (though within any government, there will be a division of responsibility, with each agency taking ultimate responsibility for the decisions that fall within its purview—often within the public sector there are several agencies with significant interests at stake). Without effective participation in the decision-making over which they have some jurisdiction, 'team members' will, of course, lack 'ownership' and 'buy-in' of the decision, and it will be difficult for the team to work smoothly. After a decision is made, the team must work together within the framework of the agreed strategy. Part of that strategy for public agencies is to convince others of the appropriateness of the actions.

But to repeat what I said above, the public might be more effectively convinced if there were more openness both in the process of decision-making and concerning the nature of the disagreements. Openness in process assures the public that the decision does not reflect the exercise of special interests. And a summary of the discussion convinces the public that all of the important arguments were considered, all sides were looked at: a judgement was made that the weight of evidence came down in favour of the course of action being undertaken. After all, governments are elected in part to make these difficult judgement calls. What the public wants to know is that there has been real deliberation. But government needs to be committed to openness *after the fact*: there must eventually be honest and open evaluations of the actions. Otherwise, there will be no basis for learning from experience.

Like the preceding argument, while worries about 'undermining credibility' and 'being a member of the team' have considerable validity, they are often exaggerated and taken too far. This is a slippery slope down which to slide. While there is a certain degree of validity in the argument, the incentives for secrecy of incumbents that I described earlier make leaders of these organizations particularly prone to invoke this argument.

Each of us in public life must weigh what we say in public and in private, mindful of the abuses to which excessive secrecy is prone. In the end, my confidence in democratic processes leads me to the conviction that there is far more scope for open disclosure, far less risk of 'undermining' the authority of institutions, than those who invoke this argument claim. Martin Feldstein, my predecessor as Chairman of the Council of Economic Advisers under Ronald Reagan, engaged in an honest discussion of the consequences of the huge deficits that were then mounting. Though he did not succeed in changing the policies, he played an important role in the formation of the consensus that eventually led to the deficit reductions of the 1990s. That there could be such an open discussion I think actually enhanced confidence in democratic processes and institutions.

The Implementation of Openness

I have tried to make a case for greater openness in government. How can such greater openness be implemented? At the same time, I have tried to describe the strong incentives on the part of those in the government for secrecy. The incentives for secrecy are great, and so too are the opportunities for evading the intent of any disclosure regulations. If formal meetings have to be open, then all decisions can be made in informal meetings. If written material is subject to disclosure, there will be an incentive to ensure that little is written down. Because of these limitations of legalistic approaches, emphasis must be place on creating a *culture* of openness, where the presumption is that the public should know about and participate in *all* collective decisions. We must create a mindset of openness, a belief that the information that public officials possess is 'owned' by the public, and that to use it for private purposes—if only in an exchange of favours with a reporter—is as much a theft of public property as stealing any other form of property.

There is a narrow set of exceptions that I have laid out in the preceding section, but these exceptions need to be highly circumscribed. The objective should be to make them as small and narrowly defined as possible. And there should be public discussion about the extent of those exceptions. One basic framework for public access to information is contained in the Freedom of Information Act passed by the US Congress in 1966. In principle, this law enables any citizen to gain access to any information in the public domain, with narrow exceptions for privacy. But such legislation can only be partially successful unless there is a real commitment to openness. Government officials may be careful in what they write down and what remains a 'mouth-to-ear' secret, precisely because they do not want to disclose important information to the public.

One of the strong incentives for secrecy is to provide cover for special interests to do their work. Requirements on disclosure of campaign contributions have been valuable—they have at least sensitized the electorate to the role, for instance, of tobacco money in affecting legislative outcomes. But I must confess that while the United States has strong disclosure requirements (including those affecting lobbyists), special interests still seem to have considerable scope. Presumably matters might have been even worse without these requirements.

The press plays an essential role in the battle for openness. But the press, as we have seen, is at the same time a central part of the 'conspiracy of secrecy'. The press must commit itself to working for openness. It is too much to expect them to disclose their secret sources inside the government, or not to seek out exclusive sources of information. There needs to be more reporting on the reporting process itself, exposing the nefarious system, if not the key players.

Non-governmental organizations, such as Amnesty, also have an important role to play in helping to create a culture of openness—and in checking the proclivity of government officials for secrecy.

Concluding Remarks

Amnesty International has long been devoted to ensuring that all governments protect basic human rights. It has been one of the most effective voices for human dignity in the world. Openness—transparency—is one of the most important instruments for achieving this goal. It is behind the cloak of secrecy that the rights of individuals are most frequently abrogated.

I have long been concerned with a special aspect of human rights and dignity: in the words of Franklin Delano Roosevelt, the right to 'freedom from hunger'. There can be no human dignity, no basic rights, when parents see their child die of starvation or their daughter sold into a life of prostitution for mere survival. There is little doubt that decisions by governments do have profound implications for this basic human right. These decisions should be made openly, and with the active and open participation of those affected by them. I am convinced that openness and participation will affect the nature of the decisions being made. FDR articulated this basic right in the midst of the greatest economic calamity of capitalism, the Great Depression. The world is now in the midst of perhaps its second greatest calamity; and for those in the affected countries, especially Indonesia, the depression which has been brought about is more severe than the depths of the Great Depression. The hopes that had soared with the Asian miracle have been dashed. Poverty rates, which had plummeted over three decades, are now steadily climbing.

It is behind the veil of ignorance that all human atrocities occur. What is happening in East Asia is a tragedy; there will be scars for years to come. I do not want to enter here into a debate over the extent to which misguided policies may or may not have contributed to this calamity. But I do want to put forward the hypothesis that more open and representative deliberation, more open and fuller discussion, would most likely have led to different policies being pursued, policies that would at the very least have subjected the poor and vulnerable to less risk. Even the limited discourse which has occurred has served a useful purpose—policies have been affected.

Greater openness can be justified on *instrumental grounds*, as means to ends—ends such as reducing the likelihood of the abuse of power. Greater openness is an essential part of good governance. A powerful case has been made that greater openness might have avoided the extremes of the Cold War. I believe that better decisions would have been made than those that emerged from the reliance on the secret wisdom of the cognoscenti. The end of the Cold War has laid bare both the failures of the culture of secrecy and undermined the necessity of continuing it further. Perhaps the greatest irony of the Cold War is that in the attempt to preserve democracy and democratic values, we adopted policies that undermined democratic processes. The culture of secrecy was like a virus, spreading from one part of the government to another, until it invaded areas where national security played no role at all.

I also believe that greater openness has an intrinsic value. Citizens have a basic right to know. I have tried to express this basic right in a number of different ways. The public has paid for the information; thus for a government official to appropriate the information that comes to his disposal in his role as a public official for private purposes is as much a theft of public property as the stealing of any other public property. While we all recognize the necessity of collective action, and the consequences of collective actions for individual freedoms, we have a basic right to know how the powers that have been surrendered to the Collective are being used. This seems to me to be a basic part of the implicit compact between the governed and those that they have selected to temporarily govern them. To be sure, there are exceptions, and I have dealt at length with these exceptions. But I have tried to argue that they are, or at least should be, limited in scope.

It also seems to me that the less *directly* accountable a governmental agency is to the public, the more important it is that its actions be open and transparent. By the same token, the more independent and the less directly politically accountable a government agency is, the greater the presumption for openness. Thus, I would argue that there is a greater obligation for openness both for independent agencies within national governments and for the international governmental institutions. Openness is one of the most important checks on the abuse of public fiduciary responsibilities.

We are at an exciting time. The end of the Cold War has provided us the opportunity—I would say, has made it necessary for us—to re-examine the role of secrecy and openness. At the same time, new technologies have provided mechanisms through which information can be more effectively shared between government and those governed. We can now have a more informed electorate than in any time in history. Further, advances in education, of a kind unthinkable a century ago, have put more and more citizens in a position to evaluate and assess the information that can so readily be made available.

We need but one step more: a commitment by government to greater openness, to promote dialogue and open discussion, to eschew secrecy in all its myriad forms. While I have outlined concrete legislation to which all governments might subscribe, I have recognized the limitation of such legislation. The incentives of secrecy are simply too great, and the scope for discretionary actions is too wide. I have therefore stressed the importance of creating a culture of openness—a task in which organizations such as Amnesty International have an essential role to play. Such openness may not guarantee that wise decisions will always be made. But it would be a major step forward in the on-going evolution of democratic processes, a true empowerment of individuals, to participate meaningfully in the decisions concerning the collective actions that have such profound effects on their lives and livelihoods.

Response to Stiglitz

B. S. Chimni

It is improbable that any democrat will argue against the Stiglitz thesis that 'there should be a strong presumption in favour of transparency and openness in government'. As he rightly observes, 'in today's world, no one argues against openness, only against *excessive openness*'. Albeit, most of the arguments which public officials use to justify excessive openness 'are simply self-serving rationalizations'. In the words of Weber, 'the pure interest of the bureaucracy in power . . . is efficacious far beyond those areas where purely functional interests make for secrecy.'[1] Indeed, 'nothing is so fantastically defended by the bureaucracy' as the concept of the 'official secret'.[2] The concept has been 'enriched' in the Third World, the subject of my comment, by the colonial experience; the bureaucracy here considers it its right and privilege to deny citizens any information with regard to the workings of the government. Unfortunately, the elected representatives are no less prone to abuse power and to enrich themselves behind the veil of 'official secrecy'. It explains the growing belief in civil society that the right to information is absolutely necessary to move from formal to participatory forms of democracy. But equally significant is the rising belief among Third World peoples that democracy is today a transnational affair and therefore it is not enough to introduce transparency and openness at the level of the nation-state without ensuring that the same norms apply to international actors, viz., states, international institutions, and transnational corporations. It is this last point I wish to elaborate in the rest of this response.

First, I would like to underline the differential transparency and openness standards practised in relation to domestic and foreign policies even in the most democratic of states. Weber explained the general phenomenon in the following way: 'everywhere that power interests of the domination structure toward *the outside* are at stake . . . we find secrecy.'[3] Thus, there is a curious sanction for the pursuit of power politics outside state boundaries. States do not feel in the same way accountable to citizens of other states as they do to their own. Indeed, both political theory and international law tolerate the fact that states may treat their own citizens and nationals of other countries by vastly different standards. This tends to legitimize greater secrecy in the conduct of international relations. It explains why the magical phrase 'national security' is routinely invoked to justify keeping the people in the dark about the conduct of foreign policy and about such key issues as defence expenditure. The phrase peremptorily excludes information from the public domain.

Second, I would like to argue that while transparency and openness in government is critical to strengthening democratic values, this goal, in the era of globalization, cannot be realized without injecting transparency and openness in the functioning of international institutions and transnational corporations. For international institutions have increasingly usurped the functions of governments, and transnational corporations have come to wield greater power than a large number of states in the international system. To take at first the case of the absence of transparency and openness in international institutions, all is not well even in the United

Nations. The Security Council, for example, has been the site of decisions taken by a small group of Northern states 'separately meeting in secret'.[4] On a different plane, the IMF/World Bank jointly stand accused, among other things, of practising secrecy in the negotiations of structural adjustment programmes (SAPs); the citizens of the country undergoing SAPs are rarely taken into confidence.[5] Of course, as Meesen points out (with reference to the IMF), this suits both:

Secrecy helps political leaders and officials of the debtor state to avoid parliamentary control and to exclude interest groups from making their pressure felt. And secrecy fits well into the technocratic approach IMF experts favour. They are not used to, and far removed from, parliamentary control.[6]

The opacity of the WTO decision-making and dispute settlement process is also extremely worrisome. The protest by a large group of Third World countries for being sidelined in the talks at the Third Ministerial Conference (Seattle, December 1999) underscores the problems with the WTO process of decision-making. Its dispute settlement process also leaves much to be desired. The Working Procedures adopted provide that 'the deliberations of the panel and the documents submitted to it shall be kept confidential'. In brief, it is not entirely appreciated that transparency will not only generate increasing trust but also ensure, in the final analysis, the consensual (re)definition and resolution of problems and responses.[7]

The need for transparency and openness in the operation of the transnational corporate sector cannot be overemphasized. While transnational corporations take the lead in demanding transparency from governments, they do not practise it themselves. Among other things, the lack of transparency allows for illegitimate labour practices, transfer pricing (depriving host states of legitimate taxes), corrupt practices (the bribing of foreign governments to procure favours), and often condemns the peoples of the Third World to the role of guinea pigs. While the ruling elite in the Third World is perhaps equally to be blamed for this state of affairs, it does not take responsibility away from the transnational corporate sector.

This is the reason that the United Nations Draft Code of Conduct on Transnational Corporations *inter alia* provides that 'transnational corporations should disclose *to the public* in the countries in which they operate . . . clear, full and comprehensible information on the structure, policies, activities and operations of the transnational corporation as a whole' (emphasis added). Unfortunately, the Northern states have for nearly a decade stalled the adoption of the Code of Conduct. Indeed, they have gone further and forced the closure of the United Nations Center for Transnational Corporations, which was striving to bring a degree of transparency to the operations of transnational corporations. On the other hand, it is somewhat heartening that international laws are being put in place (for example, the OECD Convention on Combating Bribery of Foreign Public Officials in International Business Transactions, 1997) to deter, prevent, and combat the bribery of foreign public officials in connection with international business transactions.

Finally, I would like to draw attention to the emerging new relationship between power and knowledge in the Third World as a result of international policies and programmes undermining institutions that provide the intellectual resources for opposing the practice of secrecy by governments, international institutions, and transnational corporations.

Thus, for example, SAPs tend to destroy higher education and the university system in Third World countries through the withdrawal of resources normally allocated to it (mostly in the name of promoting primary education). It, among other things, compels academics to turn towards alternative sources of funding for conducting research, mostly at the expense of their independence. What remains is knowledge produced by governmental agencies, international institutions, and corporate actors with little incentive for transparency.

In sum, what is called for is 'the extension of democracy beyond the nation-state to bring to account those global and transnational forces which presently escape effective democratic control'.[8] The move to inject greater transparency and openness of governance at the global level involves both ideological and practical tasks. At the ideological level, there is the need to unmask the pretence of governments and international institutions to be 'neutral' actors which are in hot pursuit of the common good, as opposed to sectional interests. At the pragmatic level, there is the need to: implement the proactive right to know laws; establish international decision-making processes which allow for the widest participation; devise dispute-resolution mechanisms that work in the open; adopt effective international laws to check corruption in international business transactions; contest policies that undermine institutions that are responsible for the production of critical knowledge; and finally hold international institutions and transnational corporations accountable in international law for the consequences that ensue from the lack of transparency and openness.

5

On Writing Rights

Homi K. Bhabha

Wherever you live, whoever you may be, once the lights dim in a movie theatre, or the screen lights up on your TV or PC, you become, more or less, a part of the global world. Many of the keywords of twenty-first-century political and cultural life embrace such a worldwide perspective: the global market as the touchstone of 'free enterprise'; democratic capitalism, as the watchword of the crusade against alternative, socialist systems; or, more recently, the 'Coca-Colonization' of the world, that catchword of global theorists, which suggests that from a curvaceous bottle with the profile of a 1950s Vargas model there emerges the genie of the postmodern dream: youth, entertainment, cool technologies, and hot financial markets. A time-worn, singular figure, however, bears contrary witness to the whirligig of our global age fraught, as it is, with the fever of frantic speeds, appetites for expanding size, and the vanity of vast numbers. It is the figure of the human being tethered to the spirit of writing/literature.

At the heart of Toni Morrison's latest novel, *Paradise*, there is a deep yearning for a global vision of 'home' that manifests itself across a range of places and peoples: 'From Nome to South Africa. Algonquin and Laplanders, Zulus and Druids.'[1] In what direction, at what distance, Morrison asks, might there be a 'home' of safety and dignity for the peoples of historical drift, political degradation, and cultural displacement? An answer emerges from the intuition that the spirit of human habitation lies less in space and more in a sign: it is, Morrison suggests, 'the first sign that any human anywhere had made . . . the vertical line; the horizontal one' (ibid.). From this emblem of intersection, two lines that cross to form a crucifix, the stick-figure of the human form, even the horizontal and vertical axes of writing itself, there emerges what Morrison calls the right 'to respect freely and not in fear— oneself and one another. Which was what love was: unmotivated respect' (p. 146).

At a historical diagonal to this ethic of love, Michael Ignatieff reports from the killing fields of the world's war-zones— Rwanda, Kosovo, Kabul—where there is, tragically, fear and unfreedom and the death of respect. In *The Warrior's Honour: Ethnic War and the Modern Conscience*, Ignatieff reflects on the 'ethics' of globalization. In that context, he brings us back to that hieroglyphic form, 'a vertical line; then the horizontal one', shared by the shape of writing and the human form itself. Ignatieff makes the link between the necessity of literature and the freedom of man quite explicit, and quite contemporary. 'The rhetoric of the global village, the globalization of the media', he suggests, often conceals a most basic insight: the consciousness 'that we are all Shakespeare's "thing itself"': unaccommodated man, the poor, bare forked animal. It is "the thing itself" that has become the subject—and the rationale—for the modern universal human rights culture.'[2]

In this, the year of the 50th Anniversary of the Universal Declaration of Human Rights, what is the human 'thing itself'? Who is 'one of us' as we live in what Conrad so aptly called the 'uneasy anchorages of life'? How do we stand in that 'turn' in the road, that in one direction leads to what is 'right' (law, duty, obligation, a 'human rights culture') and in another direction takes us to literature, writing, 'representation', 'the culture of mimesis', the illusion of life? Can these paths be joined? Can the culture of rights and the writing of culture be made to converse with each other, to convey, in collaboration, the human spirit? It is the linked claims of cultural respect and recognition, the joint concern of both Morrison and Ignatieff, that mark my path in this essay. From my literary perspective it is the ethical and aesthetic 'imagination' of cultural difference, and its conditions of commonality or association, that I have sought to explore. I have kept an eye turned towards narrative and discursive commitments to culture, and the obligations towards rights and writing, as enacted in that public sphere of communication where the 'politics of recognition' is increasingly invoked as a way of giving due cultural respect to emergent, minority cultures in multicultural societies.

In the realm of the 'politics of recognition', the claim to 'equal respect' is the moment when demands for 'difference' awkwardly encounter the ethics of deference. Just as you defer to another's view on the grounds of precedence, conviction, or 'experience', without sharing their views, so too do you respect the other's 'right to culture' within a pluralist, tolerant universe, without necessarily consenting to it. And if, in that deferral, there is the assertion of defiance or desperation—I defer to your authority, your experience, without assenting to it—so also do you, 'with all due respect', clear the ground, and your throat, for a conflictual or contentious engagement of terms that may disrupt the more consensual conversations of mankind. How are we to envisage the new multicultural demand for 'equal cultural respect' while maintaining that discriminating sense of aesthetic quality and the distinctions of cultural style that the study of literature rightly teaches us to respect?

Although the concept of the minority that I want to develop requires me to question some significant aspects of Charles Taylor's concept of cultural identity as a minoritarian claim, I am fully in agreement with the emphasis he places on the importance of 'recognition' as a central issue in the creation of a just society. By emphasizing 'recognition', he gives due importance to those aspects of 'cultural' representation and circulation that are too often subordinated to economic and political issues when we discuss questions of equality, obligation, or rights. And it is on the fate of 'culture', from policy to poetry, that I want to reflect in what follows.

In his justly celebrated essay *The Politics of Recognition*, Taylor suggests that there is something valid in the presumption of 'equal respect to all cultures':

All human cultures that have animated whole societies over a considerable stretch of time have something important to say to all human beings. I have worded it this way to exclude partial cultural milieux within a society, as well as short phases of a major culture . . . But when I call this claim [of equal respect] a presumption, I mean that it is a starting hypothesis with which we ought to approach the study of another culture [. . . for] we may have only the foggiest idea ex ante of in what its valuable contribution might consist . . . But merely on the human level, one could argue that cultures that have provided the horizon of meaning for large numbers of human beings, of diverse characters and temperaments, over a long period of time, are almost certain to have something that deserves our admiration and respect, even if it is accompanied by something that we have to abhor and reject.[3]

The demand for cultural respect in the context of minorities or multiculturalism, Taylor argues, depends, 'merely on the human level', on the presumption of equal value which is the framing condition of the politics of recognition: all cultures that have animated whole societies for a considerable stretch of time have something important to say to all human beings. Then, in a second move, an *après coup*, comes the condition of respect which is a kind of performative 'value'—a practice of cultural signification that has to generate cultural value in a dialogical relationship with the 'other's' culture. At this juncture, however, there is a fly in the ointment, or as we say in India, gristle in the kebab. Taylor's smooth progress from the universal 'human' value of whole societies to the cultural value that attaches to historically specific forms of cultural knowledge is based on an exclusion of a particular form of cultural identity. All cultures deserving of respect are whole societies, their 'wholeness' represented by a long, deep, historical continuity; but in order to assert that holistic assumption of cultural value, Taylor has to introduce a caveat. Returning to the quotation interrupted above we read:

I have . . . excluded partial cultural milieux within a society as well as short phases of a major culture. There is no reason to believe that, for instance, the different art forms of a given culture should all be of equal, or even of considerable, value; and every culture can go through phases of decadence (p. 66).

What is the significance of this 'exclusion' of the 'partial cultural milieux' in making a case for cultural value on the grounds of 'whole societies'? Could it be—as I think it is—that in the language of communitarian liberalism, 'whole societies', however universal their aspirations, are fundamentally imagined to be national or societal cultures? The problem with that, for the purposes of migrant or minoritarian cultures, lies in an inability to conceive of the 'cultural options of the minority' outside of the national, even nationalist, frame.

In his enormously influential *Multicultural Citizenship*, Will Kymlicka argues on these grounds that multicultural citizenship 'is not primarily the freedom to go beyond one's language or history, but rather the freedom to move around within one's societal culture'.[4] This domesticated conception of the 'good life' of multicultural citizenship must be placed in a more practical context. The way in which the presumptive universal measure of the 'whole society' turns into the prescriptive imperative to nationhood and national culture is born out in the interpretation of Article 27 of the International Covenant on Civil and Political Rights, one of the two main implementing conventions of the Universal Declaration of Human Rights. Article 27 asserts the right of minorities, 'in community with the other members of their group, to enjoy their own culture, to profess and practice their own religion, or to use their own language'.

Many member states proposed an amendment that immigrants should not be considered minorities. It was held that the presence of unassimilated minorities constituted a challenge to the unity of the nation. The inclusion in the Covenant of provisions that might 'encourage the formation of new minorities, artificially prolong the existence of present minorities and delay the integration of certain groups'[5] was accordingly opposed. Although this amendment was ultimately defeated, it was conceded that there was a general intent to suggest that 'ethnic, religious, or linguistic groups must have been established in a State over a longer period of time— i.e., evidence a certain historical stability—in order to qualify as minorities'.[6] The assumption here is that 'long periods of time', 'historical stability' and the integrity of the whole society of the State all add up to the fact that a key element in the definition of a minority is loyalty.

The sense that persists in Article 27 that minorities should 'preserve' their cultural identity rather than emerge in new social formations is argued on the grounds that minorities must contribute to the 'common good'. In a critique of Taylor on this very point, Seyla Benhabib, the feminist political philosopher, rightly points out that 'historically the strong pursuit of collective goals or "goods", commonly referred to as nationalism, has usually been at the cost of minorities— sexual, cultural or ethnic'.[7] Our concept of common and collective 'goods' requires some rethinking when we realize that the human condition of being a 'minority' is often to participate in 'a partial culture' of migratory and transitional forces that cannot be as stable and settled as the state-centred discourse of 'naturalization' envisaged in Article 27.

When a Tamil migrant woman worker in Sri Lanka becomes a refugee in Germany, she is assigned a 'status' and a 'place' in each location by international covenants and national laws, social prejudices, and communal conventions. In each situation her status as a cultural and political 'minority' is relationally renegotiated in the light of those social, institutional, and affiliative conditions of 'alterity' and 'alienness', those conventions of social normativity and 'normality' within which, and through which, she is named 'minority' or 'migrant'.

The individuals of partial cultural milieux (let's just refer to them as partial cultures or minority cultures) may pursue customs or found institutions that give us, or them, a perfectly 'self-conscious' sense of cultural traditions or communal histories. There is, however, a profound sense of the partial and the processual in the self-fashioning of political subject-hood and cultural identification. Our recognition of ourselves as 'rights-bearing individuals' is a result of the willing act of 'human artifice', as Hannah Arendt calls it, whereby 'We are not born equal; we become equal as members of a group on the strength of our decision to guarantee ourselves mutually equal rights.'[8] In arguing, *pace* Taylor, for the restoration or recuperation of the excluded 'partial milieux' as a significant site of 'minority culture', I am also suggesting that the notion of a 'whole culture', so often invoked in multicultural debate, may be no more than a stalking horse. Which leads us to the fundamental question in the context of these essays: do the 'partial cultural milieux' have any practical resonance for the politics of recognition, in a national or global context?

In a recent issue of *The Nation*, Manning Marable, an African American cultural historian, has argued for the growing relevance of the 'partial milieux' in the struggle for racial justice and cultural rights in the United States:

The leviathan of institutional racism and its racial stereotypes have mutated into new forms of inequality. The frontlines in the battle for racial justice for African Americans are increasingly located in our prisons, in community-based coalitions struggling against political brutality and in efforts to organize the unemployed and welfare recipients forced into workfare programmes.[9]

If we move from the national to the more global context, then, as economic historian Saskia Sassen argues in her recent volume *Globalization and Its Discontents*, the partial decentralization of the sovereignty of the state in the transnational world opens up the theatre of international law to 'a space where women . . . can come out of the invisibility of aggregate membership in a nation-state by partly working through non-state groups and networks [where] the needs and agendas of women are not necessarily defined by state-borders.'[10] In Britain, David Held's monumental study *Democracy and the*

Global Order proposes an interesting form of cosmopolitan polity where, under the umbrella of democratic law, 'sovereignty can be stripped away from the idea of fixed borders and territories and be thought of as, in principle, malleable time-space clusters . . . drawn upon in diverse self-regulating associations, from states to cities and corporations.'[11]

Whereas Taylor suggests that from the 'merely' human level we might assume that the 'value' of cultural difference is conditional upon there being a 'whole society' measured in large numbers of people over a long period of time, it is my view that behind the 'universal' language of the merely human there is a very specific idea of a 'national' culture that becomes the inevitable basis of cultural judgement and cultural justice.

We need not, of course, dismiss the appeal to the 'merely human'. After all, we quite properly invoke the merely or purely 'human' as a horizon of moral hope and political courage when we talk of human rights in a national and international perspective. But as a literary pedant, allow me to suggest that the word 'merely', as in 'merely human', has an intriguing double meaning. 'Mere' stands for the pure, unadulterated apprehension of 'humanity' as an almost metaphysical or spiritual value, beyond history, culture, or politics. However, in its archaic meaning, 'mere' is also a word for a boundary, a frontier, a border. We continually shuttle between these two meanings in the making of culture—the human as an ethical or moral horizon beyond everyday life, and the human as constituted through the process of historical and social time. The 'merely human' might then provide a more relativistic or diverse sense of humanity, a 'culture' of humanity. The 'human', as a cultural category, frequently signifies a process of translation: it reveals a realm of cultural experience that exists somewhere between the individual and the public sphere, in between the 'passions and the interests', the 'human' as part of a historical narrative—located in space and time—and then humanity as a form of ethical apprehension and aesthetic intimation that points beyond the present to provide us with a means of judging the conditions of our life and proposing other goals and values. In complex multicultural societies, the 'culture of humanity' requires that we continually translate the 'merely' human, the more metaphysical sense of meaning and identity, into 'mere humanity' as the border between various social and historical forces that produce the 'human' as a multicultural category.

According to Joseph Raz, in conditions of 'affirmative multiculturalism' one cannot be free of tension in the creation of community; one is always required to face irresolvable and irreconcilable cultural choices in constituting the 'good life' for ourselves and others:

Tension is an inevitable concomitant of accepting the truth of value-pluralism [in the context of affirmative multiculturalism]. And it is a tension without stability, without a definite resting-point of reconciliation of the two perspectives, the one recognizing the validity of competing values and the one hostile to them. There is no point of equilibrium, no single balance which is correct and could prevail to bring the two perspectives together. One is forever moving from one to the other from time to time.[12]

Such a tension tears at the very heart of the choices with which history confronts human beings. In the poem that follows, the 'mereness' of the person, crossing cultural and historical borders, 'moving from one to the other, from time to time', is finally envisaged in the trope of the mermaid. The word mermaid is derived from the same root as the 'mere', or borderline nature of humanity, that I have just been talking about. In this poem Adrienne Rich explicitly addresses the problems of the politics of recognition. Writing from the perspective of what I have called the partial milieux, Rich suggests that to belong to a movement, in the collective or political sense of the word, demands a renewed sense of self-recognition that disturbs the language of self and Other, of individual and group, in its search for a discourse of passion in which to inscribe the notion of 'rights':

Old   backswitching   road   bent   toward   the   ocean's
light
Talking   of   angles   of   vision   movements   a   black
or a red tulip
                opening
Times of walking across a street   thinking
not I have joined the movement   but   I   am
stepping in this deep current
Part of my life washing behind me   terror I
couldn't swim with
part of my life waiting for me   a part
I had no words for
I need to live each day through   have them
and know
    them all
though I can see from here where I'll be standing
at the end.

                                    _ _ _ _ _ _ _ _ _ _ _ _ _ _ _ _

_ _ _ _ _ _ _ _ _ _ _ _ _

When does a life bend toward freedom?   grasp its
direction?
How   do   you   know   you're   not   circling   in   pale
dreams, nostalgia, stagnation

but entering that deep current   malachite,
colorado
requiring all your strength wherever found
your patience and your labour
desire pitted against desire's inversion
all your mind's fortitude?
Maybe through a teacher: someone with facts with
numbers   with poetry
who wrote on the board: IN EVERY GENERATION ACTION
FREES OUR DREAMS
Maybe   a   student: one   mind   unfurling   like   a
redblack   peony
....
....
....

And   now   she   turns   her   face   brightly   on   the   new
morning in

                                                   the   new
classroom
new   in   her   beauty   her   skin   her   lashes   her   lively
body:
Race,   class ....all
that...but   isn't   all   that   just
history?
Aren't people bored with it all?

She could be
myself at nineteen   but free of reverence for past
ideas
ignorant of hopes piled on her   she's a mermaid
momentarily precipitated from a solution
which could stop her heart   She could
swim or sink
like a beautiful crystal.[13]

By emphasizing politics as movement, Rich turns it into a negotiated (un)settlement (if I might coin a phrase) between the subject as first person—I—confronted by its split double—You—that is future's part, the politicized 'person to come'. Rendering the first-person subject uncertain of its own experience ('How do you know you're not circling. . . .?') opens up the possibility of a minority politics that is very different from the binary polarization of identities—Self/Other; majority/minority—that are familiar to the traditional mode for imagining political contradiction and conflict. It then becomes possible to open up to a wider world of differences in a more inclusive politics to which there is no access without a painful 'bending' of freedom; a subject that must learn to confront its own desires, 'desire pitted against desire's inversion' as an agonistic struggle with its own motivations, just as it is preparing to do battle with the 'enemy'—class, race, or gender—in the world outside. Such a productive, if anxious, representation of 'different' social causes allows for a community of rights and interests where the coming together of subjects is part of a 'side-by-side' process of solidarity rather than an assertion of the abstract 'equality' or identity between sovereign subjects of difference. The *faux naive* phrase, 'Race, class . . . all that . . . but isn't all that just history?' makes this a text of the pedagogy of our times. Withholding the 'naming' of her politics until the end allows us to think about politics as a process of making connections between partial cultural milieux. The 'subject' of the poem is, quite literally, the sphere of the proximity of differences—race, class, gender, generation—as they emerge in a range of intersecting public spaces: the street, the academy, the political party. Structuring human and syntactic relations as chiasmatic doubles, the poem performs a mode of interweaving the 'one-in-the-other': hope and ignorance, mothers and daughters, political sisters and intergenerational strangers, vain historic hopes and 'past ideas'. The process of revision and regeneration will not stop. Where the 19-year-old woman stands now, mermaid of the partial milieux, caught in the uneasy anchorage of flight and fall, there Rich stood too, and stands again.

It is Robert Lowell who gives us a portrait of 'herself at nineteen', in this poem dedicated to Rich:

> . . . comes the season of your rash fling at playing bourgeois. . . .
> Now thin, one loose lock tossed . . . the splendid must fall,
> *Montaigne, you bastard! We've robbed the arsenal*
> to feed the needy, Toussaint, Fanon, Malcolm,
> The revolution's *mutilés de guerre,*
> shirtless ones dying, killing on the rooftops—we too,
> disabled veterans, how long will we bay with the hounds
> and beat time with crutches? your groundnote was joy . . .[14]

She too was a mermaid once, and in that 'solution' of verse, is nineteen once more . . . stepping in, malachite, colorado . . .

What Rich's poem represents with such dramatic clarity and delicacy is the fact that demands for 'minority' representation and recognition—be it race, class, gender, generation—are made from the perspective of identities that are intercultural. The poem opens up the space of what I called a chiasmatic, diagonally crossed, lateral 'side-by-side' solidarity where differences do not aspire to be represented in sovereign autonomy; Rich made it difficult for us to rank 'class' above race, or gender above generation.

Through poetry, Rich makes a significant point about the intercultural demand for 'recognition' that James Tully, the political philosopher, discusses at some length in *Strange*

Multiplicity, his Seeley lectures delivered at Cambridge. Tully argues that the norm of the independent nation-state is so deeply a part of the thinking of contemporary constitutionalism that we too easily assume that 'every culture worthy of recognition is a nation', thereby misrecognizing that the modern age is more appropriately recognized as being intercultural rather than multicultural:

Consequently from the outset citizens are to some extent on a negotiated, intercultural and aspectival [rather than essentialist] 'middle ground' or common ground . . . The politics of cultural recognition takes place on this intercultural common ground, as I shall call this labyrinth composed of the overlap, interaction and negotiation of cultures over time.[15]

What is culturally new about the multicultural or minority claim to recognition and respect? Taylor, again in concert with much public opinion, answers this question about the demand for social justice—the comparability and parity of conditions of cultural production and participation—by extending his notion of the 'whole society' in an evolutionary direction:

But at least in the intercultural context, a stronger demand has recently arisen: that one accord equal respect to actually evolved cultures. The further demand that we are looking for here is that we all recognise the equal value of different cultures; that we not only let them survive, but acknowledge their worth.[16]

Taylor attributes this notion 'of equal respect for already evolved cultures' to the influence of Frantz Fanon, the psychoanalyst from Martinique who became one of the foremost leaders of the Algerian revolution. Although I would suggest that Fanon's colonial genealogy is substantially different from the conditions of late twentieth-century liberal multicultural states, Taylor sees enough similarity to make the connection explicit (ibid.: pp. 64–5):

What is new therefore is that the demand for recognition is now explicit . . . One of the key authors in this transition is Frantz Fanon . . . who argued that in order to be free . . . [the subjugated] must first of all purge themselves of these depreciating self-images. . . . The idea, that a struggle for a changed self-image, which takes place both within the subjugated and against the dominator has . . . become crucial to certain strands of feminism, and is also a very important element in the contemporary debate about multiculturalism.

For Fanon it is precisely the status of culture as an 'achieved' or 'evolved' condition that must be most relent-lessly questioned in conditions where social discriminations and hierarchical structures are part of the 'sentimentality' and the governmentality of everyday life. In *Racism and Culture*, for instance, Fanon makes a passionate case against accepting the accredited modes of 'respecting the culture of native populations'. For the culture of authenticity sponsored by the colonial State produces 'archaic, inert institutions . . . patterned like a caricature of formerly fertile institutions . . . a cultural mummification that leads to a mummification of individual thinking', one that defines the 'other' without appeal 'under the appointment of reliable men [who] execute certain gestures, [and] is a deception that deceives no-one'.[17] Fanon is equally sceptical of nationalist or nativist 'authen-ticity' and its patriotic recoding of a cultural tradition:

Rediscovering tradition, living it as a defence mechanism, as a symbol of purity, the decultured individual leaves the impression that the mediation takes vengeance by substantializing itself. This

falling back on archaic positions . . . [this] culture put into capsules
. . . is revalorized. It is not reconceived, grasped anew, dynamized
from within. It is shouted. (p. 52)

Fanon's cultural politics of recognition attempts to go beyond
the national perspective of 'whole person or the whole society' with which I began. What discriminatory, authoritarian
cultures do is not obliterate 'difference', but create a state of
continued cultural agony where the minority cultures of
'difference' or the 'diversity' of communal interests, rights
and competing 'goods' are always 'partially' or marginally
recognized—kept alive in an agony of disarticulation and
displacement. 'The aim sought is rather a continued agony
than a total disappearance of the colonized culture', Fanon
writes, acknowledging the colonial variant of the partial
cultural milieux.

Fanon suggests that the great tragedy of discriminatory
knowledges—racism or sexism—is that they deny the possibility of entering an ethical and political world where respect
emerges from negotiating cultural difference through fully
entering into the cultural contradiction and conflict that
exists in another culture. The only way to achieve a mutual
respect between cultures, Fanon suggests, is to recognize that
we can only form solidary connections with other cultures by
relating to each other with a full awareness of our own limits,
our contradictions, our unevenness, our 'mere humanity'—by
which, of course, I mean our sense of ourselves on the borderline of difference and change: 'Once the colonial status is
irreversibly excluded . . . the two cultures can then affront
each other, [and then] enrich each other' (p. 54). To
reconstruct and respect your own cultural 'difference' must
lead you, painfully and provocatively, to salvage the Other
culture's dis-respect, or vice versa:

From the moment you and your people are liquidated like so many dogs you have to retain your importance . . . You must therefore weigh as heavily as you can upon the body of your torturer in order that his soul lost in some byway, may find itself once more.

Returning again to the poetry of Adrienne Rich:

Talking   of   angles   of   vision   movements   a   black
or a red tulip
                              opening
Times of walking across a street   thinking
not I have joined the movement but   I   am
stepping in this deep current . . .[18]

'Stepping in' also happens to be Toni Morrison's term in her new novel *Paradise* for entering into the dark waters of historical memory and emerging with a respect for writing and narrative. 'Stepping in' is an act of reparation, an embodiment of grace, whose passage through language turns into insight. 'Stepping in to find the pinpoint of light. Manipulating it, widening it, strengthening it.' And so intense were the steppings in, that it became 'a question of language. Lone called it "stepping in". Consolata said it was "seeing in". Thus the gift was in sight.'[19]

And it is such 'insight' into language and time that allows one to survive with respect. For it is the miracle of Morrison's fiction to dignify the slightest signs of life and liberty; to bend low, to dig deep, to seek the merest stirring of self-respect, dignity, independence, integrity, insight, yes, insight, as it inhabits the ordinary people who become extraordinary, the everyday which turns into an ec-static freedom. For Morrison, narrative is the pre-eminent realm of human and social inter-est. In its inventions, narrative invests language with the 'right' to explore and endure, to survive and savour a complex revision in the community of meaning and being. We have almost come full circle, for in our end is our beginning: the two intersecting, diagonal lines, the axes of writing itself, the stick figure of the human being.

The great gift of literature lies in endowing the language of equality and rights with the 'right to narrative'—to tell stories that create the web of history, and change the direction of its flow. For narrative is both speech and action, as Hannah Arendt pointed out in *The Human Condition*, and it is the very means by which we reveal each other to ourselves. By the 'right to narrate', I mean to suggest all those forms of creative behaviour that allow us to represent the lives we lead, question the conventions and customs that we inherit, dispute and propagate the ideas and ideals that come to us most naturally, and dare to entertain the most audacious hopes and fears for the future. The right to narrate might inhabit a hesitant brush stroke, be glimpsed in a gesture that fixes a dance movement, become visible in a camera angle that stops your heart. Suddenly in painting, dance, or cinema you rediscover your senses, and in that process you understand something profound about yourself, your historical moment, and what gives value to a life lived in a particular town, at a particular time, in particular social and political conditions.

The right to free thought and speech is fundamental to the right to narrate. It travels in the same direction, in its peculiar, messy combination of subjective and objective factors, individual needs and group obligations, actual words and symbolic acts. To protect the 'right to narrate' is to protect a range of democratic imperatives: it assumes that there is an equitable access to those institutions—schools, universities, museums, libraries, theatres—that give you a sense of a collective history, and the means to turn those materials into a narrative of your own. Such an assured, empowered sense of 'selfhood', the knowledge that to tell your story is to know that there is a 'public culture' in which it will be heard and could be acted upon, depends upon the nation's guardianship of what Article 5 of the International Convention on Economic, Social and Political Rights defines as 'the right to take part in cultural life'.

Narrative is not simply a social virtue; it is a moving sign of civic life. Those societies that turn their back on the right to narrate are societies of deafening silence: authoritarian societies, police states, xenophobic countries, nations traumatized by war or economic hardship; societies under the boot of death, in the grip of the destruction of freedom. When you fail to protect the right to narrate, you are in danger of filling the silence with sirens, megaphones, hectoring voices carried by loudspeakers from podiums of great height over people who shrink into indistinguishable masses . . . The right to narrate assumes that there is a commitment to creating 'spaces' of cultural and regional diversity, for it is only by acknowledging such cultural resources as a 'common good' that we can ensure that our democracy is based on dialogue and conversation, difficult though it may be, between the uneven and unequal levels of development and privilege that exist in complex societies. The upholding of the right to narrate must not only be done; it must be seen to be done.

Writing in November 1945, W. E. B. Dubois, that monumental figure of African American moral and political reconstruction, was able to envision a community of the partial cultural milieux, with which I want to end:

[We] must conceive of colonies in the nineteenth and twentieth centuries as not something far away from the centres of civilization

. . . [they are] the local problems of London, Paris, New York. They are not something which we can consider at our leisure but part of our own local present economic organization. Moreover, while the center of the colonial system (and its form and pattern) is set in the localities which are definitely called colonies and are owned politically and industrially by imperial countries, we must remember also that in the organized and dominant states there are groups of people who occupy the quasi-colonial status: laborers who are settled in the slums of great cities; groups like Negroes in the United States who are segregated physically and discriminated spiritually in law and custom . . . All these people occupy what is really a colonial status and make the kernel and substance of the problem of minorities.[20]

The quasi-colonial stance is the ironic grace granted to the peoples of the multicultural 'demand' whose duty is not only to repair their own world, but by virtue of their partial presence—not their public virtue—to move beyond it, towards the transnational or global order. This is very different, however, from the current condition of 'globalization' in terms of the trade agreements of late capitalism, industrial arrangements facilitated by the inequities of North and South, and rapid technological transfers between privileged, cosmopolitan elites—many of which forget the history of the quasi-colonial.

This notion of globalization as the latest triumph of modernity—or postmodernity—is complicit with what I have described as the vanity of 'whole societies' which are now celebrated paradoxically in a 'totalized/totemic fragmentation'. The desire to respect the agency of survival, the continued agony and agonism of cultural difference, teaches us that 'humanity' or humanness is itself a translational and transitional category. By this, I am suggesting neither a form of cultural pluralism nor a rampant social constructivism. Pluralism believes that each culture has its values that are total-ized within itself; constructivism suggests that each instance of value and identity is constituted in, and confined to, its par-ticular 'social construction'. In both cases there is a closing 'off' of the kind of partial cultural milieux that I have proposed.

To translate the 'human' is to place the human being on the 'crossroads' in a dialogical space where as 'human value' or 'cultural freedom' or 'self-consciousness', it demands that each moment of recognition is a difficult 'double-exposure' to time and history. We have to relate to a memory of the past that is proleptic, literally dying to be reborn; and to protect ourselves from a vain and vaunting future that believes that its time has irrevocably arrived, that the present is its exclusive destiny and its isolate domain.

Response to Bhabha

Charles Taylor

It would appear that Homi Bhabha and I are talking past each other. So it might be useful if I cleared up the misunderstanding before addressing his very interesting remarks.

The cross purposes seem to centre on the expression 'partial milieux', which I used in the *Politics of Recognition* and which he takes up. My use of this was in the context of the following argument: I think there is a presumption that human cultures that have animated societies across great stretches of time have something important to say to us. The context in which I make this point is obviously that in which people are tempted to make globalizing negative judgements. This is unfortunately our situation, as we can see, *inter alia*, from the current tendency to demonize Islam in much of the Western media and even educated opinion.

To turn this around, and speak of the civilization I know most about, that which emerges from Latin Christendom, I am saying that anyone who would offer a blanket dismissal of this from the outside would be both presumptuous and blind. But—and here was my caveat—it by no means follows that all 'partial milieux' in this civilization are worthy of admiration. I am not saying that my outsider is bound to approve of, say, the Spanish Inquisition or the Nazi Party. Again, it would be presumptuous and blind to say that this civilization had no painting worth seeing; but it doesn't follow that all periods in all parts of Europe were great moments for painting.

Such was my—I think—obvious point. Professor Bhabha has somehow understood me as saying that 'partial milieux' are in some way always less interesting, which of course makes nonsense of my argument. I was never arguing for a hierarchy of value between wholes and parts; just making the rather anodyne point that the residence of certain qualities in a whole doesn't argue its existence in each one of its parts, although it must evidently exist in *some*.

Anyway, the conclusion that I am suspected of coming to—that ' "whole societies" . . . are fundamentally imagined to be national or societal cultures'—not only doesn't even remotely follow from my argument, but is certainly not what I believe. There is even something vaguely comic about attributing this kind of view to a Canadian federalist living in Quebec, who has by definition spent the last 30 years in an existential struggle for the opposite side.

This brings me to my own confession of failure. Clearly my *Politics of Recognition* paper lent itself to confusion. I believe the important message in all these cross purposes (and Professor Bhabha's is by no means the first) is that while multiple, or as people tend to say 'multicultural' societies are ubiquitous today, the way in which this multiplicity works out—the problems, the struggles, the dilemmas, the injustices—can be very different from case to case. This was the largely unspoken background of my paper, and so I felt I could talk about two very different situations—that of Canada and that of the US—only to find that the arguments and considerations are frequently run together, as though they were meant to apply to the same situation. This is, of course, particularly the case in the US, because hegemonic powers always have trouble imagining that life is different across their borders.

This is what would make any general principle, giving

priority to 'whole societies' over 'partial milieux', rather absurd; and equally so, the opposite principle. States are important because they are still the major loci of what fragile democratic control we have, whether acting on their own, or (increasingly and of necessity) acting in concert. But in order to be these loci of democracy, they have to recognize their multiple, in some cases even multinational, nature. This means that they have to learn to weigh less heavily on the semi-agonistic conversation which is underway between the 'partial milieux' (in Bhabha's sense) that live within them. And an important part of this is opening space in the political identity.

It is a crucial feature of more open political identity spaces that they allow room for complexity, ambiguity, and 'hybridity' (if I may appropriate Bhabha's term) in personal identities. Or rather, they allow all of these to flourish, instead of forcing us back into the last-ditch defence of tightly defined, monolithic, primordial allegiances. Here is where Homi Bhabha's work has been extraordinarily rich and helpful to all of us who are working in this field. In a really fruitful conversation we end up being on more than one side; we are in our own position, but can also be drawn into that of the interlocutor. When we relax our stance as ideological polemicists, we all are liable to have this experience, but it needs to be articulated.

And for this purpose, the language of traditional political theory—rights, citizenship, the demand for equal recognition, class, race, colonialism, etc.—is terribly inadequate. Part of the problem with our contemporary philosophical language is its surrender to an exclusive Kantianism. But this is only part of it. Much more crippling is its phenomenological poverty. In the heat of ideological polemic, one can be drawn into putting one's whole life into these terms. They lend themselves to revendication and struggle.

But an important part of what we are is crushed and repressed in this subsumption. This is what is so well captured in the poem by Adrienne Rich that Bhabha quotes: 'part of my life waiting for me a part I had no words for'. Of course, there will always be parts we never have words for. But retrieving the crushed and denied facets of our lives from oblivion is an unavoidable task for a fully human life; and that means that there is always something further to articulate.

not I have joined the movement but   I am
stepping in this deep current
Part of my life washing behind me   terror I
couldn't swim with

It is crucial to the human condition that this articulation can't be done properly alone. We live with designated, inescapable interlocutors which our history and situation have given us. By 'inescapable' I mean, not that we can't shut them out, but that we can only do this at the cost of a polemical stance which also requires that we suppress something important in us. This could even be considered a defining characteristic of the condition of hybridity in which so many of us find ourselves in our time.

The inescapable interlocutor is in a position to do us damage, to keep us in a sense chained; since we can only break free by leaving part of us behind. That is why these myriad semi-agonistic conversations have to work themselves free from the struggles that exclusion arouses. That is what mutual recognition means, something which is to be understood in a Humboldtian rather than a Hegelian manner.

The Hegelian theory might tempt us into thinking that

there is some general formula for this recognition, something like the 'we' that becomes an 'I', and the 'I' that becomes a 'we' (as he puts it in the *Philosophy of Spirit*). But in fact, each conversation, each agon, has its own dense and contradictory shape. We need thick narratives, as Bhabha notes. But this means more than the 'right to narrate'. It certainly includes this, but there is more to it than that. We also need the language that will allow us to say those things that have been locked inside us by the deafness of the interlocutor.

This is where Bhabha's work has been so extraordinarily interesting and valuable. We can see this in his essay in this volume. He finds language, words which are saying the as yet unsaid; more, what we are having the greatest difficulty saying. And this found language becomes the occasion for a further elaboration pushing us some distance on into the inarticulate no-go zones of our inherited exclusions.

6

Citizens of the World

K. Anthony Appiah

When my father died, my sisters and I found a draft of the
final message he had meant to leave us. It began with a
reminder of the history of our two families, in Ghana and in
England, his summary account of who we were. But then he
wrote: 'Remember that you are citizens of the world.' And he
went on to tell us that this meant that, wherever we chose to
live—and, as citizens of the world, we could surely choose to
live anywhere that would have us—we should make sure we
left that place 'better than you found it'. 'Deep inside of me',
he went on, 'is a great love for mankind and an abiding desire
to see mankind, under God, fulfil its highest destiny.'

That notion of leaving somewhere 'better than you found
it' was a large part of what my father understood by citizenship. It wasn't just a matter of belonging to a community; it
was a matter of taking responsibility with that community for
its destiny. As his long-term practical commitment to the
United Nations and a host of other international organizations showed, he felt this responsible solidarity with all
humanity. But he was also intensely engaged with many nar-
rower, overlapping communities. You could learn this by
glancing at the account my father wrote of his life, which he
called the 'autobiography of an African patriot'. What he
meant by this epithet was not just that he was an African and a
patriot of Ghana, which was true, but that he was a patriot of
Africa, as well. He felt about the continent and its people what

he felt about Ghana and Ghanaians: that they were fellows, that they had a shared destiny, that they should hold together. And he felt the same thing, in a more intimate way, about Ashanti, the region of Ghana he and I grew up in, the residuum of the great Asante empire that had dominated our region before its conquest by the British.

Growing up with this father and an English mother, who was both deeply connected to our family in England and fully rooted in Ghana, where she has now lived for nearly half a century, it has never seemed to me hard to live with many such loyalties. Our community was Asante, was Ghana, was Africa, but it was also (in no particular order) England, the Methodist church, the Third World: and, in his final words of love and wisdom, my father wanted to remind us that it was also humankind.

My sisters and I have homes in four distinct countries—I in America, and they in Namibia, Nigeria, and Ghana—but wherever we live, we are connected to Ghana and to England, our family roots, and to other places by love and friendship and experience. Each of us has lived for a time in at least one other country outside Ghana and England. And what strikes me about our experience—apart from the fact that it is one that is reproduced in many, many families today—is not the difficulty of these relocations but how easy they have largely been. I gather from many responses in many places over the years, that it is tempting to think of experiences such as ours as somehow especially modern, and, therefore, as raising new and special difficulties. But in trying to think about why living with these many overlapping loyalties has been so natural and so easy, I have been reassured by the reflection that our little family experiment actually belongs to one of the oldest patterns of the species.

In every region of the world, throughout recorded history, men and women have travelled great distances—in pursuit of trade, of empire, of knowledge, of converts, of slaves—shaping the minds and the material lives of people in other regions with objects and ideas from far away. Alexander's empire moulded the politics but also the sculpture of Egypt and North India; the Moguls and the Mongols shaped the economies but also the architecture of great swathes of Asia; the Bantu migrations populated half the African continent, bringing language and religion but also iron-working and new forms of agriculture. The effects are clear in religion: Islamic states stretch from Morocco to Indonesia; Christianity is strong in every continent, borne often by missionaries in the wake of empire, while Judaism has travelled to every continent with barely a hint of evangelism; and Buddhism, which long ago migrated from India into much of East and South East Asia, can now be found in Europe and Africa and the Americas as well.

But it is not just religions that travel: Gujaratis and Sikhs, and people whose ancestors came from many different parts of China or of Africa, live in global diasporas. The traders of the Silk Route changed the style of elite dress in Italy. The Ming porcelain found in Swahili graves follows the path of Admiral Cheng Ho, whose fifteenth-century expeditions ended with the establishment of 'relations between the Ming court and official figures at Mogadishu, Malindi, Mombassa, Zanzibar, Dar es Salaam and Kilwa'.[1] There is an endless parade of examples: the Mande merchants of the Sahel; the English, Dutch, Italian, and Iberian sailors of the Western Age of Adventure; the Polynesian navigators who first populated the Pacific. The nomadic urge is deep within us. The ancestors of the human population outside Africa probably left a mere 100,000 years or so ago. It has not taken us very long to cover the planet. We have always been a travelling species.

So the interpenetration of societies and forms of life is a very old phenomenon, one that is natural to us (and that has produced, no doubt, much bloodshed and violence and suspicion, as well as much productive and friendly exchange). In the human past, there have been places that largely kept themselves apart for long periods from neighbours and from strangers; and even since the beginning of European expansion at the start of the sixteenth century, in many places, in Europe as elsewhere, it was possible to live a long life without thinking much beyond the nearest town. It was already true by the nineteenth century that the economic lives of every inhabitant of these, British, islands were profoundly dependent on events in other countries, even other continents: but that was a fact you did not need to notice.

In our century, however, the balance has shifted. The ratio of what is settled to what has travelled has changed everywhere. Ideas, objects, and people from 'outside' are now more and more obviously present everywhere than they have ever been. Calling this process 'globalization', as we often do, is all very well, but that tells us very little either about what is novel in it or about its significance. For, as I have suggested, you could describe the history of the human species as a process of globalization: the globalization, if you like, of the *longue durée*, in fact, of the longest humanly possible *durée*, that of the period within which we have been fully human.

But, in our historical myopia, we more normally use the term to speak of recent events. We reflect, in the language of globalization, on the way in which CNN and the BBC have come to have audiences around the planet and on the creation of global products, from Nestlé's powdered milk to

Mercedes-Benz cars, from Coca-Cola to Microsoft Windows, from the Beatles to Michael Jackson. Globalization surfaces as the theme of discussions of the internationalization of legal norms in the sphere of trade through the WTO; in the sphere of human rights, through the treaties that have followed in the wake of the UN's Declaration of Human Rights, and in work on the development of transnational accounting norms in commerce or of systems of cross-national commercial arbitration. Globalization can mean the increasing dominance of English as the language of business or the spread of liberal democracy or the growth of the World Wide Web. And we hear it spoken of both by those who celebrate and by those who deplore the fluidity of capital flows, whose material preconditions lie in the same information technology that has made the internet possible.[2] Planes and boats and trains, satellites and cables of copper and optic fibre, and the people and things and ideas that travel all of them, are, indeed, bringing us all ever more definitively into a single web. And that web is physical, biological, electronic, artistic, literary, musical, linguistic, juridical, religious, economic, familial.

In this broad context, it has seemed to some increasingly natural to think of our species, as my father did, as a community—which is part of what is meant, no doubt, by that now-tired phrase 'the global village'. This formulation was coined to be paradoxical. For, however much we are now connected, the relations between us—from Bombay to Birmingham, from Rio to Rome, from Accra to Adelaide— are hardly similar to those of village life. The only place I have ever lived that might have been called a village is a place called Minchinhampton, not too many miles west of here: we used to 'go up' the village to the post office, or the chemist, the butcher, the church, the pub, or to the doctor. When I went to school at Blue Boys, up by the dairy, nearly 40 years ago, we could walk back home in a quarter of an hour, and, on the way, we would meet people whose names and families we knew and who knew our names, and the names of our parents and grandparents, an aunt and uncle, some cousins. But even 30 or 40 years ago, many of those who lived in Minchinhampton took buses and cars to work in the Stroud valley or towards Dursley or Cirencester or Bristol, and the place was already full of people we did not recognize; and my own presence—the brown son of a mother born not far away in Lechlade but also of a Ghanaian father—reflected an intrusion from afar. Now, as the housing estates have grown up along the road towards Cirencester, and Stroud's suburbs have reached towards Minchinhampton's common, Minchinhampton may not yet have the anonymity of New York or London, but it is decisively a town, a collection of neighbourhoods; and even within the neighbourhoods people often seem to pass each other as strangers.

The word 'village' evokes, at least for me, a face-to-face community, a place whose inhabitants can walk past the houses and name their fellow villagers; people who see each other on the street, down the pub, on the farm, in the shops, 'up the village'. Fewer and fewer people live in such places, not just in the North but also in the South. The street where I spent most of my childhood is not in Minchinhampton but in Kumasi, in Ghana, in the country's second city. But it was a city of neighbourhoods, each of which felt a little like the village of my imagination. When I was a child, it was a new street—we were the first people to live in our house, which my parents built. And my grandfather, who lived opposite, was one of the first people to have built a modern house in that area. But we knew everyone on the street, a community of a few hundred people, and, if you had asked me, I think I would have said when I was eight or ten that I would be able to go back and find them when I grew up. In fact, the majority have moved on, as I have, in a way that would have been unimaginable for my grandfather: Eddie, from across the street, who never finished school, called to wish me a Happy New Year from Japan; Frankie, my cousin from next door to Eddie, lives in England; Mrs Effah still lives next door, but visits her children in the United States; even my mother and sister have moved across the city.

Urbanization has proceeded apace everywhere across the globe; and suburbanization has changed the shape of the *urbs* of Europe and North America. When urban migrants in the South move to cities and towns, they move, first, if they are lucky, to places where they have connections, and those connections reach back into the rural settlements from which they came. But soon they are joined together with people from a region—Igbo people, say, in Lagos, or Baianos in Rio or Bengalis in Bombay—as well as with people whose languages and traditions are even less familiar. If they hold on to an identity, it is unlikely to be a village identity: it will be a town, a region or a language, in part because that is something that they have in common with more people, in part because towns, regions, and languages are things the strangers who are their new neighbours in the city might have heard of.

Our increasing interconnectedness—and our growing awareness of it—have not, then, made us into denizens of a single village. Our most basic social identities—the identities that are called 'tribal' in Africa, for example, or the ethnic groups of the Balkans or the modern multicultural city—are no longer village identities. Everyone knows you cannot have face-to-face relations with six billion people. But you cannot have face-to-face relations with a hundred thousand or a million or ten million people (with your fellow Serbs or Swahilis or Swedes) either; and we humans have long had practice in identifying, in towns, cities, and nations, with groups on this grander scale.

Rome, after all, in the years around the birth of Christ, already had a population of nearly a million people; and being a citizen of that city and its empire was, as St Paul famously insisted, a substantial thing. To be *civis Romanus* was to be bound together with other Romans not by mutual knowledge or recognition, but by language, law, and literature. Increasingly, since the eighteenth century, people all around the planet have grown into national affiliations that extend over territories that would take weeks or months to traverse on foot, covering thousands of villages, towns, and cities, millions of people, and, often, dozens of languages, or scores of barely mutually intelligible dialects.

These nations have absorbed some of the central functions of the old Greek *polis*: they are the sources of law for their inhabitants, for example, and they define their identities when they travel away from home. If the citizens of modern nations are also subjects, it is because their nation is subjected, just as an adult non-slave male in a Greek *polis* could be subjected by the subjection of his city. When modern nations are free, they are also sovereign, as the free *polis* was. There is no recognized higher secular authority. And so, despite the differences, it is, I think, not unnatural that we have come to call the public business of these nations 'politics'.

Still, as I have been insisting, nations differ from the *polis* so substantially in scale (there is no space large enough to encompass in a single gathering the free citizens of almost all of them) that relations between citizens must, of necessity, be relations between strangers. If nationals are bound together, it is on the Roman model, by what I just called 'language, law, and literature'; and if they share an experience of events, it is not *in propria persona*, but through their shared exposure to narrations of those events: in folktale and novel and movie, in newspapers and magazines, on radio and television, in the national histories taught in modern national schools.

Narrative was central to earlier forms of political identity, too: the Homeric poems for the Greek city-states; the Augustan poetry of Virgil (but also of Horace) for a cultivated Roman elite; the epic of Sundiata for Malinke societies in West Africa; the Vulgate for mediaeval Christendom; the story of Shaka for the Zulu nation. If there is something distinctive about the new national stories, perhaps it is this: that they bind citizens not in a shared relation to gods, kings, and heroes, but as participants in a common story. Modern political communities, that is, are bound together through representations in which the community itself is an actor; and what binds each of us to the community (and thus to each other) is our participation, through our national identity, in that action. Our modern solidarity derives from stories in which we participate through synecdoche. If the citizens of the world are to be a global community, here is one potential source of solidarity that is, so to speak, already on the right scale.

The trouble with borrowing a rhetoric of fellow feeling from the nation, however, is that the national story is so much a story of a nation among nations, an *inter*-national narrative. And the standard national story creates solidarity by contrasting what *we* do with what *they* do, usually, as we all know, to *their* disadvantage. If there is no agent outside the human community, no antagonist to its protagonist, can we tell stories that will bind us together?

I have posed the question as one of imaginative identification and worried that the human species might fail to engage our sympathies because, to put it crudely, solidarity may require enemies. But perhaps this is the wrong place to start. Nations are also sources of law, of public norms, of regulation, and order. If we are to be a global community, should we not take the direct route and become a single polity? Why not transfer sovereignty to the global level, thus creating a single state? Why should the world not be a single *polis*?

This will seem like the right moment, no doubt, to introduce the recently much bruited idea of the cosmopolitan. 'Cosmos', after all, is just the Greek for 'world', so a cosmopolitan should, etymologically at least, be someone who thinks that the world is, so to speak, our shared home-town, reproducing, in effect, something very like the paradox of the global village.

I am not equipped, I fear, to summarize the history of this idea, or perhaps I should say, this word. Cosmopolitanism as an ideal in the West is conventionally regarded as a legacy of Stoicism, a movement of which Zeno of Citium (334–262 BC), the Cypriot rather than the Eleatic, is conventionally regarded as the founder. But Zeno seems to have begun within the broad framework laid out by the Cynics, who had been the first to coin the (deliberately paradoxical) expression *kosmou politçs* 'citizen of the cosmos'. The paradox would have been clear to anyone in the classical Greek world. A citizen—a *politçs*—belongs to a particular *polis*: a city to which he or she owes loyalty; the *kosmos* for Cynics and for Stoics is the world, not in the sense of the earth, but in the sense of the universe. But for most of their contemporaries, to be a *politçs* of one place was exactly not to be a *politçs* of any other. Talk of citizenship in the *kosmos* reflected a rejection of the call of local loyalties—reflected, in fact, the general Cynic hostility to custom and tradition—and so it was more than a mere appeal to a universal human solidarity. It would be as if someone asked you where your home was and you said 'anywhere' or 'everywhere', to which it would be natural to reply that, in that case, you did not have a home at all.

So it is interesting and important that, by and large, what we nowadays mean by cosmopolitanism is not, in fact, the proposal that we should create a world state to govern our world community. And that was, at least as far as I know, very much the case with the Stoics. Certainly Marcus Aurelius, one of the most enduring of the later Stoics, whose *Meditations* are still widely available (in paperback!) today, ends the last book of that great work with a paragraph that begins:

O man, citizenship of this great world-city has been yours. Whether for five years or five score, what is that to you? Whatever the law of that city decrees is fair to one and all alike.[3]

Now if anyone had ever been in a position to set out to put into place a world government, it would have been Marcus Aurelius. He was, after all, one of the last great emperors of the greatest empire of the Classical West. But the world-city he was talking about reflected a sense of spiritual rather than political confraternity. Here *kosmos* really means the universe because, as one of his many translators once put it, 'just as to the Athenian Athens was the "dear city of Cecrops", to the philosopher the universe is the dear city of God.'[4]

Marcus Aurelius is, in this respect, as I say, like many modern cosmopolitans (and here I am happy to include myself). Far from being disposed towards world government, we hold to a vision that accepts, even celebrates, the diversity of social and political systems in the world, taking pleasure in the existence and the products of peoples and places other than our homes. Our acceptance of other nations, societies, and styles of life is not a reflection of indifference to people elsewhere: while accepting a variety of political arrangements, we care deeply that all nations and communities should respect certain fundamental human needs and grant certain fundamental rights. But we are not convinced that a unitary world sovereign is necessary to that end: and, indeed, we worry that such a literal cosmopolis would threaten many of the values that are fundamental to the cosmopolitan vision.

To be a citizen of the world, in this sense, is, indeed, to be concerned for your fellow citizens, but the way you live that concern is often just by doing things for people in particular places. A citizen of the world can make the world better by making some local place better; it is just that that place need not be the place of her literal or original citizenship. Which is why, when my father told us we were citizens of the world, he went on to tell us that we should work, for that reason, for the good of the places where—whether for the moment or for a lifetime—we had pitched our tents.

What is distinctive about cosmopolitans is that we display our concern for our fellow humans without demanding of them that they be or become like ourselves. Cosmopolitanism is humanist, thinking no human alien; but it resists those forms of universalizing humanism, like Victorian mission Christianity or the colonial *mission civilisatrice*, that manifest love for others by attempting to impose their own purportedly superior ways. That is why cosmopolitanism is no friend to cosmopolis. It is because a world-state risks imposing exactly the sort of uniformity that cosmopolitanism resists. And the same impulses that lead us to respect differences across societies lead us to insist on rights to difference within states, so that our cosmopolitanism abroad goes with a form of multiculturalism at home. If multiculturalism can be made to work for modern nation-states, then perhaps a cosmopolis could be constructed that was multicultural, too: and then the cosmopolitan might have less reason to worry about the project of world government.

But my aim today is not to discuss the pros and cons of world government or how it can be constructed in ways that respect the cosmopolitan impulse.[5] Rather, what I want to do is to develop an account of the cosmopolitan respect for differences and to explore what that respect requires when we are engaged in moral debate across the boundaries between nations. The answers here have obvious consequences for what would be required if we were to move towards the integration of the political systems of the many nation-states. But one of my aims today is to show that cosmopolitans can already exercise a citizenship of the world even without any changes in political institutions.

Early on in Laurence Sterne's *A Sentimental Journey*, an 'old French officer' observes that:

Le POUR, et le CONTRE se trouvent en chaque nation; there is a balance, said he, of good and bad every where; and nothing but the knowing it is so can emancipate one half of the world from the prepossessions which it holds against the other—that the advantage of travel, as it regarded the *sçavoir vivre*, was by seeing a great deal of men and manners; it taught us mutual toleration; and mutual toleration, concluded he, making me a bow, taught us mutual love.[6]

Here is an English writer of the old canon writing in English but also French about a journey to France at a time when she was at war with England; which should remind us how easily cosmopolitan educated men and women in Europe were before the nineteenth century. Cosmopolitanism of this sort begins by urging that we should know others, with their differences, and believes that this will lead us to toleration, perhaps even to 'mutual love'.

But this way of making the argument raises an immediate problem. For it starts with an acknowledgement that there is good and bad in each place. And if that is so, won't treating people in other places as fellow citizens require us, indeed, to love the good but also to seek to eradicate the bad? Why love the French as they are, rather than helping them to become better? Why not take advantage, at the same time, of the ways in which they can improve us? Cosmopolitanism embraces Difference, with a capital D: but why not embrace the Good, with a capital G? Of course, we can learn from other kinds of people and from other societies, just as they can learn from us. But if we do that, we shall inevitably move towards a world of greater uniformity. Differences will remain, naturally, but they will remain precisely in the spheres that are morally indifferent: cosmopolitanism about these spheres will be fine, but surely only because they are, from a moral point of view, of secondary importance. This is what I am going to call universalistic cosmopolitanism: a celebration of difference that remains committed to the existence of universal standards.

But there is another way to go. That is to argue against universal standards—what I just now called the Good, with a capital G—and to defend difference because there is no Archimedean point outside the world of contesting localities from which to adjudicate. This has its less attractive exponents: ASEAN despots who defend the intolerance of their regimes against Amnesty International's critiques by arguing that human rights campaigns are just another colonial attempt to impose Western norms upon 'Asian values'; or those who defend female genital mutilation (FGM) as an expression of 'African values'. But it surely also has its more engaging defenders: who want to keep a space for forms of life threatened by the economic and political hegemony of the industrialized world.

Thinking about these debates can help us to distinguish two ways in which we might justify tolerance for illiberal practices that are grounded in local traditions. Most people feel very differently about male and female 'circumcision'. The circumcision of male infants has very little to be said for it as a medical procedure; and even if it did, it is a form of irreversible bodily alteration that might, on general liberal grounds, be best left to men to decide on for themselves. Something similar might be said for the piercing of the earlobes of infant girls. Yet, surely, attempts to impose this view on the billions of people who practise one or the other would be an unjustified invasion of societies where these practices are tied to a sense of 'identity'. It is here that the two possible lines of response come apart.

One line is just to endorse an anti-universalistic cosmo-politanism. Liberalism is just *our* local framework; Confucianism and many African traditional religions provide others, each of which is, as they say, 'equally valid'. This will allow us to permit male circumcision, but only at the cost of allowing FGM as well. I have very little sympathy with this line of approach myself. It requires us to define hermetically sealed worlds, closed off from one another, within which everyone is trapped into a moral consensus, inaccessible to arguments from outside. And what are we to say, then, of the African women who are opposed to FGM? Or of Indonesians who have struggled to speak freely? I would rather argue that the harm done by involuntary male circumcision, say, was too small to offset the value that it derives from the wider meanings in which it is embedded. That would allow us to distinguish it from FGM and Indonesian limitations on free expression, because these latter, however well rooted in local traditions, are too burdensome to be justified by their contributions to the meanings of particular African or Southeast Asian identities.

I cannot explore here in all its richness the debates about moral relativism. But if cosmopolitanism is to be defended, we must start by deciding which route to follow: shall we follow a universalism that is sensitive to the ways in which historical context may shape the moral significance of a practice, or an anti-universalism that protects difference at the cost of sealing each community into a moral world of its own?

Let me try to situate the scepticism that grounds so many recent anti-universalistic arguments, by exploring it in the form of the sceptical anti-universalism made familiar by Richard Rorty. This begins with what he calls 'ironism', which combines the acknowledgement of the historical contingency of our own central beliefs and desires—which he dubs our 'final vocabulary'—with 'radical and continuing doubts' about our own starting points. This ironism is, as I am sure you will recognize, a pretty regular feature of the contemporary academy, though it is also as well to remember that the world is full of people (inside the university as well as outside) whose doubts, if any, about the grounding of their own moral positions are, to put it mildly, far from manifest.

Rorty's ironism is grounded in the experience of being 'impressed by other vocabularies . . . taken as final by people or books' that one has encountered and the conviction that nothing in his own final vocabulary can either 'underwrite or dissolve' these doubts, because *his* vocabulary is no closer to reality than anyone else's.[7] It is grounded, then, in a sceptical response to the exposure to those other nations with which the cosmopolitan venture, as Sterne's French officer articulates it, begins.

This sceptical anti-universalism is not, of course, just Rorty's: it is reflected in Lyotard's story of postmodernity as the end of meta-narratives and, in my view, in the formal fragmentation of postmodern literary texts. All of these moves have been glossed in various ways as rejections of the Enlightenment. And in such a context an older humanism, with the notion of a human essence, a human nature that grounds the universality of human rights, has indeed come to seem to many simply preposterous.

But the argument here has not always managed to avoid muddle. A critique of the Enlightenment on Rorty's grounds—one that combines anti-realism in metaphysics and scepticism in epistemology—has been combined, dare I say, inconsistently with a critique whose foundations are, so to speak, '*plus universaliste que le roi*'. Often, that is, attacks on something called 'Enlightenment humanism' have been attacks not on the universality of Enlightenment pretensions but on the Eurocentrism of their real bases: Hume's or Kant's or Hegel's inability to imagine that a 'Negro' could achieve anything in the sphere of 'arts and letters' is objectionable not because it is humanist or universalistic but because it is neither. A large part of the motivation for this recent anti-universalism has been a conviction that past universalism was a projection of European values and interests: this is a critique that is best expressed by saying that the actually existing Enlightenment was not Enlightened; it is not an argument that Enlightenment was the wrong project.

If you want, as I do, to hold on to the idea that the

ethnocentrism of the Enlightenment was wrong, but still share the radical and continuing doubts of Rorty's ironist, you must find, I believe, a different response than his to the cosmopolitan experience of being 'impressed by other vocabularies'. I prefer, that is, to speak with the Enlightenment: to think of dialogue—all dialogue, not just the dialogue across nations that cosmopolitans favour—as a shared search for truth and justice.[8] I am impressed by other vocabularies not so much, as Rorty is, because they threaten my current convictions as because they may have something to teach me.

At the end of his paper on 'Justice as a Larger Loyalty', Rorty says:

I think that discarding the residual rationalism that we inherit from the Enlightenment is advisable for many reasons. Some of these are theoretical and of interest only to philosophy professors . . . Others are more practical. One practical reason is that getting rid of rationalistic rhetoric would permit the West to approach the non-West in the role of someone with an instructive story to tell, rather than in the role of someone purporting to be making better use of a universal human capacity.[9]

The 'universal human capacity' in question is 'reason': and what Rorty wants 'us' to do in 'our' dialogue with the 'non-West', rather than trying to show them that our 'Western' use of the universal capacity of reason has revealed more truths and a better way to live, is to suggest instead that among our 'shared beliefs and desires there may be enough resources to permit agreement on how to coexist without violence'.[10] That, then, is Rorty's proposal. I shall return to it after sketching my own.

People from other parts of the world attract our moral attention; through them we see the 'balance of good and bad' in a particular position, and our sympathy is engaged. In the past, in a humanist narrative, this would have been glossed as the discovery of our common humanity: and these responses to others could have been defended in that tradition as a source of insight into that human nature. Yes, they are different and we rejoice in that: but we can rejoice in it in the end only because it is human difference. (Strains of the 'Ode to Joy' in the background here . . . 'Alle Menschen werden Brüder . . .' und so weiter.)

This—I agree with Rorty here—is the wrong conclusion. To find the right one, let me begin by filling in the caricature of the view that we have both rejected. On that older view, there was an objective human nature: there were objective needs and interests, grounded in both our animal and our rational natures, and it was in these common natures that our common human rights were somehow based. The task one faced, then, in addressing a society other than one's own—a people whose moral views were Other—was to point them to that common nature and show how it grounded these moral claims. Principles were universal: what was local was their application. This was a form of moral realism; the view that the universe, not human sentiment, determines what is right and good. And for the moral realist, of course, if the universe is on my side, it will naturally be opposed to those Others who disagree with me.

Many problems were identified over the years with this project. One was that it appeared to commit what G. E. Moore dubbed the 'naturalistic fallacy', the mistake Hume purportedly identified in trying to derive an 'ought' from an 'is', confusing facts and values, the True and the Good. After two centuries of Humean philosophy, we are now being urged from many philosophical directions to give up the fact–value opposition and accept some form of moral realism. Moral facts, on these views, are in as good a shape as facts about the birds and the bees. Rorty seems to want to go the other way, here, giving up the idea that the universe determines what the facts are, so that values are in no worse shape than facts. This is a philosopher's debate that I have a stake in. About this I think he is wrong.

But the debates over realism about the True and the Good carry no special weight in the context of a dialogue between Rorty's 'West' and the 'non-West', or, to be slightly more concrete, between 'human rights' and 'Asian values'. For, if the naturalistic fallacy is a mistake, then the old humanist argument is a bad foundation for belief in human rights, *even within the West*. 'Of course,' the humanist will agree, 'if my moral realism is mistaken, I have no argument to make to these Others for the correctness of my views; but that is because, if moral realism is incorrect, *nobody* has any reason to believe in human rights, not even me.'

The problem I want to raise for dialogue across societies arises even if moral realism is correct. And if the position I am caricaturing as the older humanism had ever seriously faced real other societies, this very untheoretical problem would have reared its ugly head.

I happen to believe that there is such a thing as a universal human biology, that there is a biological human nature. I would say, for example, that it is defined by the more than 99% of our genes that we all share, by the fact that our closest common ancestor may have lived a little more than 100,000 years ago. Such central events as the old triad of 'birth, copulation and death' are, in obvious ways, reflections of that biology. So I don't think what's wrong with the older argument is the appeal to a human essence.

The problem that becomes clear in real cases is that the interests that people have in virtue of our shared biology do not exist outside their symbolic contexts. We give birth not to organisms but to kin; we copulate not with other bodies but with lovers and spouses; and the end of the organic life has a meaning that depends crucially not only on questions of fact (Is there a life beyond?) but also on questions of value (Do we have, in our society, the notion of a life that is, in some sense completed?). A shared biology, a natural human essence, does not give us, in the relevant sense, a shared ethical nature.

And once you enter into a genuine dialogue with people who hold views other than your own about these matters, you are going to discover that there is no non-question-begging way of settling on a basis of facts, whether moral or non-moral, from which to begin to discuss. There are no guaranteed foundations. It does no good here to say, with the moral realist, that whether we can persuade people of the correctness of our view of the good for them is a separate issue from whether our view is correct. I too think that is right; but that is, so far, just a theoretical question, an issue for philosophers. For making that distinction does not free us from the problem I am trying to delineate, which is, as I want to insist, a *practical* problem.

In real life, ethical judgements are intimately tied up with metaphysical and religious belief and with beliefs about the natural order. And these are matters about which agreement may be difficult to achieve. (It's hard to persuade people there are, on the one hand, no electrons or, on the other, no witches.) Real dialogue will quickly get stymied in these circumstances because interlocutors who disagree at *this* level are likely to treat each other's claims as 'merely hypothetical' and are thus not likely to engage with them seriously.

The result is that if we in fact take up dialogue across gaps of belief, experience, imagination, or desire, we will end up unable to find real agreements at the level of principle. More than this, we shall often end up failing to agree not about principle but about what is to be done. A disagreement of principle about why we should save this child from drowning does not practically have to be resolved, if in fact we agree that the child must be saved. But what if you believe that the child is meant to die because an ancestor has called her and I do not?

What I want to suggest, however, is that there was something wrong with the original picture of how dialogue should be grounded. It was based on the idea that we must find points of agreement at the level of principle: here is human nature, here is what human nature dictates. What we learn from travel, but also from reading novels or watching films from other places, is that we can identify points of agreement that are much more local and contingent than this. We can agree, in fact, with many moments of judgement, even if we do not share the framework within which those judgements are made, even if we cannot identify a framework, even if there are no principles articulated at all. And, to the extent that we have problems finding our way into novels, or films or neighbourhoods, they can occur just as easily with novels and films and places around the corner, as they do with those from far away.

Rorty does not notice this, I think, because he supposes that debates within the West are different from debates across a Western–non-Western divide. And that is because he believes—as his provocative articulation of his position as 'ethnocentrism' suggests—that something called 'Western culture' (Rorty's 'we', without qualification, is almost always 'the West') does for conversations within the West what the universe was supposed to do for my humanist. For Rorty, what he calls 'Western culture', historically contingent as it may be, is what 'we' all share, it is the sea 'we' navigate together, the air 'we' all breathe. If I wanted to put sharply what I think is wrong with this formulation, I would say that I find it much easier to converse with the Queen Mother of Asante than I would to spend time discussing almost anything with a Republican Senator in the United States. I do not believe in the homogeneity of this cold Western air, or in its difference at every point from the air of the 'warm South'.

I have managed to write until now without using the word 'culture', except twice in the last few sentences to invoke a notion that Rorty uses, which brings the word in only in quotation marks. And I have been able to do so because I have become increasingly convinced that culture, like the luminiferous ether of nineteenth-century physics, doesn't do much work. I spoke a little while ago about 'dialogue across societies' and, perhaps, you thought this was just a periphrastic way of invoking cross-*cultural* dialogue. But if it is true that there are difficulties in cross-cultural dialogue, in this sense, they are often no more and no less substantial than dialogues within societies: between James Baldwin and Margaret Mead; between Sterne's world and me; between Toni Morrison and Shakespeare. Treating international difference, between what Rorty calls 'the West' and 'the non-West', as an especially profound kind of something called 'cultural difference' is, in my view, a specially profound and characteristically modern mistake. I reread *Sentimental Journey* prior to writing this paper and it struck me as a much stranger book than any African novel I have read recently; it was harder work, it needed more footnotes, there were more sentences I had to read twice. The sexual politics of Sterne's casual libertinage (the libertinage, I should remind you, of a priest of the Church of England) is stranger to me than anything in Chinua Achebe's gender politics. How does it help, in these circumstances, to speak of Western culture as something that undergirds 'our' response to Sterne, or of Igbo culture as a barrier to 'our' grasping Achebe?

It would be a long task to think through why we have come to invoke 'culture' as the name for the gap between us here and them there. But we should acknowledge how much our—which in this case means 'your'—sense of 'them' (the Igbo of Achebe's novels, the Yoruba of Soyinka's plays, my Asante forbears and contemporaries) is the product of a disciplinary artifact. Anthropology, our source of narratives of otherness, has a professional bias towards difference. Who would want to go out for a year of fieldwork 'in the bush' in order to return with the news that 'they' do so many things just as we do? We don't hear about cross-cultural sameness for the same reason we don't hear about all those non-carcinogenic substances in our environment: sameness is the null result.

I want to defend a kind of cosmopolitanism. But not as the name for a dialogue among static closed cultures, each of which is internally homogeneous and different from all the others; not as a celebration of the beauty of a collection of closed boxes.

The humanism I have caricatured was right in thinking that what we humans share is important. But it was wrong, I think, as Rorty does, about the boundaries of what we share. Far from relying on a common understanding of our common human nature or a common articulation (through principles) of a moral sphere, we often respond to the situations of others with shared judgements about particular cases. We in our settings are able to find many moments where we share with people from different settings a sense that something has gone right or gone wrong. It isn't principle that brings the missionary doctor and the distressed mother together at the hospital bedside of a child with cholera: it is a shared concern for this particular child. And you do not need to be a missionary or an ethnographer to discover such moments: it happens also when we read. What we find in the novel, which is always a message in a bottle from some other position, even if it was written and published last week in your home town, derives not from a theoretical understanding of us as having a commonly understood common nature—not, then, from an understanding that we (we readers and writers) all share—but from an invitation to respond in imagination to narratively constructed situations. In short, what makes the cosmopolitan experience possible, in reading as elsewhere, is not that we share beliefs and values because of our common capacity for reason. In the novel, at least, it is not 'reason' but a different human capacity that grounds our sharing: namely, the grasp of a narrative logic that allows us to construct the world to which our imaginations respond. That capacity is to be found up the Amazon, the Mississippi, the Congo, the Indus, and the Yellow Rivers, just as it is found on the banks of the Avon and the Dordogne.

I am insisting on agreement about particulars rather than about universals and on the role of the narrative imagination in our response to fictions, then, because I see them as neglected elements in our accounts of our responses to people who are different from ourselves. I do not deny that agreement about universals occurs, too. Nor do I agree with Rorty that the gift for narrative is the only one, or the most important one, that we share. Here is a point, in fact, where our philosopher's disagreement about rationalism makes a difference: for 'rationalistic rhetoric' claims that in all encounters human beings are struggling with similar mental apparatus to understand a single world. Not only do I believe, unlike Rorty, that this is just how things are, I think, despite Rorty, that thinking this way helps in disagreements with others, whether those others are down the street today or across oceans or centuries from ourselves. Rorty supposes that the rationalist is bound to think that 'we' are right and 'they' are wrong: but if there is one world only, then it is also possible that *they* might be right. We can only learn from each other's stories if we share both human capacities and a single world: relativism about either is a reason not to converse but to fall silent. Rorty wants to speak to others, to enlarge our 'Western' sympathies: discarding what he calls our 'residual rationalism' strikes me as being of no help in this project we share. Even on pragmatist grounds, he ought, I think, to be on my side.

Cosmopolitanism imagines a world in which people and novels and music and films and philosophies travel between places where they are understood differently, because people are different and welcome to their difference. Cosmopolitan- ism can work because there can be common conversations about these shared ideas and objects. But what makes the conversations possible is not always shared culture (though, if the word 'culture' is to be kept for anything, there will no doubt be shared cultures and conversations based on them); not even, as the older humanists imagined, universal principles or values (though sometimes people from far away can discover that their principles meet); nor yet shared under- standing (though sometimes people with very different experiences end up agreeing about the darndest things). What works in meetings with other human beings across gaps of space, time, and experience is enormously varied. For novels and films, for example, it is the capacity to follow a narrative and conjure a world: and that, it turns out, there are people everywhere more than willing to do.

The cosmopolitan agenda focuses on conversations among places: but the case for those conversations applies for conversations among cities, regions, classes, genders, races, sexualities, across all the dimensions of difference. For we do learn something about humanity in responding to the worlds people conjure with words in the narrative framework of the novel, or with images in the frame of film: we learn about the extraordinary diversity of human responses to our world and the myriad points of intersection of those various responses. If there is a critique of the Enlightenment to be made, it is not that the *philosophes* believed in human nature, or the universality of reason: it is rather that they were so dismally unimaginative about the range of what we have in common.

The position I have come to may seem to be uneasily placed between the impulses I have dubbed universalistic and anti-universalistic. I have said that what two people or two societies have in common as a basis for dialogue will generally include a hodgepodge of particular and general: narrative imagination, the capacity for love and reason, some principles, judgements about the rightness and wrongness of particular cases, the appreciation of certain objects. But that dodges such key questions, as whether there really are Asian values that differ from Western values, for example, in placing a lesser moral weight on individuality than on the collective. The key question isn't whether what we can share is various (it is) but whether or not it includes respect for certain fundamental moral values, among them, in particular, the fundamental human rights.

And, to insist on a point, I am not concerned only with whether we all have these rights. I believe we do, but then I would, since, to the extent that there is something called the West, I am pretty firmly intellectually ensconced in it. I am concerned with what I called the practical question of whether we can expect everybody in the world (or at any rate almost everybody, once they give us a reasonable degree of attention) to come round to *agreeing* that we have those rights.

This is, of course, too large a question to answer here. It is, in a certain sense, a question whose answer is developing before our eyes. We are watching a world in which people are facing each other with different ideas about what matters in human life, and influences are travelling, through the media and popular culture and evangelism and, no doubt, in many other ways. But in order to think clearly about what is at stake here, it is important to be clear about what picture of rights we are endorsing.

So, in this final part of this essay, I want, first, to sketch a picture of rights that fits with cosmopolitanism, because it combines universal and particular in the world of values. And then, in closing, I shall try to show you why I will not be so surprised if it commends itself to people in many places, all sorts and conditions of women and men.

The roots of the cosmopolitanism I am defending are liberal: and they begin from liberalism's fundamental insistence on the equal dignity of all people, their equal entitlement to respect. It is not easy to say in a short compass what this entails, and, indeed, it seems to me that exploring what it might mean is liberalism's historic project. But we have already learned some lessons about what a life of dignity requires in the modern world.

One slightly older lesson was expressed with great force by John Stuart Mill, in the third chapter of *On Liberty*, which might almost be summarized in this single sentence: 'If a person possesses any tolerable amount of common sense and experience, his own mode of laying out his existence is best, not because it is the best in itself, but because it is his own mode.'[11] The chapter is entitled 'On individuality, as one of the elements of wellbeing', and it is a powerful articulation of an ideal that is to be found, in various relatively familiar formulations, in a range of modern thinkers from Oscar Wilde[12] and Nietzsche to Sartre and Michel Foucault. Foucault put it tersely once by saying 'we have to create ourselves as a work of art'.[13] Nietzsche's formulation is both more elegant and more substantial, though he adds in a dash of illiberal and unnecessary elitism:

One thing is needful. To 'give style' to one's character—a great and rare art! It is practiced by those who survey all the strengths and weaknesses of their nature and then fit them into an artistic plan until every one of them appears as art and reason and even weaknesses delight the eye. Here a large mass of second nature has been added; there a piece of original nature has been removed— both times through long practice and daily work at it. Here the ugly that could not be removed is concealed; there it has been reinterpreted and made sublime.[14]

But perhaps its most familiar expression is in the words of that great American philosopher Frank Sinatra:

> I've lived a life that's full.
> I've traveled each and ev'ry highway;
> But more, much more than this, I did it my way.[15]

This life was good—the singer has 'too few' regrets 'to mention'—not just because it was full but because it was lived his way. If my choosing it is part of what makes my lifeplan good, then imposing on me a plan of life—even one that is, in other respects, a good one—is depriving me of a certain kind of good.

This liberal thought fits well with cosmopolitanism, because it suggests that people should be left to find their own way in the world, and that we should value the different ways they will choose. Liberalism is about freedom because freedom is a precondition for a dignified human existence: and it is such a precondition because a human life is something for which each person is him or herself responsible. Liberalism values individuals and celebrates, with cosmopolitanism, the great variety of what individuals will choose when given freedom.

Liberalism of this stripe is thus different from libertarianism—the view that the less government we have the better—because it is consistent with the former, but not with the latter, to value government as a provider of the materials for self-creation. But it is also likely to seem to be a hopeless starting point for founding a global project, because it is likely to seem to beg the question against the claims that have been made from many directions that the West is 'too individualist'.[16]

So it is important to see that the individual whose self-creation is being valued here is not, in the justly censorious sense of the term, individualist. Many people around the world, including many within the West, would object to a liberalism that was premised upon a deep unsociability. But nothing I have said is inconsistent with the recognition of the many ways in which we human beings are naturally and inevitably social. First, because we are incapable of developing on our own, because we need human nurture, moral and intellectual education, practice with language, if we are to develop into full persons. This is a sociality of mutual dependence. Second, because we naturally[17] desire relationship with others: friends, lovers, parents, children, the wider family, colleagues, neighbours. This is sociality as an end. And third, because many other things we value—literature, and the arts, the whole world of culture; education; money; and, in the modern world, food and housing—depend essentially on society for their production. This is instrumental sociality. But there is a deeper sense in which this picture recognizes the social construction of the individual self; and to make that point, which draws on the lessons of the multicultural liberalism of someone like Charles Taylor, it is helpful to introduce the more recent vocabulary of 'identity'.

The contemporary use of the word 'identity' to refer to such features of people as their race, ethnicity, nationality, gender, religion or sexuality, first achieved prominence (and perhaps had its origin) in the work of Erik Erikson. This use of the term 'identity' reflects, of course, the conviction that each person's identity—in the older sense of who he or she truly is—is deeply inflected by such social features. And it is an undeniable fact of modern life that people have increasingly come to believe that this is so. In political and moral thinking nowadays it has become commonplace to suppose that a person's projects can reasonably be expected to be shaped by such features of their identity and that this is, if not morally required, then at least morally permissible. We understand the woman who organizes her life and her affiliations around her gender, or the gay man who sees his sexuality as shaping the meaning of his life.

Identity has at least two dimensions. There is a collective dimension, the intersection of the sorts of identities we have been discussing; but there is also what one might call a personal dimension, consisting of other socially important features of the person—intelligence, charm, wit, greed—that are not themselves the basis of forms of collective identity. Not every aspect of the collective dimension will have the general power of sex, gender, and sexuality or of nationality, ethnicity, and religion. What the collective dimensions have in common is that they are what the philosopher Ian Hacking has dubbed 'kinds of person'. Hacking's key insight about 'kinds of person'—men, gays, Americans, Catholics, but also butlers, bakers, and philosophers—is that they are brought into being by the creation of names for them.[18] So he defends what he calls a 'dynamic nominalism', arguing 'that numerous kinds of human beings and human acts come into being hand in hand with our invention of the categories labeling them.'[19]

Hacking begins from the philosophical truism that, in intentional action, people act 'under descriptions'; that their actions are conceptually shaped. (What I do is dependent on what I think I am doing. To use a simple example, I have to have a wide range of concepts for my writing my name in a certain way to count as 'signing a contract'.) It follows that what I can do depends on what concepts I have available to me; and among the concepts that may shape my action is the concept of a certain kind of person and the behaviour appropriate to a person of that kind.

Hacking offers as an example Sartre's brilliant evocation, in *Being and Nothingness*, of the Parisian *garçon de café*:

His movement is quick and forward, a little too precise, a little too rapid. He comes towards the patrons with a step a little too quick.

He bends forward a little too eagerly, his eyes express an interest too solicitous for the order of the customer.[20]

The idea of the *garçon de café* lacks the sort of theoretical commitments that are trailed by many of our social identities: black and white, gay and straight, man and woman. So, it makes no sense to ask of someone who is employed as a *garçon de café* whether that is what they really are. Because we have expectations of the *garçon de café*, it is a recognizable identity. But those expectations are about the performance of the role; they depend on our assumption of intentional conformity to the expectations.

With other identities, however—and here the familiar collectives of race, ethnicity, gender, and the rest come back into view—the expectations we have are not based simply on the idea that those who have these identities are playing out a role. Rightly or wrongly, we do not normally think of the expectations we have of men or of women as being simply the result of the fact that there are conventions about how men and women behave.

Once labels are applied to people, ideas about people who fit the label come to have social and psychological effects. In particular, these ideas shape the ways people conceive of themselves and their projects. So the labels operate to mould what we may call '*identification*', the process through which individuals intentionally shape their projects—including their plans for their own lives and their conceptions of the good life—by reference to available labels, available identities. In identification, I shape my life by the thought that something is an appropriate aim or an appropriate way of acting for an American, a black man, a philosopher. It seems right to call this 'identification' because the label plays a role in shaping the way the agent takes decisions about how to conduct a life, in the process of the construction of one's identity.

Thus, every collective identity seems to have the following sort of structure:

a label, 'L' associated with *ascriptions* by most people (where ascription involves descriptive criteria for applying 'L') which lead to *expectations* about how Ls will behave; and *identifications* by Ls (where identification implies a shaping role for the label in the intentional acts of the possessors, so that they sometimes act *as an L*); and, finally, consequences, in the way that people treat Ls (so that sometimes they are treated *as an L*).

These 'as an Ls'—acting as an L, being treated as an L—connect identities to conceptions of what Ls are (or should be) like.

To see what is going on here, it may be helpful to consider two different pictures of what is involved in shaping one's individuality. One, a picture that comes from romanticism, is the idea of finding one's self, of discovering in reflection or in a careful attention to the world, a meaning for one's life that is already there, waiting to be found. This is the vision we can call *authenticity*: it is a matter of being true to who you already really are. The other picture, the *existentialist* picture, is one in which, as the doctrine goes, existence precedes essence: which is just a fancy way of saying that you exist first and then have to decide what to exist *as*, who to be, afterwards. On an extreme version of this view, we have to make a self up, as it were out of nothing, like God at the Creation, and individuality is valuable because only a person who has made a self has a life worth living. But neither of these pictures is right.

The authenticity picture is wrong because it suggests that

there is no role for creativity in making a self, that it is all already fixed by our natures. And the existentialist picture is wrong because it suggests that there is only creativity, that there is nothing for us to respond to, nothing out of which to do the construction. The reasonable middle view is that constructing an identity is a good but that the identity must make some kind of sense. And for it to make sense, as the examples of race or gay identity suggest, it must be an identity constructed in response to facts outside one's self, things that are beyond one's own choices. Self-construction, to make human sense, must draw on what history has given each of us.

And thinking about what history has, in fact, given us, as materials for our identities, will allow us to answer the worry I raised about the unsociability of the liberal self. For the language of identity allows us to remind ourselves how much it is true that we are, in Charles Taylor's elegant formulation, 'dialogically' constituted: beginning in infancy, it is in dialogue with other people's understandings of who I am that I develop a conception of my own identity. We come into the world 'mewling and puking in our mother's arms' (as the Bard of Avon so genially put it) capable of human individuality, but only if we have the chance to develop it in interaction with others. An identity is always articulated through concepts (and practices) made available to you by religion, society, school, and state, mediated by family, peers, friends. Dialogue shapes the identities we develop as we grow up: but the very material out of which we make it is provided, in part, by our society, by what Taylor has called our language in 'a broad sense', which 'cover[s] not only the words we speak, but also other modes of expression whereby we define ourselves, including the "languages" of art, of gesture, of love, and the like'.[21] It follows that the self whose choices liberalism celebrates is not a pre-social thing—not some authentic inner essence independent of the human world into which we have grown—but rather the product of our interaction from our earliest years with others.[22]

As a result, individuality presupposes sociability, not just a grudging respect for the individuality of others. A free self is a human self, and we are, as Aristotle long ago insisted, creatures of the *polis*, social beings. To have individuality as a value is not, therefore, to refuse to acknowledge the dependence of the good for each of us on relationships with others. Indeed, as I have suggested, without relationships we could not come to be free selves, because we could not come to be selves at all. But a free self isn't just dependent on others at the start. Throughout our lives part of the material that we are responding to in shaping our selves is not within us but outside us, out there in the social world. Many people—most, in fact—shape their identities as partners of lovers who become spouses and fellow-parents.

I hope I have persuaded you that you already think that identity, as I have been explaining it, matters. But how does identity fit into our broader moral projects?

One view is this: There are many things of value in the world. Their value is objective, they are important whether or not anybody recognizes they are important. But there is no way of ranking these many goods or trading them off against one another, so there is not always, all things considered, a best thing to do. As a result, there are many morally permissible options. One thing identity provides is another source of value, which helps us make our way among those options. To adopt an identity, to make it mine, is to see it as structuring my way through life. That identity has built into it that which helps me think about my life: one such simple pattern, for example, is the pattern of a career, which ends, if we live long enough, with retirement. But identities also create forms of solidarity: if I think of myself as an X, then sometimes the mere fact that somebody else is an X too may incline me to do something with or for them; where X, here, might be 'woman', 'black', 'American'. Now solidarity with those who share your identity might be thought of as, other things being equal, always a good thing: so there is a universal value of solidarity but it works out in different ways for different people, because different people have different identities. Or it might be thought to be a good thing, as well, because we enjoy it and because, other things being equal, it is good for people to have and to do what they enjoy having and doing.

But, as we have seen, there are also values that are internal to an identity, that make sense for someone who has it, and which, for someone who has that identity, are among the values they must take into account, but which are not values for people who do not have that identity. If they did not have that identity, that thing would not be a value for them. Take the value of ritual purity as an example, as conceived of by some orthodox Jews. They think they should keep kosher because they are Jewish: they don't expect anyone who is not a Jew to do so, and they may not even think it would be a good thing if they did. It is a good thing only for those who are or those who become Jewish: and they do not think that it would be a better world if everybody did become Jewish. The covenant, after all, is only with the children of Israel.

Similarly, we might think that the identity of being a nationalist in a struggle against colonial domination might make it valuable for you to risk your life for the liberation of your country, as Nathan Hale did, regretting that he only had *one* life to give. If you were not a nationalist, you might still die advancing your country's cause; and then, while some good came of it, the good that came of it would not be, so to speak, a good for you. We might regard your life as wasted, just because you did not identify with the nation you had died for.

There are thus different ways in which identity might be a source of intrinsic value, intrinsic in the sense of being a source of value rather than being something that realizes other values. First, if an identity is yours, it may determine certain acts of solidarity as valuable, or it may be an internal part of the specification of your satisfactions and enjoyments. It is good for me to help you deal with your HIV infection as a fellow American, or as another gay person. Or: I gain enjoyment from giving money to the Red Cross after a hurricane in Florida as an act of solidarity with other Americans or with other Cuban-Americans.

Second, it may make certain acts or achievements have a value for me they would not otherwise have had: would not have had if I had not had that identity. When a Ghanaian team wins the African Cup of Nations in soccer, that is of value to me in virtue of my identity as a Ghanaian. If I am Catholic, a wedding in a Catholic Church is of value to me because I am a Catholic. Whatever it would be worth to me if I were not a Catholic, it would have to matter to me in a different way.

This picture of self-creation places identity at the heart of human life: and liberalism, I am suggesting, takes this picture seriously and tries to construct a state and society within which it is possible. But the cosmopolitan impulse is central to this view, too, because it sees a world of cultural and social variety as an essential precondition for the self-creation that is at the heart of a meaningful human life. And all of this, remember, is the working out of the notion that we are creatures equal in dignity.

Scepticism about the genuinely cosmopolitan character of the view I have been defending may flow in part from the thought that it seems so much a creature of Europe and its liberal tradition.[23] So it may be as well to insist in closing that my own attachment to these ideas comes, as much as anything, from my father, who grew up in Asante, at a time when the independence of its moral climate from that of European Enlightenment was extremely obvious. Of course, he also went on to live in London for many years and acquired there the training of an English lawyer; and, of course, the school he went to in Ghana was a Methodist school, a colonial variant of the English boys' public school, where he was taught to think morally through Cicero and Caesar as much as through the New Testament. It would be preposterous to claim, in short, that he came to his cosmopolitanism or his faith in human rights and the rule of law unaffected by European cultural traditions.

But it would be equally fatuous to deny that the view he arrived at had roots in Asante (indeed, as one travels the world, reviewing the liberal nationalisms of South Asia and Africa in the mid-century, one is struck not only by their similarities but also by their local inflections). Two things, in particular, strike me about the local character of the source of my father's increasing commitment to individual rights: first, that it grew out of experience of illiberal government; second, that it depended on a sense of his own dignity and the dignity of his fellow citizens that was almost entirely the product of Asante conceptions.

The first point about experience, is crucial to the case for liberalism. It is the historical experience of the dangers of intolerance—religious intolerance in Europe in the seventeenth century, for example, for Locke; racial intolerance in the colonial context, for Gandhi (or for my father)—that often lies behind the scepticism about the state's interventions in the lives of individuals that itself underlies much liberal sentiment. My father saw the colonial state's abuses of his fellows and, in particular, the refusal to pay them the respect that was their due; he was imprisoned, later, by Kwame Nkrumah, without trial (and then released after a year and a half in detention with as little explanation as when he was arrested). As a lawyer and a member of the opposition, he travelled Ghana in the years after independence defending people whose rights were being abused by the postcolonial state.

The political tradition of liberalism is rooted in these experiences of illiberal government. That liberal restraint on government recommends itself to people rooted in so many different traditions is a reflection of its grasp of a truth about human beings and about modern politics.

Just as the centrality of murderous religious warfare in the period leading up to Locke's *Treatises* placed religious toleration at the core of Locke's understanding of the liberalism he defended, so the prime place of the persecution of political dissenters in the postcolonial experience of tyranny has made protection of political dissent central to the liberalism of those who resist postcolonial states in Africa.[24] (My father worried little about the state's entanglement with religion; once, I remember, as the national television came to the end of its broadcast day, my father sang along with the national hymn that they played some evenings, the religious twin of the more secular national anthem that they played on others. 'This would be a much better national anthem', he said to me. And I replied, ever the good liberal, 'But the anthem has the advantage that you don't have to believe in God to sing it sincerely.' 'No one in Ghana is silly enough not to believe in God', my father replied.[25] And, now, I think he was right not to be worried about the entanglement: there is no history of religious intolerance in Ghana of the sort that makes necessary the separation of church and state; a genial ecumenism had been the norm at least until the arrival of American TV evangelism.)

But more important yet, I think, to my father's concern with individual human dignity was its roots in the preoccupation of free Asante citizens, both men and women, with notions of personal dignity, with respect and self-respect. Treating others with the respect that is their due is a central preoccupation of Asante social life, as is a reciprocal anxiety about loss of respect, shame, and disgrace.[26] Just as European liberalism—and democratic sentiment—grew by extending to every man and (then) woman, the dignity that feudal society offered only to the aristocracy, and thus presupposes, in some sense, aspects of that feudal understanding of dignity, so Ghanaian liberalism, at least in my father's form, depends on the prior grasp of concepts such as *animuonyam* (respect). It is clear from well-known Akan proverbs that respect was precisely not something that belonged in the past to everybody:

Agya Kra ne Agya Kwakyerçmç, emu biara mu nni animuonyam.
(Father Soul and Father Slave Kyerçmç, neither of them has any respect; that is, whatever you call him, a slave is still a slave.)

The point, however, is that just as *dignitas*, which was once, by definition, the property of an elite, has grown into human dignity, which is the property of every man and woman, so *animuonyam* can be the basis of the respect for all others that lies at the heart of liberalism.[27] Indeed, *dignitas* and *animuonyam* have a great deal in common. *Dignitas*, as understood by Cicero, reflects much that was similar between republican Roman ideology and the views of the nineteenth-century Asante elite; it was, I think, as an Asante that my father recognized and admired Cicero, not as a British subject.

A single case should not convince you that the prospects for a cosmopolitan liberalism are as rosy as I believe they are. But I am buoyed not only by this singular example, but also by the enthusiasm that the claims of the fundamental human rights meet not from governments, of course, but from millions of ordinary people around the world. Because we are, already, fellow citizens of a world. We do not have to wait for institutional change to exercise our common citizenship: for to engage respectfully in dialogue with others around the world about the questions great and small that we must solve together, about the many projects in which we can learn from each other, is already to live as fellow citizens, as Marcus Aurelius and Laurence Sterne's French officer did. I have been arguing that there is a great diversity in the starting-points we have for these conversations, the shared points of entry from which we can proceed. This is as true of conversations between Confucians from Shanghai and Pentecostalists from Peoria, as it is for conversations between people who differ in class and gender, or profession, or along a whole range of dimensions of identity. From these conversations we can be led to common action—for our shared environment, for human rights, for the simple enjoyment of comity. Respectful interchanges, common action: these we can take up with our fellow citizens, because we start with a common concern for our own dignity and a growing conviction of the worth of others. Because there are points of attachment for the project of dignity in so many places within my own society and around the world, I look forward with confidence to the process of the globalization of a cosmopolitan liberalism.

'In the course of my life I have seen Frenchmen, Italians, Russians etc.; I even know, thanks to Montesquieu, that one can be Persian; but *man* I have never met . . .'[28] So wrote Joseph de Maistre—no friend to liberalism—in his *Considérations sur la France*. It is a thought that can, ironically, be made consistent with a liberal cosmopolitanism; a thought that may even lead us to the view that cosmopolitanism is, in certain ways, inconsistent with one form of humanism. For a certain sort of humanist says that nothing human is alien: and we could gloss this as saying that the humanist respects each human being *as* a human being. Maistre is suggesting that we never really come to terms with anybody as a human because each actual person we meet, we meet as a French person, or as a Persian, in short, as a person with an identity far more specific than fellow human.[29] Exactly, the cosmopolitan says. And a good thing too. But we do not have to deal decently with people from other cultures and traditions *in spite of* our differences; we can treat others decently, humanely, *through* our differences. The humanism I have rejected requires us to put our differences aside; the cosmopolitan insists that sometimes it is the differences we bring to the table that make it rewarding to interact at all. That is, of course, to concede that what we share can be important, too; though the cosmopolitan will remind us that what we share with others is not always an ethnonational culture: sometimes it will just be that you and I, a Peruvian and a Slovak, both like to fish, or have read and admired Goethe in translation, or responded with the same sense of wonder to a postcard of the Parthenon, or believe, as lawyers with very different trainings, in the ideal of the rule of law.

That is, so to speak, the anglophone voice of cosmopolitanism. But, in the cosmopolitan spirit, let me end with a similar thought from my father's, no doubt less familiar, tradition: *Kuro korô mu nni nyansa*, our proverb says: In a single *polis*[30] there is no wisdom.

Response to Appiah

Richard Rorty

I agree with Anthony Appiah that 'a world of cultural and social variety' is 'an essential precondition for the self-creation that is the heart of an individual human life'. But I am not sure about his next sentence: 'And all of this, remember, is the working out of the notion that we are creatures equal in dignity.'

In a liberal cosmopolitan global society of the sort Appiah and I both hope for, all human beings will be treated as having dignity. But I do not see much point in saying that they are now, before such a society has been achieved, all equal in dignity. This doubt is a result of my more general suspicion of arguments of the form 'We ought to seek to establish a utopia of the following sort, because such-and-such is presently the truth about us.' My attitude is: let's try to figure out what kind of utopia we want, and let the truths about us be whatever we have to believe in order to work together for its creation. To put it crudely, let your view of human dignity fall out from your politics; don't milk your politics out of such a view.

I am not sure that this disagreement about precedence is of any importance. I am also not sure that any of the other philosophical issues about which Appiah says that he and I disagree matter. When it comes to facts and values, we both agree that 'moral facts are in as good a shape as facts about the birds and the bees', whatever that shape may be. I take the equality of status here to mean that true moral beliefs are true in exactly the same sense as are true beliefs about birds. Appiah may wish to analyse this sense in terms of correspondence to reality, I do not. But surely it is the equal status that matters, not the nature of truth?

At another passage in his essay the question of correspondence to reality comes up more explicitly. There Appiah says that he and I disagree about whether 'in all encounters human beings are struggling with similar mental apparatus to understand a single world'. I do not see any reason to doubt this claim, though I would rephrase it. As a faithful follower of Donald Davidson, I believe that anybody who can use one human language can learn to talk with users of any other human language about anything (my version of 'similar mental apparatus') and that most of everybody's beliefs about everything must be true (my version of 'understanding a single world'). But I doubt that this rephrasing matters for any purposes other than avoiding various tiresome issues that only philosophers discuss.

So when Appiah says that 'even on pragmatic grounds' I ought to be on his side, and to agree that 'we share both human capacities and a single world', my response is that we are already on the same side on all the issues that could have a practical import. We both agree that conversation can put anything up for grabs, and should be allowed to do so. The residual issue between the traditional representationalist view of mind and language (which I take it Appiah favours) and my Davidsonian/Wittgensteinian/Derridean non-representationalist view is hard to relate to practice. I have sometimes tried to establish such a relation by claiming that the latter view makes intellectual life a trifle harder for fanatics and authoritarians than the former. But I would not stake much on this claim. It is hard to imagine willingness to cooperate in inquiry, and in other social projects, as hanging on the outcome of debates between, say, Davidson and Searle, or Wittgenstein and Kripke.

Can I say, as Appiah does, that the Enlightenment was right to view 'the dialogue that cosmopolitans favour as a shared search for truth and justice'? Sure, if the latter phrase just means a shared search for agreement about what to believe and do in various circumstances. If it means more than that, I would claim, the 'more' is going to be pretty hard to make relevant to practice.

Having said about all I have to say about the issues I am inclined to brush aside as 'merely' philosophical, let me now turn to some other matters. I am sorry to have given Appiah the impression that I believe there to be, between 'the West' and 'the non-West' an especially profound kind of something called 'cultural difference'. I do not believe this, but I have to admit that some passages in a paper Appiah quotes ('Justice as a Larger Loyalty') suggest that I do. My only excuse is that the paper was prepared for an East–West Philosophy Conference; loose talk about whether the twain might ever meet was more or less built into the occasion.

On the other hand, I do feel pride in and loyalty towards the European Enlightenment (and, more generally, the tradition of secular cosmopolitanism that blossoms in the work of Sterne and Voltaire). I can see what Appiah means when he says that he finds it easier to talk to the Queen Mother of the Asante than with somebody like Senator Helms. I suspect I would too. But the fact that the geographical region we call 'the West' is not very homogeneous is no reason for admirers of the Stoics and the *philosophes* not to indulge in a bit of regional boosterism. If the utopia of which Appiah's and my dreams comes into existence, both groups of thinkers will be looked back to with affectionate gratitude.

Appiah says that he does not agree with me that 'the gift for narrative is the only one, or the most important one, that we [human beings] share.' I agree that it is not the only one. We also, to take the most obvious example, share a gift for argument—for what Brandom calls 'playing the game of giving and asking for reasons'. My hunch that the gift for narrative may be the most important one comes from my belief that narratives are a better source of hope than arguments, and that cooperating to construct a utopia is more a matter of shared hope rather than of shared belief.

Appiah says that 'our modern solidarity derives from stories in which we participate through synecdoche'—a point with which I heartily agree—and goes on to raise the question 'If there is no agent outside the human community, no antagonist to its protagonist, can we tell stories that bind us together?' This seems to me a good and important question, but I think there is a straightforward answer to it. Science-fiction stories, in which our descendants encounter societies of intelligent aliens—some better than us, some worse than us—fill the need for inspiring narratives about our species, rather than just about our tribe or nation. The size of the science-fiction sections in the bookstores suggests the hunger than people have for such narratives. Reading these stories plays a very large role in helping us to keep on hoping that human history may yet prove to be story of progress.

The most pessimistic of these stories suggest that we have already made too many mistakes: that things now can only get worse. The more optimistic science-fiction stories tell of a Terran federal republic in which fanaticism, racism, and homophobia have vanished, and in which the sort of liberal cosmopolitanism Appiah describes has been achieved. I doubt that we can overestimate the importance of such stories for the human future. Only if lots of young people in every country are gripped by such stories, and thereby come to dream some of the same dreams, are we likely to get anything like Appiah's utopia.

Endnotes

Notes to Introduction

1. Edmund Burke, *Reflections on the Revolution in France*, edited by J. G. A. Pocock (Cambridge: Hackett, 1987), p. 54.
2. Quoted in Eric Foner 'Introduction' in Thomas Paine, *Rights of Man* (Harmondsworth: Penguin, 1985), p. 7.
3. The phrase has recently been appropriated and been used to great effect by Richard Rorty. See, for example, his 'Human Rights, Rationality and Sentimentality' in Stephen Shute and Susan Hurley (eds.), *On Human Rights, The Oxford Amnesty Lectures 1993* (New York: Basic Books, 1993).
4. William Blake, 'London' in *Songs of Innocence and Experience* (Oxford: Oxford University Press, 1967), p. 150.
5. Quoted in the *New York Times*, 7 January 2001, p. 5.
6. Quoted in the *New York Times*, 23 August 2000, p. A8.
7. Quoted in 'Wired News', 12 September 2000.
8. Jay R. Mandel and Louis Ferleger, 'Preface', *The Annals, AAPSS*, 570, July 2000, p. 14.
9. Quoted in the *Guardian*, 27 January 2001, p. 28.
10. Though one certainly should not underestimate the importance of building institutions that can protect rights at the supranational level. See, for example, Benjamin R. Barber, 'Can Democracy Survive Globalization?', *Government and Opposition*, Summer 2000, pp. 275–301 and David Held, Daniele Archibugi, and Martine Köhler (eds.), *Re-Imagining Political Community: Studies in Cosmopolitan Democracy* (Cambridge: Polity, 1998).

Notes to Chapter 1

1. Part two, ch. iii. The 2,600 income distribution observations have been 'filtered to give high-quality data', including 682 observations from 108 countries.

2. Calculated from data on the top 100 transnational corporations in *United Nations, World Investment Report 1998* and *World Investment Report 1995*.

3. Susan George, *The Lugano Report* (London: Pluto Press, 1999).

4. Both cited in Howard M. Wachtel, 'The Mosaic of Global Taxes', published in French in *Le Monde Diplomatique*, October 1998.

5. 'Amid Restructuring, Seoul Predicts a Surge in Investment' and 'Foreigners Buy Record Total of Thai Assets', *International Herald Tribune*, 5 January 1999.

6. [Editor's note]: W. H. Auden's celebrated line is from 'September 1 1939', a poem he subsequently disavowed (he later pointed out that one had to die in any case). It can be found in E. Mendelson (ed.), *The English Auden: Poems, Essays and Dramatic Writings 1927–1939* (London: Faber, 1977), pp. 245–7.

Notes to the Response

1. Charles A. Reich, 'The New Property', *Yale Law Journal*, 73 (1964), p. 764.

2. Michael D. Reagan, *The Managed Economy* (New York: Greenwood Press, 1963), p. 190.

3. Ibid., p. 193.

4. Ibid., pp. 194–5.

5. Milton Friedman, 'Introduction to the Fiftieth Anniversary Edition', in F. A. Hayek, *The Road to Serfdom* (Chicago: Chicago University Press, 50th anniversary edition, 1994), p. ix.

6. Gunnar Myrdal, *Asian Drama: An Inquiry into the Poverty of Nations* (New York: Pantheon, 1968), p. 709.

7. Ibid., p. 727.

8. Ibid., p. 728.

9. See Folker Frobel, Jurgen Heinrichs, and Otto Kreye, *The New International Division of Labour: Structural Unemployment in Industrialised Countries and Industrialisation in Developing Countries* (Cambridge: Cambridge University Press, 1977).

10. Quoted in Henry A. Davis, *Project Finance: Practical Case Studies* (London: Euromoney Publications, 1996), p. 178.

Notes to Chapter 2

1. Reuters, 'U.N. Agencies Tell of Damage in Iraq', *New York Times*, 7 January; Betsy Pisik, 'Strikes Hit Iraqi Schools, Hospitals . . .', *Washington Times*, 8 January 1999.

2. *New Republic*, editorials, 2 May 1981; 2 April 1984. Tom Wicker, *New York Times*, 14 March 1986; editorial, *Washington Post National Weekly*, 1 March 1986. For a review of the spectrum that reached the general public, see Noam Chomsky *Necessary Illusions* (South End Press, 1989), and *Deterring Democracy* (Verso, 1991; extended edition Vintage, 1992).

3. Juan Hernández Pico, *Envío*, UCA, Jesuit University, Managua, March 1994.

4. Ruben Ricupero, statement published in *Third World Resurgence*, Penang, 95, 1998.

5. Paul Jeffrey, *National Catholic Reporter*, 11 December 1998, citing Honduran Bishop Angel Garachana. On the effects of deforestation and US development programmes, see also Sara Silver, 'Coffee Growers Find Less is More', *Austin American-Statesman*, 27 December 1998; Dudley Althaus, 'Deforestation Contributed to Tragedy by Mitch in Honduras, Experts Claim', *Houston Chronicle*, 30 December 1998 (*Central American Newspak*, 13, p. 23, December–January 1999).

6. Nitlapán-Envío team, 'A Time for Opportunities and Opportunists', *Envío*, 17 December 1998, p. 209. See also David Gonzales: 'Mitch Who? U.S. Stalls Mercy Flights: Aid to contras by express, disaster relief by boat', *New York Times*, 16 December 1988, New York City section, p. 27.

7. Reuters, 'French to Clear Unearthed Land Mines', *Peacework*, AFSC, Cambridge, Mass., December 1998.

8. On the 'secrecy', see Noam Chomsky, *At War with Asia* (Pantheon, 1970), reporting from the scene; Edward Herman and Noam Chomsky, *Manufacturing Consent* (Pantheon, 1988), reviewing the record.

9. Barry Wain, 'The Deadly Legacy of War in Laos', *Asia Wall Street Journal*, 24 January 1997; Padraic Convery, 'Living a Footstep away from Death', *Guardian Weekly*, 4 October 1998; Marcus Warren, 'America's Undeclared War Still Killing Children', *Sunday Telegraph*, 20 April 1997; *Accident Massacre*, Ronald Podlaski, James Forsyth, and Veng Saysana, Humanitarian Liaison Services, Warren Vermont, 1997; *A Deadly Harvest*, Mennonite Central Committee Bombie Removal Project, and Keith Graves, 'US Secrecy Puts Bomb Disposal Team in Danger', *Sunday Telegraph*, 4 January 1998; Matthew Chance, 'Secret War Still Claims Lives in Laos', *Independent*, 27 June 1997; Matthew Pennington, 'Inside Indochina', *Bangkok Post*, 20 February 1996, citing the Cambodian Mines Action Center. Fred Branfman, 'Something Missing: A Visit to the Plain of Jars', *Indochina Newsletter*, Cambridge, Mass., no. 4, 1995; a Lao-speaking IVS volunteer, Branfman did far more than anyone to try to expose the crimes in the Plain of Jars from the 1960s.

10. See, e.g. Reuters, 'Bomb Kills Seven Vietnamese Children', 10 April 1997. The deaths and 34 casualties in a school ground received 40 words in the *Wall Street Journal*, 60 in the *Boston Globe*, zero in the *New York Times*.

11. Amnon Kapeliouk, *Yediot Ahronot*, 7 April 1988. David Lamb: 'Agent Orange Said to Enter Vietnam Food Chain', *Los Angeles*

Times, 31 October 1998. Barbara Crossette, *New York Times*, 18 August 1992, Science section. Peter Waldman, 'In Vietnam, the Agony of Birth Defects Calls An Old War to Mind', *Wall Street Journal*, 17 February 1997.

12. Barbara Crossette, 'Indochina's Missing: An Issue That Refused to Die', *New York Times*, 14 August 1991; *New York Times*, 6 January 1992.

13. David Sanger, 'Hanoi to Assume Debts Owed U.S. by Saigon Rulers', *New York Times*, 11 March 1997.

14. *New York Times*, 24 October 1992.

15. News conference, 24 March 1977.

16. Nicholas Kristof, 'Burying the Past: War Guilt Haunts Japan', *New York Times*, 30 November 1998; Peter Grier, 'Lessons from Monet to Pinochet', *Christian Science Monitor*, 4 December 1998. On these issues, see Noam Chomsky, *Year 501* (South End Press, 1993), ch. 10; 'Hamlet without the Prince', *Diplomatic History*, 20.3, Summer 1996, symposium on Robert McNamara's memoirs; 'Memories', *Z* magazine, July/August 1995. On public opinion, see the regular surveys by the Chicago Council on Foreign Relations, John Rielly (ed.), *American Public Opinion and U.S. Foreign Policy*, the most recent in 1999.

17. Mary Ann Glendon, 'Knowing the Universal Declaration of Human Rights', 73 *Notre Dame Law Review* 1153, 1998. Thomas Paine, *Rights of Man*, pt. ii, 1792. Bruce Kicklick (ed.), *Thomas Paine, Political Writings* (Cambridge University Press, 1989).

18. *The United Nations and Human Rights 1945–1995*, UN Blue Books Series, vol. vii, Department of Public Information, UN New York, 1995.

19. 'Respect for Human Rights, the Secret of True Peace'. See Arthur Jones, 'Pope Blasts Consumerism as Human Rights Threat', *National Catholic Reporter*, 8 January 1999. In the national press, the message was briefly reported but not its content (*Washington Post* and *New York Times*, 2 January 1999;

the last sentence of the *NYT* report alluded to the content). The Vatican message had received some limited earlier mention. A database search found scattered references, including one in the national press: Reuters, *New York Times*, 16 December 1998, p. 19. The general issues received some coverage when the Pope visited Mexico a few weeks later. See Alessandra Stanley, 'Pope is Returning to Mexico with New Target: Capitalism', *New York Times*, 22 January, also 24 January. Richard Chacón and Diego Ribadeneira, *Boston Globe*, 24, 25 January 1999.

20. Alessandra Stanley, *NYT*, 22 January 1999, above.

21. Vyshinksky quoted by David Manasian: 'Human-Rights Law: the conscience of mankind', *Economist*, 5 December 1998; Kirpatrick by Joseph Wronka, 'Human Rights', in R. Edwards (ed.), *Encyclopedia of Social Work* (NASW, Washington, 1995), pp. 1405–18. See also his *Human Rights and Social Policy in the 21st Century* (University Press of America, 1992), and 'A Little Humility, Please', *Harvard International Review*, Summer 1998. Abrams, Statement, UN Commission on Human Rights, on Item 8, 'The Right to Development', 11 February 1991.

22. Amnesty International London, *United States of America: Rights for All*, October 1998. See interview with Pierre Sané, Secretary-General of Amnesty International, by Dennis Bernstein and Larry Everest, *Z* magazine, January 1999, a rare departure from the general dismissal, far at the dissident extreme.

23. For a sample of what was known at the time, see my article in Cynthia Peters (ed.), *Collateral Damage* (South End Press, 1992), and Noam Chomsky, *Deterring Democracy* (Verso, 1991). On biological warfare facilities, see Charles Glass, *New Statesman*, 17 February 1998; his discoveries in 1988 as ABC TV Middle East correspondent were officially denied, now trumpeted as proof that Saddam must be destroyed. For a careful analysis, particularly of Britain's role, see Mark Phythian, *Arming Iraq: How*

the U.S. and Britain Secretly Built Saddam's War Machine (Northeastern University Press, 1997). On agriculture and the record generally, see Jonathan Randal, *After Such Knowledge, What Forgiveness? My Encounters with Kurdistan* (Westview, 1999). On the US Senators, see Miron Rezun, *Saddam Hussein's Gulf Wars* (Praeger, 1992).

24. Moshe Zak, editor of *Ma'ariv, Jerusalem Post*, 4 April 1991; Ron Ben-Yishai, *Ha'aretz*, 29 March 1991; Shalom Yerushalmi, *Kol Ha'ir*, 4 April 1991. See *Deterring Democracy*, 1992, Afterword.

25. Serge Schmemann, 'The Critics Now Ask: After Missiles, What?', *New York Times*, 18 December 1998.

26. Randal: *After Such Knowledge*, op. cit. Also Vera Saeedpour, 'Kurdish Times and the New York Times', *Kurdish Times* (Brooklyn), published by Cultural Survival, Summer 1988, sampling also other journals; for review in a broader context, see *Necessary Illusions*, App. V.3.

27. On Turkey and the Kurds, see Randal, *After Such Knowledge*, op. cit. Human Rights Watch, *Forced Displacement of Ethnic Kurds from Southeastern Turkey*, October 1994, and *Weapons Transfers and Violations of the Laws of War in Turkey*, November 1995; David McDowall, *The Destruction of Villages in South-East Turkey*, Medico International and Kurdish Human Rights Project (KHRP), June 1996; John Tirman, *Spoils of War: the Human Cost of America's Arm Trade* (Free Press, 1997); KHRP, *1998 Annual Report*, April 1999, reviewing Court judgements during 1988; KHRP and Bar Human Rights Committee of England and Wales, *Policing Human Rights Abuses in Turkey*, May 1999.

28. J. Patrice McSherry, 'The Emergence of "Guardian Democracy"', *NACLA Report on the Americas*, November/December 1998. Carothers, 'The Reagan Years', in Abraham Lowenthal (ed.), *Exporting Democracy* (Johns Hopkins University Press, 1991); *In the Name of Democracy* (University of California Press, 1991).

29. Carothers, 'Dithering in Central America', *New York Times Book Review*, 15 November 1998.

30. See Noam Chomsky, '"Consent without Consent": Reflections on the Theory and Practice of Democracy', *Cleveland State Law Review*, 44.4, 1996. McKinley, see Louis Pérez, *The War of 1898* (University of North Carolina, 1998).

31. Adam Isacson and Joy Olson, 'Just the Facts: A quick tour of U.S. defence and security assistance to Latin America and the Caribbean', *International Policy Report*, December 1998. *National Security Strategy of the United States*, The White House, March 1990; for more extensive quotations, see Noam Chomsky, *Deterring Democracy*, 1991, ch. 1. On arms sale, see Lora Lampe, 'The Leader of the Pack', *Bulletin of the Atomic Scientists*, January/February 1999; on the earlier record, William Hartung, *And Weapons for All* (HarperCollins, 1994).

32. Lawrence Mishel, Jared Bernstein, and John Schmitt, *The State of Working America 1998–1999* (Cornell, 1999). On inequality, working, legal mandate, see ibid., and Phineas Baxandall and Marc Breslow, *Dollars and Sense*, January–February 1999 (citing OECD: *Annual Employment Outlook*, 1998). Second decile, Edward Wolff's research, cited by Aaron Bernstein: 'A Sinking Tide Does Not Lower All Boats', *Business Week*, 14 September 1998. On Reaganite criminality, see 'The Workplace: Why America Needs Unions, But Not The Kind It Has Now', *Business Week*, 23 May 1994. On illegal resort to trade agreements to undermine unions, see labour historian Kate Bronfenbrenner, *Final Report: The Effects of Plant Closing or Threat of Plant Closing on the Right of Workers to Organize*, a study undertaken under NAFTA rules, withheld by the Clinton Administration. See Editorial, 'Class War in the USA' and 'We'll Close', excerpts from Bronfenbrenner's study, *Multinational Monitor*, March 1997. On corporate manslaughter in England and its impunity, see Gary Slapper, *Blood in the Bank* (Ashgate, 1999).

33. Sources cited in Noam Chomsky, 'United States and the

"Challenge of Relativity"' in Tony Evans (ed.), *Human Rights Fifty Years On: A Reappraisal* (Manchester University/St Martin's, 1998).

34. See Noam Chomsky, *Deterring Democracy*, ch. 4.

35. Among many recent examples, Gerald Baker, *Financial Times*, 14 December 1998, also noting potential flaws in the miracle; Reed Ableson, *New York Times*, 2 January 1999.

36. James Bennet, 'At a Conference on Wall Street Diversity, the President Finds His Own Stock Soaring', *New York Times*, 16 January 1999.

37. Greenspan, 22 July 1997, Congressional Hearings, quoted by Edward Herman in 'The Threat of Globalization', *New Politics*, 26, Winter 1999. Gene Koretz, 'Which Way are Wages Headed?', *Business Week*, 21 September 1998. 1994 survey, Robert Pollin and Stephanie Luce, *The Living Wage* (New Press, 1998). On unionization and wages, see Mishel *et al.*, op. cit, and earlier studies in this biennial series of the Economics Policy Institute.

38. Louis Uchitelle, 'The Rehabilitation of Morning in America', *New York Times*, 23 February 1997.

39. Joseph Stiglitz, 'Some Lessons from the East Asian Miracle', *World Bank Research Observer* 11.2, August 1996; 'An Agenda for Development in the Twenty-First Century', *Annual World Bank Report on Development Economics*, World Bank, 1998; Wider Annual Lectures 2, UN University and World Institute for Development Economics Research, May 1997. Felix, 'Is the Drive Toward Free-Market Globalization Stalling?: Review Essays', *Latin American Research Review* 33.3, 1998.

40. Eichengreen, *Globalizing Capital: A History of the International Monetary System* (Princeton University Press, 1996).

41. On the documentary record on Indochina, see Noam Chomsky, *For Reasons of State* (Pantheon, 1973); *Rethinking Camelot* (South End Press, 1993). For a careful and judicious scholarly review, see George Kahin, *Intervention* (Knopf, 1986).

42. *Proceedings of the ASIL* 13, 14 (1963), cited by Louis Henkin, *How Nations Behave* (Council on Foreign Relations, Columbia, 1979), pp. 333–4. Marc Trachtenberg, 'Intervention in Historical Perspective', in Laura Reed and Carl Kaysen (eds.), *Emerging Norms of Justified Intervention* (American Academy of Arts and Sciences, 1993), citing 1961 Acheson Report, Kennedy Library.

43. State Department Legal Adviser Abraham Sofaer, *The United States and the World Court*, US Department of State, Bureau of Public Affairs, *Current Policy* 769 (December 1985), statement before the Senate Foreign Relations Committee. Shultz, 'Moral Principles and Strategic Interests', State Department Bureau of Public Affairs, *Current Policy* 820, address at Kansas State University, 14 April 1986. For further quotes and context, and further sources for the above, see Noam Chomsky, *Necessary Illusions* (South End Press, 1989).

44. Albright quoted by Jules Kagian, *Middle East International*, 21 October 1994; Secretary of Defense William Cohen quoted by Philip Shenon in: 'U.S. Asserts It Will Consider Raids Unless Iraq Backs Down', *New York Times*, 2 December 1998.

45. Jane Perlez, 'Trickiest Divides Are Among Big Powers at Kosovo Talks', *New York Times*, 11 February 1999. Former Bush Administration National Security Council official Richard Haas of the Brookings Institution, quoted by Jonathan Landay in: 'How a NATO Strike on Serbs Could Set Precedent', *Christian Science Monitor*, 21 January 1999.

46. George Jones, *Daily Telegraph*, 29 June 1993.

47. Marcia Kurop, 'Shakeup Plan for UN Unlikely to Satisfy US', *Christian Science Monitor*, 16 July 1997.

48. *Survey of Current Business*, 76 (12), December 1996, Washington DC, US Deparment of Commerce.

49. Morton Horwitz, *The Transformation of American Law 1870–1960* (Oxford University Press, 1992).

50. 'Looking for New Leadership', *Newsweek International*, 1 February 1999.

51. See Noam Chomsky, *Profit over People* (Seven Stories, 1998).

52. Alan Story, 'Property in International Law', *Journal of Political Philosophy*, 6.3, 1998, pp. 306–33.

53. Christopher Hill, *Liberty Against the Law* (Penguin, 1996), citing Barnabe's *Journal* (1638).

54. Center for Responsive Politics, cited in *Dollars and Sense*, January–February 1999.

55. Bernays, *Propaganda* (Liveright, 1928). See Alex Carey, *Taking the Risk Out of Democracy* (University of New South Wales Press, 1995/University of Illinois Press, 1997); Elizabeth Fones-Wolf, *Selling Free Enterprise: The Business Assault on Labor and Liberalism, 1945–1960* (University of Illinois Press, 1995); Stuart Ewen, *PR!: A Social History of Spin* (Basic Books, 1996). On the general context, see Noam Chomsky, 'Intellectuals and the State', reprinted in *Towards a New Cold War* (Pantheon, 1982), and 'Force and Opinion', reprinted in *Deterring Democracy*.

56. Hutchins Commission quoted in William Preston, Edward Herman, and Herbert Schiller, *Hope and Folly: the United States and UNESCO 1945–1985* (University of Minnesota Press, 1989). Human Rights Watch, *The Limits of Tolerance: Freedom of Expression and Public Debate in Chile*, November 1998.

57. Stuart Ewen, *Captains of Consciousness: Advertising and the Social Roots of the Consumer Culture* (McGraw-Hill, 1976); Bagdikian, *The Media Monopoly* (Beacon [5th edn.] 1997).

58. Bruce Knecht, 'Magazine Advertisers Demand Prior Notice of "Offensive" Articles', *Wall Street Journal*, 30 April 1997.

59. Dan Schiller, *Digital Capitalism* (MIT, 1999).

60. Preston, in Preston *et al.*, *Hope and Folly*, op. cit.

61. Herbert Schiller, *Information Inequality: the Deepening Social Crisis in America* (Routledge, 1966); Edward Herman and Robert McChesney, *The Global Media* (Cassell, 1997); Dan

Schiller, *Digital Capitalism*, op. cit.; McChesney, *Rich Media, Poor Democracy* (University of Illinois Press, 1999).

62. Marshall Clark, 'Cleansing the Earth', *Inside Indonesia*, October–December 1998. On MAI, see Noam Chomsky, *Profit over People* (Seven Stories, 1998).

Notes to Chapter 3

1. Peter Fitzpatrick, 'Globalism', paper presented at Conference on the Future of Human Rights, Warwick University, 14 December 1998.

2. TRIPS covers copyrights, patents, trademarks, industrial designs, trade secrets (undisclosed information), integrated circuits (semiconductors), geographical indications, etc.

3. *The Cambridge Encyclopedia*, 2nd edn., ed. D. Crystal, 1994, defines *dharma* as 'the universal law that applies to the universe, human society and the individual. As the moral law, it is both a general code of ethics applicable to all, and a moral law specific to an individual's station in life.'

4. See Doug Cassell, 'The Right To Food: Has Uncle Sam Become Uncle Scrooge?', *Worldview Commentary*, 123, 20 November 1996.

5. Vandana Shiva, *Globalization of Agriculture and the Growth of Food Insecurity* (New Delhi: Research Foundation for Science, Technology, and Ecology, 1996), p. 10.

6. 27 January 1998.

7. Vandana Shiva, *Mustard or Soya? The Future of India's Edible Oil Culture* (New Delhi: Navdanya, 1998).

8. Vandana Shiva and Afsar H. Jafri, *Seeds of Suicide: The Ecological and Human Costs of Globalization in Agriculture* (New Delhi: Research Foundation for Science, Technology, and Ecology, 1998).

9. Steven Gorelick, *Small is Beautiful, Big is Subsidised*, International Society for Ecology and Culture, 1998.

10. Cited in Joel Bleifuss, 'Recipe for Disaster', in *In These Times*, 11 November 1996.

11. '"Cargill, The New East India Company": A Profile of the Largest Grain Tender in the World' (New Delhi: RFSTNRP, 1993).

12. Vandana Shiva, *Betting on Biodiversity: Why Genetic Engineering Will Not Feed the Hungry* (New Delhi: Research Foundation for Science, Technology, and Ecology, 1998), p. 58.

13. *The Biotech Reporter*, January 1997.

14. *RAFI News*, 13 March 1998.

15. *Inside US Trade*, 15 (25), June 20 1997.

16. Letter from US Agribusiness to the US Secretary of Agriculture, 12 June 1997.

17. George Monbiot, 'Food Fascism', *Guardian*, 3 March 1998.

18. World Bank Report No. 18089–IN: *India 1998 Macro-Economic Update: Reforming for Growth and Poverty Reduction*.

19. Gandhi preached 'domestic production and boycott of foreign goods as part of the campaign for independence' (*The Collins English Dictionary*).

20. 'Ram Rajya' is a metaphor for good governance (the rule of the god Rama, as described in the epic *Ramayana*); 'Rome Rajya' refers to the Catholic missionaries.

21. Cited in *International Herald Tribune*, 26 January 1999.

22. The 16th-century mosque Babri Masjid, in Ayodhya, Uttar Pradesh, India, was destroyed on 6 December 1992 by Hindu fundamentalists, who consider the site to be the birthplace of the god Rama. The BJP (Janata) party and Vishwa Hindu Parishad were accused of fomenting this action, and the police services of failing to take any action to prevent the demolition.

23. During the tour of India by the Pakistani cricket-team in 1999, pitches were at times vandalized by Hindu fundamentalists objecting to the tour.

24. The subject of Deepa Mehta's film *Fire* (premiered in Toronto

in 1999), which included a loveless arranged marriage and a lesbian relationship between two sisters-in-law, was objectionable to Hindu fundamentalists.

25. Hindutva is the term for the politics of Hindu fundamentalism.

Notes to Chapter 4

1. See Amartya Sen, 'Ingredients of Famine Analysis: Availability and Entitlements', *Quarterly Journal of Economics*, 96 (3), August 1981.

2. See D. P. Moynihan, *Secrecy. The American Experience* (New Haven: Yale University Press, 1998).

3. A minister to Louis XIV cunningly described taxation as follows: 'The art of taxation consists in so plucking a goose as to obtain the largest amount of feathers with the least possible amount of hissing.' See *Newsweek*, 69, 16 April 1984.

4. See A. B. Atkinson and J. E. Stiglitz, 'The Design of Tax Structure: Direct Versus Indirect Taxation', with A. Atkinson, *Journal of Public Economics*, 6, July–August 1976.

5. See William Greider, *Who Will Tell the People? The Betrayal of American Democracy* (New York: Simon & Schuster 1992), ch. 2, 'Well-Kept Secrets', for the role of secrecy in the S&L crisis.

6. See J. E. Stiglitz: 'S&L Bailout', in J. Barth and R. Brumraught, Jr (eds.), *The Reform of Federal Deposit Insurance: Disciplining the Government and Protecting Taxpayers* (New York: HarperCollins, 1992).

7. Banks have an incentive to sell assets that have increased in market value, thus increasing their 'book' value, while retaining assets that have decreased in value, so that they will not have to recognize losses.

8. There is a certain irony in that, a few years later, the Treasury levelled charges of lack of transparency in the accounting standards of some Asian countries and complained of government

interference, when only a few short years before they had evaded the same principles.

9. In the late 1970s, the Justice Department got an injunction against *The Progressive* magazine publishing an article on how to make nuclear bombs. The case was dropped seven months later when it was demonstrated that the story was based entirely on publicly available materials. See Ted G. Carpenter, *The Captive Press: Foreign Policy and the First Amendment* (Washington: Cato Institute, 1995).

10. Would the strong advocacy role of the US Treasury, including its Deputy Secretary, be changed if the large fees that a Wall Street firm was likely to realize from the privatization had been brought out in the open? Would its behaviour and that of others have been affected if the names of the lobbyists had been publicly released? I cannot but suspect that the answer to both questions is yes. Indeed, some senior administrative officials were seemingly so worried about the future fallout from the looming scandal that they tried to distance themselves from the decision-making process—others were left to sign the relevant documents. Whether or not such allegations are, in the end, proved true, the culture of secrecy inevitably gives rise to such suspicions, innuendo, and distrust.

11. For further discussion, see P. Orszag, *Privatization of the US Enrichment Corporation: An Economic Analysis*, London School of Economics, Ph.D. Dissertation, 1997; Nurith C. Aizenman, 'National Security for Sale', *Washington Monthly*, 17–23 December 1997; and the *New York Times*: 'Mishandling Russian Uranium', 11 June, A24, 1997; 'Selling Uranium Plant to Enrich the Private Sector?', 2 July, D2, 1998; 'Nuclear Security for Sale', 20 July, A14, 1998.

12. See Sissela Bok, *Secrets* (New York: Pantheon, 1982), for a comprehensive overview.

13. See Thomas Emerson, *Toward a General Theory of the First Amendment* (New York: Vintage Books, 1967) and *The System*

of Freedom of Expression (New York: Vintage Books, 1970), for a survey.

14. 'And though all the winds of doctrine were let loose to play upon the earth, so Truth be in the field, we do injuriously, by licensing and prohibiting, to misdoubt her strength. Let her and Falsehood grapple; who ever knew Truth put to the worse, in a free and open encounter?' Milton's argument was later echoed by Jefferson in his 1779 Virginia 'Bill for Establishing Religious Freedom' which argued in part that truth 'is the proper and sufficient antagonist to error, and has nothing to fear from the conflict unless by human interposition disarmed of her natural weapons, free argument and debate; errors ceasing to be dangerous when it is permitted freely to contradict them.'

15. Letter from James Madison to W. T. Barry, 4 August 1822, in Saul Padover (ed.), *The Complete Madison* (New York: Harper, 1953). Quoted in Carpenter, above, p. 1.

16. 'Without publicity, all other checks are fruitless: in comparison of publicity, all other checks are of small account. It is to publicity, more than to everything else put together, that the English system of procedure owes its being the least bad system as yet extant, instead of being the worst.' See Bentham (1838–43), vol. iv, p. 317. Quoted in E. Halévy, *The Growth of Philosophic Radicalism* (London: Faber & Faber, 1972), p. 403.

17. Mill argues '(t)he peculiar evil of silencing the expression of an opinion is, that it is robbing the human race; posterity as well as the existing generation; those who dissent from the opinion, still more than those who hold it. If the opinion is right, they are deprived of the opportunity of exchanging error for truth: if wrong, they lose, what is almost as great a benefit, the clearer perception and livelier impression of truth, produced by its collision with error.' See J. S. Mill, 'On Liberty' [1859], in J. S. Mill, *Three Essays* (Oxford: Oxford University Press, 1975), p. 24.

18. 'As between one form of popular government and another, the advantage in this respect lies with that which most widely diffuses the exercise of public functions; . . . by opening to all classes of private citizens, so far as is consistent with other equally important objects, the widest participation in the details of judicial and administrative business; as by jury trial, admission to municipal offices, and above all by the utmost possible publicity and liberty of discussion, whereby not merely a few individuals in succession, but the whole public, are made, to a certain extent, participants in the government, and sharers in the instruction and mental exercise derivable from it.' See J. S. Mill, *Considerations on Representative Government* [1861], in H. B. Acton (ed.) *J. S. Mill: Utilitarianism, On Liberty and Considerations on Representative Government* (London: J. M. Dent and Sons, 1972), p. 262.

19. Agency problems arise in the private sector as well, and thus lead to attempts by the bureaucracy to keep information from others. 'Every bureaucracy seeks to increase the superiority of the professionally informed by keeping their knowledge and intentions secret.' See H. H. Gerth and C. W. Mills (eds.), *From Max Weber: Essays in Sociology* (New York: Galaxy, 1958), p. 233. Weber gave the authoritative treatment of the role of secrecy in bureaucracy.

20. See Albert O. Hirschman, *Exit, Voice and Loyalty: Responses to Decline in Firms, Organizations and States* (Cambridge, Mass.: Harvard University Press, 1970).

21. For a discussion of market incentives for disclosure, and the need for government intervention, see, e.g. J. E. Stiglitz: 'Incentives, Risks and Information: Notes towards a Theory of Hierarchy', *Bell Journal of Economics*, 6, 2, 1975, pp. 552–79; 'Information and Economic Analysis', in Parkin and Nobay (eds.), *Current Economic Problems* (Cambridge: Cambridge University Press, 1975), pp. 27–52; 'The Private Uses of Public Interests: Incentive and Institutions', *Journal of Economic*

Perspectives, 12, Spring 1998, pp. 3–22; and S. Grossman: 'The Informational Role of Warranties and Private Disclosure about Product Quality', *Journal of Law and Economics*, 24, 1981, pp. 461–84.

22. A key issue, as society increasingly faces complicated and technical issues, is how to integrate expertise, democratic accountability, and representativeness. See, e.g. J. E. Stiglitz: 'Central Banking in a Democratic Society', *De Economist* (Netherlands), 146, no. 2.

23. See D. Mueller (ed.), *Perspectives on Public Choice: A Handbook* (Cambridge: Cambridge University Press, 1997).

24. In more technical terms, the practice of secrecy leads to an inefficient Nash equilibrium.

25. While this process seemed transparent to those within the Administration—we knew which reporters were in the 'purchase' of which members of the Administration—outsiders were confronted with an impossible job of screening out the 'propaganda'. Some officials were particularly adept at managing the press; indeed, there were many instances when they seemed to manage the press better than they managed their own agencies.

26. See A. Edlin and J. E. Stiglitz: 'Discouraging Rivals: Managerial Rent-Seeking and Economic Inefficiencies', *American Economic Review*, 85, 5, 1995, and A. Shleifer and R. W. Vishny, 'Management Entrenchment: The Case of Manager-Specific Investments', *Journal of Financial Economics*, 25, 1989, pp. 123–9.

27. In arguing against the Alien and Sedition Acts at the end of the 1700s, James Madison noted how the incumbents 'will be covered by the "sedition-act" from animadversions exposing them to disrepute among the people' while the challengers would have no such protection, so he asked 'will not those in power derive an undue advantage for continuing themselves in it; which by impairing the right of election, endangers the

blessings of the government founded on it?' See Madison, 'The Virginia Report of 1799–1800, Touching the Alien and Sedition Laws'. In L. Levy (ed.), *Freedom of the Press from Zenger to Jefferson* (Indianapolis: Bobbs Merill, 1966), p. 225.

28. See Bok, *Secrets*, op. cit., ch. iv, 'Secret Societies'.

29. In affirming the *New York Times*'s right to publish the *Pentagon Papers*, Supreme Court Justice Hugo Black wrote, 'In my view, far from deserving condemnation for their courageous reporting, the *New York Times*, *The Washington Post* and other newspapers should be commended for serving the purpose that the Founding Fathers saw so clearly. In revealing the workings of the government that led to the Vietnam war, the newspapers nobly did precisely that which the founders hoped and trusted they would do.' See *New York Times*, 1 July 1971, 'Supreme Court, 6–3, Upholds Newspapers on Publication of Pentagon Papers'. Furthermore, a public opinion poll conducted in the weeks after the disclosure of the Pentagon Papers reflected that 58% of the public felt the newspapers did the right thing (whereas 29% felt they had been in the wrong) in publishing the top-secret papers. See Roper Centre, *Public Opinion Online*, 1989, poll originally conducted by Louis Harris and Associates, University of Connnecticut.

30. I am indebted to Alan Blinder for this articulation.

31. On the delicate issues of whistle-blowing, see C. Peters and T. Branch, *Blowing the Whistle: Dissent in the Public Interest* (New York: Praeger, 1972) and Bok, op. cit.

Notes to the Response

1. H. H. Gerth and C. W. Mills (eds.), *From Max Weber: Essays in Sociology* (London: Routledge & Kegan Paul, 1970), p. 233.

2. Ibid.

3. Ibid., emphasis in original.
4. M. W. Reisman, 'The Constitutional Crisis in the United Nations', *American Journal of International Law*, 87, 1993, pp. 83–100.
5. *Towards An Economic Platform for the South* (Geneva: South Centre, 1998).
6. K. M. Meesen: 'IMF Conditionality and State Sovereignty', in Detlev C. Dicke (ed.) *Foreign Debts in the Present and a New International Economic Order* (Fribourg: Fribourg University Press, 1986), p. 126.
7. E. B. Haas, *When Knowledge is Power: Three Models of Change in International Organizations* (Berkeley: University of California Press, 1990), p. 209.
8. D. Held and D. Archibugi (eds.), *Cosmopolitan Democracy: An Agenda for a New World Order* (Cambridge: Polity, 1995), p. 232.

Notes to Chapter 5

1. Toni Morrison, *Paradise* (London: Vintage, 1999), p. 145.
2. Michael Ignatieff, *The Warrior's Honour: Ethnic War and the Modern Conscience* (London: Vintage, 1999), p. 5.
3. Charles Taylor, 'The Politics of Recognition' in *Multiculturalism: Examining The Politics of Recognition*, ed. Amy Gutmann (Princeton: Princeton University Press, 1994), pp. 66–74.
4. Will Kymlicka, *Multicultural Citizenship: A Liberal Theory of Minority Rights* (Oxford: Clarendon Press, 1995), p. 90.
5. Francesco Capotorti, *Study on the Rights of Persons Belonging to Ethnic, Religious, and Linguistic Minorities*, United Nations, New York, 1991, p. 33.
6. Manfred Nowak quoted in Jelena Pejic, 'Minority Rights in International Law', in *Human Rights Quarterly*, 19 (3), August 1997, p. 672.

7. Seyla Benhabib, *The Claims of Culture. Equality and Diversity in the Global Era* (Princeton University Press, forthcoming).

8. Hannah Arendt, *Origins of Totalitarianism*, 3rd edn (London: George Allen & Unwin, 1967), pp. 300–1.

9. *The Nation*, 14 December 1998.

10. Saskia Sassen, *Globalization and its Discontents* (New York: New Press, 1995), pp. 99–100.

11. David Held, *Democracy and the Global Order: From the Modern State to Cosmopolitan Governance* (Cambridge: Polity 1995), p. 234.

12. Joseph Raz, *Ethics in the Public Domain, Essays in the Morality and Law of Politics* (Oxford: Clarendon Press, 1994), p. 165.

13 Adrienne Rich, 'Movement', in *Dark Fields of the Republic. Poems 1991–1995* (New York: W. W. Norton, 1995), pp. 61–2.

14. Robert Lowell, 'Child-Pastel of Adrienne Rich', in *History* (New York: Farrar, Straus, Giroux, 1977), p. 154.

15. James Tully, *Strange Multiplicity: Constitutionalism in an Age of Diversity* (Cambridge: Cambridge University Press, 1995), p. 14.

16. Taylor, 'The Politics of Recognition', p. 64.

17. Frantz Fanon, 'Racism and Culture', in *Toward the African Revolution*, trans. by Haakon Chevalier (Harmondsworth: Penguin, 1970), p. 44.

18. Rich, 'Movement', p. 61.

19. Morrison, *Paradise*, p. 247.

20. W. E. B. Dubois, *Color and Democracy: Colonies and Peace* (New York: Harcourt, Brace and Co., 1945), p. 184.

Notes to Chapter 6

1. John Reader, *Africa: A Biography of the Continent* (London: Penguin, 1998), p. 329.

2. As Saskia Sassen has taught me, the globalization of capital in this sense is perfectly consistent with its operations remaining

heavily dependent upon national systems of public and private regulation. See Saskia Sassen, *Globalization and its Discontents* (New York: The New Press, 1998).

3. Marcus Aurelius, *Meditations*, trans. with an introduction by Maxwell Staniforth (Penguin: London and New York, 1964).

4. Staniforth in his introduction to the *Meditations*, op. cit., p. 18. It might be objected that Staniforth is a rather Christianizing reader of Marcus Aurelius. To which it might be replied that Western Christianity is a rather Stoicized religion.

5. If it were, I would begin by urging us to 'unbundle' sovereignty and think about assigning institutional responsibilities for different tasks at different levels, and creating multiple sites for the resolution of conflicts among levels. I should argue not so much for a separation as for a diffusion of powers.

6. Laurence Sterne, *A Sentimental Journey* (Worlds Classics, Oxford: Oxford University Press, 1968), pp. 62–3.

7. Richard Rorty, 'Justice as a Larger Loyalty', in Phengh Cheah and Bruce Robbins (eds.), *Cosmopolitics* (Minneapolis: University of Minnesota Press, 1998), p. 73.

8. But the justification for this way of thinking must come in what it yields (I share Rorty's pragmatism, here). So let me be clear that some of what will be yielded by the approach I favour would be yielded by Rorty's approach as well.

9. Rorty, op. cit., p. 57.

10. Op. cit., p. 55.

11. John Stuart Mill, *On Liberty* (Amherst, New York: Prometheus Books, 1986), pp. 77–8.

12. 'Do you want to know the real drama of my life? It's that I have put my genius into my life. All I have put into my works is my talent.' Oscar Wilde as quoted in André Gide, *Oscar Wilde*, 'In Memoriam', 1910.

13. This remark comes from an interview and its wider context deserves quotation: 'I think that from the theoretical point of

view, Sartre avoids the idea of the self as something that is given to us, but through the moral notion of authenticity, he turns back to the idea that we have to be ourselves—to be truly our true self. I think the only acceptable practical consequence of what Sartre has said is to link his theoretical insight to the practice of creativity—and not to that of authenticity. From the idea that the self is not given to us, I think there is only one practical consequence: we have to create ourselves as a work of art. In his analyses of Baudelaire, Flaubert and so on, it is interesting to see that Sartre refers the work of creation to a certain relation to oneself—the author to himself—which has the form of authenticity or inauthenticity. I would like to say exactly the contrary: we should not have to refer the creative activity of somebody to the kind of relation he has to himself, but should relate the kind of relation one has to oneself to a creative activity.' Michel Foucault, *Ethics, Subjectivity and Truth*, ed. Paul Rabinow (New York: The New Press, 1997), p. 262.

14. Friedrich Nietzsche, *The Gay Science*, ed. Walter Kaufmann. (New York: Vintage, 1974), bk. 4, p. 232.

15. Revaux/Francois/Anka.

16. There are other important objections, of course, which I do not have time to consider. One of these is that the basic choices involved in self-creation seem arbitrary. I take this up in a forthcoming paper on 'Three problems for liberalism'.

17. I mean it is natural to us only in the sense that a normal human upbringing produces creatures with such desires.

18. Ian Hacking, 'Making Up People', in Thomas C. Heller, Morton Sosna and David E. Wellby (eds), *Reconstructing Individualism* (Stanford, Stanford University Press, 1986). As he would be the first to acknowledge, this insight is already present in what sociologists call 'labeling theory'. See Mary McIntosh, 'The Homosexual Role', in Edward Stein (ed.), *Forms of Desire: Sexual Orientation and the Social Constructionist Controversy* (New York: Routledge, 1998), pp. 25–42.

19. Hacking, 'Making Up People', op. cit., p. 87.

20. Hacking, 'Making Up People', op. cit., p. 81.

21. *Multiculturalism: Examining 'The Politics of Recognition'*. An essay by Charles Taylor, with commentary by Amy Gutmann (ed.), K. Anthony Appiah, Jürgen Habermas, Steven C. Rockefeller, Michael Walzer, Susan Wolf (Princeton, NJ: Princeton University Press, 1994), p. 32.

22. See my 'Identity, Authenticity, Survival: Multicultural Societies and Social Reproduction', in *Multiculturalism: Examining 'The Politics of Recognition'*, op. cit., pp. 149–64.

23. I should explicitly record my opposition to the view that this origin in any way discredits these ideas, either for non-Europeans or, for that matter, for Europeans. The issues I want to explore have to do with the ways in which these views can be rooted in different traditions. I am not interested in the nativist project of arguing for these principles in the name of authentically Asante (or African) roots. The issues raised in the following paragraphs are thus historical, not normative.

24. Such historical context is important, I think, because, as Michael Oakeshott once observed, political education should instil in us 'a knowledge as profound as we can make it, of our tradition of political behaviour'. Michael Oakeshott 'Political Education' in *Rationalism in Politics and Other Essays* (Indianapolis: Liberty Fund, 1991), p. 61. We might say: liberal institutions are to be recommended, in part, as a practical response to the circumstances of modern political life.

25. My father's thought clearly wasn't so much that there aren't any atheists in Ghana but that their views don't matter. Locke, of course, agreed: 'those are not at all to be tolerated who deny the being of a God. Promises, covenants, and oaths, which are the bonds of human society, can have no hold upon an atheist. The taking away of God, though but even in thought, dissolves all.' 'A Letter Concerning Toleration', in *Political Writings of John*

Locke, ed. with an introduction by David Wootton (New York: Mentor, 1993), p. 426.

26. There are scores of proverbs on this theme in *Bu Me Bo: The Proverbs of the Akan*, the more than seven thousand Akan proverbs that Peggy Appiah, my mother, will be publishing with my assistance next year.

27. The European history is taken up in Charles Taylor, *Sources of the Self: the Making of the Modern Identity* (Cambridge, Mass.: Harvard University Press, 1989).

28. Joseph de Maistre, *Considérations sur la France* (2nd edn., London: Bâle, 1797), p. 102. 'J'ai vu, dans ma vie, des Français, des Italiens, des Russes, etc.; je sais même, grâce à Montesquieu, qu'on peut être Persan: mais quant à l'homme, je déclare ne l'avoir recontré de ma vie . . . '

29. If you communicate on the Internet, think about how difficult it is not to imagine your e-mail correspondents (who present, after all, only strings of unspoken words) as having, for example, a specific race, gender, and age.

30. Kurô is usually translated as 'town': but towns were relatively self-governing in the Asante past, so *polis* looks like a translation that gets the right sense.

Index

Note: 'n.' after a page reference indicates the number of a note on that page.